GROWING UP AND GROWING OLD
IN ANCIENT ROME

Throughout history, every culture has had its own ideas on what growing up and growing old means, with variations between chronological, biological and social ageing, and with different emphases on the critical stages and transitions from birth to death.

This volume is the first to highlight the role of age in determining behaviour, and expectations of behaviour, across the life span of an inhabitant of ancient Rome. Drawing on developments in the social sciences, as well as ancient evidence, the authors focus on the period c.200BC–AD200, looking at childhood, the transition to adulthood, maturity, and old age. They explore how both the individual and society were involved in, and reacted to, these different stages, in terms of gender, wealth and status, and personal choice and empowerment.

Original, lively and accessible, this study opens up the subject of age and the Roman life course in a way that is tangible to the reader, and which includes and draws on current controversies and debates in ancient history. It will be important for anyone studying Roman life.

Mary Harlow is a lecturer in Roman history at the University of Birmingham, where she holds a Leverhulme Special Research Fellowship (2000/2001). Her research interests include gender, the Roman family and dress in late antiquity. She is also an associate lecturer with the Open University.

Ray Laurence is a lecturer in Roman history and archaeology at the University of Reading. His previous books include *Roman Pompeii: Space and Society* (Routledge 1994), and *The Roads of Roman Italy: Mobility and Cultural Change* (Routledge 1999). He is also co-editor of *Cultural Identity in the Roman Empire* (Routledge 1998, pb 2001) and *Travel and Geography in the Roman Empire* (Routledge 2001).

GROWING UP AND GROWING OLD IN ANCIENT ROME

A life course approach

Mary Harlow and Ray Laurence

London and New York

First published 2002
by Routlege
11 New Fetter Lane, London EC4P 4EE

Simultaneously published in the USA and Canada
by Routledge
29 West 35th Street, New York, NY 10001

Routledge is an imprint of the Taylor & Francis Group

© 2002 Mary Harlow and Ray Laurence

Typeset in Garamond by Saxon Graphics Ltd, Derby
Printed and bound in Great Britain by Biddles Ltd, Guildford and King's Lynn

British Library Cataloguing in Publication Data
A catalogue record for this book is available from the British Library

Library of Congress Cataloging in Publication Data

Harlow, Mary, 1956–
Growing up and growing old in Ancient Rome: a life course approach/
Mary Harlow and Ray Laurence.
p. cm.
Includes bibliographical references and index.
1. Developmental psychology–Rome. 2. Rome–History–Republic, 265-30 B.C. 3.
Rome–History–Empire, 30 B.C.-284 A.D. I. Laurence, Ray, 1963-II. Title.

BF713.H366 2002
305.2'0937–dc21   2001040368

ISBN 0-415-20201-9 (pbk)
ISBN 0-415-20200-0 (hbk)

CONTENTS

LIST OF ILLUSTRATIONS

Plates

Figures

PREFACE

Seldom are books on ancient history written by more than one author. When we do find books with two names on them, they tend to be edited collections of essays or collections of translated texts. Typically, the historian works on her own to produce a monograph with the aid of experts who read and comment on the manuscript. However, there are some topics that cannot or should not be approached in this manner. To our minds, human ageing is one of those. The subject is topical in the current changes to the demographic structures of Western populations, which may result, for example, in the abolition of the retirement age. It also requires a sensitivity that causes two heads to be better than one. The dialogue between the authors has been enjoyable and stimulating, causing them to understand more clearly the process by which they individually write history.

This dialogue has caused restraint at some points and at others created the conditions for a bolder or more forthright text. Its intention is to focus on age and the life course in antiquity and to open these subjects up to scrutiny. It is not a book about daily life, nor is it a book about the Roman family, though both are central to the thesis. The origins of the book lie in the teaching in Reading of an undergraduate course – the Roman Life Cycle, received enthusiastically in 1996–7 and again in 1998–9. Much has been learnt from our students in Birmingham and Reading, who have pointed out alternative perspectives or simply revealed that they perceive their immediate family being over one hundred people. It is a book that could not have been written without the work of other Roman social historians over the last fifteen years, most notably that of Richard Saller and Susan Treggiari. The rate of change and publication in this area should not be under-estimated: since the completion of this text two additional books have been published – Suzanne Dixon's *Reading Roman Women* and her edited collection *Childhood, Class and Kin in the Roman World*. The intention is not to summarise their work, or that of others, but to suggest we can take the subject of Roman social history further by focusing on the issue of age – in a similar way our subject in the past benefited from the catalyst of a new found interest or focus on the now mainstream topics of gender and the body.

Mary Harlow wishes to thank the Leverhulme Trust for financial support over part of the period in which this book was written and Birmingham University for a semester of study leave. Ray Laurence acknowledges the financial support of the Research Endowment Trust Fund of the University of Reading, which granted a term's teaching replacement to complete the book. He is also grateful to Louise Revell for replacing his teaching and to his colleagues, who were landed with an assortment of administrative tasks during his absence. Gillian Clark, Janet Huskinson, Chris Wickham and Graham Shipley read parts of the volume in draft and provided comments for which we are grateful. Karen Cokayne read Chapter 9 and her vast knowledge of old age and theories of the life course have been of benefit in that chapter and elsewhere. Both authors look forward to the publication of her Ph.D. thesis on old age. Susan Fischler kindly allowed us to read an early draft of her forthcoming article 'From Puella to Matrona', for which we thank her. Ingrid Lander kindly checked the proofs for inconsistencies and lapses into illiteracy. None of the above are in any way responsible for any errors or misconceptions that remain.

The tables in Appendix A are taken from Richard P. Saller, *Patriarchy, Property and Death in the Roman Family*, 1994, and appear by permission of Cambridge University Press. Figures 1.1 and 1.2 are from T.G. Parkin, *Demography and Roman Society*, 1992, John Hopkins University Press. Every effort has been made to obtain permission to reproduce copyright material. If any proper acknowledgement has not been made, we would invite copyright holders to inform us of the oversight. All the plates in the volume are from photographs taken by the authors.

1

INTRODUCTION

Ageing in antiquity

The fact of the matter is that there is a general lack of vital statistics
from the ancient world

(Parkin 1992: 59)

Human ageing and the life course

Our intention in writing this book is to open the subject of age and the
Roman life course for discussion. What is here is not our last word on the
subject, but is written with the intention of making this area of historical
research accessible to students at university and to those outside the subject
of Classics, as well as to informed ancient historians. From the 1980s
onwards, there has been a concerted effort to search for or discover the Roman
family (Bradley 1991; Dixon 1992; Rawson 1986, 1991, 1997). This work
has defined the family at Rome through a careful study of the literature, epigraphy and above all law. At the same time, Richard Saller (1994) simulated
the structure of the Roman system of kinship to elucidate the changing structure of the Roman family according to the age of an individual. This work
has provided the basic structure for our discussion of changes in the age of
individuals at Rome. Our concern, though, is not with the family itself but
with the individual and the view of the individual's actions according to their
position in the life course. What we wish to identify are underlying codes of
behaviour or the expectations of others when viewing the actions of a person
according to their age (see Ryff 1985 on the subjective experience of the life
course). We emphasise the role of the individual and individual action,
because we wish to be aware of variation in the life course. There is little
surviving evidence for the reconstruction of the life courses of those who were
not from the elite, and it has to be recognised that the recovery of the experience of age in antiquity is limited to this influential group. However, the
experience of age and ageing would vary within this group itself according to
the variation of family structure that was shaped through the birth and death
of its members.

The focus is on the experience of the individual acting within the expectations of his or her family and the observation of outsiders. Here, we attempt
to resist the temptation of creating a standard life course from birth to death,
in favour of an emphasis on different experiences in the relationship between

1

Plate 1.1 Marcus Aurelius: young and old. The first image shows Marcus Aurelius as a young man with a recently grown beard, whereas the second image displays him in old age with a full beard, lined eyes and a furrowed brow.

independent adults and dependent young and old. This variation is apparent in cases known to both the authors and readers of this volume. For example, a brother and sister were born two years apart. The sister married at twenty-one and had three children before she was thirty; whereas the brother married at the age of forty-two and had his first child. Technically, both the brother's and sister's children are the next generation, but in terms of chronological age there is a discrepancy of twenty-one years between the cousins. Hence, within an individual family, there is a massive variation of the age of parenting as well as the age of its members. Many of these variations are hidden by social categories, for example mother, father, granny or grandpa, that are the signifiers of the construction of identity regardless of chronological age. Hence, to study the life course of a society we need not depend entirely on chronological age for the construction of the characteristics of the individual; instead these are seen in conjunction with the changing familial roles of that person.

Today, ageing is seen as the key subject in the human sciences and humanities. The reason for this is partly that the changes in the demographic structure of the West have resulted in a significant increase in the number of old people as a proportion of the total population in the last fifty years. At the same time, our characterisation of other age-related categories has been questioned. For instance, the construction of children as innocent and protected is hard to maintain in the light of a series of media stories that

2

involve physical violence and assault by minors. It is no longer possible to simply accept that the categories child, adolescent, adult and old simply exist across time. Just as the categories female and male are culturally constructed to create a difference and to preserve a male dominance in terms of power; children, adolescents and the old are defined in a similar fashion as not adult or in a state of becoming or unbecoming adult. How these categories are defined can vary across cultures and through time. Hence, to our mind, it is imperative for ancient historians to join the debate on ageing for the benefit of their own subject and to make a contribution to the debate that is occurring in the social and biological sciences (e.g. Pilcher 1995; Medina 1996). Moreover, it is now recognised that the modern West's concepts and social expectations have been shaped through the reception and adoption of ideas rooted in antiquity (Wyke and Biddiss 1999). The modern conception of age is no exception, but discussion of this topic would fill at least another volume.

The term *life course* needs some explanation. It encapsulates the temporal dimension to life that begins at birth and ends in death with numerous stages and rites of passage along the way. However, the life course is not simply a description of biological ageing. It is culturally constructed and need not exactly follow biological or mental development in humans. Every culture has its own version of the life course, with a different emphasis on critical stages and transitions. Thus, we are born not simply into the social structure of a society, but also into the life course of that society. The individual follows the life course of a society, but their reaction to it or involvement in the stages can vary according to status, gender, personal choice and empowerment. In other words, the agent will act within the structure of the life course to a set of expectations of that agent by others within that society. Here, we follow Giddens' structuration theory (1984: 1–40) that empowers individuals differently according to their place within the structure of society with respect to their wealth, status and cultural perspective. The life course is very much a cultural perspective and part of an organising structure of a society, but the experience of ageing is also strongly influenced by the wealth or status (including gender) of the individual at Rome.

Life cycle is another term that we need to clarify. It is a term used by biologists to describe the events from birth through to death and the production of the next generation of a species. This can be used to describe the life cycles of anything from slime moulds to mammals. We need at this point to refer to the work of Bonner (1993), a biologist who spent a life time studying the seven-day life cycles of slime moulds and who has lucidly investigated the wider frame of the life cycle. He suggests that the individual adult can be viewed in a number of ways, most easily in terms of their stage of life as adult as opposed to larva or pupa. But, in many ways, an individual in terms of a wider time frame is in fact part of a life cycle – a human is an individual within a succession of life courses or generations. Thus, we should view the individual life course as part of a succession of similar life courses that biologically and culturally reproduce a society through time. To us, this cumulative patterning of life courses is the life cycle of a society. Unlike the life course, it does not end with death but is reproduced in the next generation and has a fundamental link to what we commonly regard as the temporal frame of history or the *longue durée*.

Both the life course and the life cycle are terms that relate a human present to its past and future and can be seen as temporal structures to create meaning and certainty in the human perspective of existence. A person's age within the life course sets out a position with reference to their past, and presents them with an expectation of future events. In fact, we would argue that the life course is an expected future at birth that structures a person's aspirations whether parent or child. In contrast, the life cycle of generations creates a longer view of time, via ancestry back into the past and into the future with the presumption of future generations. What is created is a structure for the past and the future. In reality, life courses could be cut short through death at any stage. At Rome, relatively few survived to old age, but that did not prevent the development of an expectation of a life into old age. These conceptions of temporality were as significant as the day-to-day changes or the *longue durée* of change across several generations. At Rome, these were represented by the secular cycles of one hundred and ten years, and were celebrated with the expectation that no one would see the rites of this festival more than once (on the festival see Beard, North and Price 1998: 201–6). Importantly, within the festival, there was an emphasis on a new beginning – the expected future experiences of the young. Significantly, the life course was a means to reproduce the age and social structure of Roman society from one generation to another – i.e. from father to son or mother to daughter. It asserts the power of parents or adults over their children and other dependants, as well as gender roles. In turn, these children become adults and utilise the same techniques and structures for reinforcing their position and power within the family structure. It is therefore also a means to reinforce key ideological positions and to maintain certainty and the status quo. In other words, the life course was a technology of power to ensure a consistency in ideology and behaviour across the generations at Rome.

The book arises from recent scholarship on the family and gender in antiquity and, in fact, could not have been written prior to the investigation of this area over the last twenty years (notably Bradley 1991; Dixon 1992; Gardner 1986; Gleason 1995; Hallett and Skinner 1997; Kertzer and Saller 1991; Rawson 1986, 1991, 1997; Rousselle 1988; Saller 1994; Treggiari 1991a; Wiedemann 1989; Williams 1999). There had been a tradition of publication on the daily life of the Romans with an implicit comparison with the modern practices and family structures of the nineteenth and twentieth centuries. This comparison is at times crude, incorporating an assumption that we today have become more civilised than those at Rome. A slave society, with the spectacles of the amphitheatre and a lack of democratic freedom or women's rights, is not to our cultural taste, even though the modern West views the culture of Rome as a key element in its own historical and cultural tradition. This has often led to the creation of Rome as a model horror into which our own society might descend. Alternatively, Rome has been used discursively as a means to promote discussion or to release anguish with reference to modern society. Few today would read Jerome Carcopino's interpretation in his section 'Feminism and Demoralisation' in *Daily Life in Ancient Rome* without a wry smile. The 'presentism' of his views, which are personal, is easily identifiable. We as authors are very conscious of the need to control the comparative genre, which can produce explanations that identify a difference between Rome and ourselves. At the same time, although we see our analysis of the life course as relevant to the contemporary debate on human ageing, we wish to identify differences within the categorisation of the key stages of the life course: infant, child, puberty, adulthood and old age.

For those reading this book from beyond the discipline of Ancient History, we refer them in the first instance to Jo-Ann Shelton's *As the Romans Did: A Sourcebook in Roman Social History* (1988) and Jane Gardner and Thomas Wiedemann's *The Roman Household: A Sourcebook* (1991) to gain access to primary evidence for human ageing at Rome. References in the text to classical sources follow standard conventions as listed in the *Oxford Classical Dictionary*: for example, Cicero's *Letters to Atticus* is abbreviated as Cic.*Att*; the numbers following the reference give the paragraph or line number of the section referred to. The reader is strongly encouraged to examine these at first hand, either in translation or in the original language. These primary sources lie at the heart of our interpretation of ageing and the meaning of age at Rome. We hope that readers outside our subject will be able to see the primary evidence for themselves, evaluate our strategies of interpretation and contribute to future discussion within this field of study. We should also make it clear that the temporal period we are dealing with chronologically stretches from about 200 BC through to AD 200.

The seemingly natural categories of child, adolescent and elderly are all terms that identify individuals as not adult. They all signify states and stages of dependence, whereas an adult is seen as independent of their parents, and only becomes dependent upon their children in old age. The categories of the dependent and the independent individual seem to characterise age in order to assert the power of the adult over both young and old (Hockey and James 1993). The transition from one stage of life to another is culturally fixed. In Britain, children become independent when they are eighteen – they can vote, effectively claim welfare benefits, etc. However, this transition has little to do with their biological stage of development. The age of eighteen (the age of enfranchisement in Britain) occurs at the end of biological growth, but the age of sixteen (the minimum legal age of marriage and sexual activity in Britain) occurs at a chronological age beyond sexual maturity. This highlights how the categorisation of the stages of life does not follow a biological logic, but is constructed within the discourse of age and maturity. The contrast with ancient Rome here is quite striking. There, marriage for girls could occur before menarche at the age of twelve or thirteen, while for males it occurred well into their twenties. This comparison demonstrates a difference in the construction of the transition to a married state within the life course across cultures. Hence, at the outset of this book, it needs to be understood that there need not be anything biologically natural about the way we construct the different categories of infant, child, adolescent, adult and old.

Death and life

Ancient historians have a tendency to be interested not only in the things that can be known from the Roman world, but also in those things that cannot be known. A classic case is life expectancy two thousand years ago. At first sight there appears to be a wealth of data. The tombstones from across the Roman empire record the ages of the deceased they commemorate. For example, the parents of Hatera Superba record on her memorial that she died at the age of one year, six months and twenty-five days (*CIL*6.19159). The information is desperately personal, with the parents choosing to record even the number of days their daughter had lived. The age of death should not be seen as simply a statistic: it is far more than that. It is a cultural response to a daughter's death. If she had died prior to teething at about six months, her parents would not have commemorated her life in the same way (Plin.*HN*7.68); similarly, if she had lived and married it would probably have been her husband who was mentioned in the inscription. Equally, other parents may not have commemorated their daughter's death at this age with a monumental inscription. The point is that the funerary epitaph is personal, and refers to a specific instant in the life course of the deceased. This affected the way in which the individual was commemorated by their kin or loved ones.

These decisions about the commemoration of an individual cause the age of death as recorded on a funerary monument to be a personalised statement, which cannot be utilised statistically in combination with other inscriptions recording the ages at death to calculate a pattern of life expectancy. Ancient historians have suggested that if we were to find the average age of death recorded in funerary inscriptions across the empire we would then know the average life expectancy of the population (Parkin 1992: 5–8). However, the geographical variation across the Roman empire of such data suggested that what was recorded was a pattern of epigraphic commemoration that was culturally determined, rather than an actual pattern of longevity (Hopkins 1966). The epigraphic samples reveal a habit of age rounding to the Roman numeral V and X, presumably for reasons of typography and stonecutting. More importantly, the inscriptions expose patterns of commemoration that reveal the relationships of kin to the deceased, as Richard Saller (1994) has shown. These patterns, it should be stated, are intimately connected to the

Roman conception of the life course and the stage of life of the deceased. For example, we find that parents predominantly commemorate sons until their twenties – after which commemoration by a wife becomes more prominent. Similarly, daughters were commemorated by parents almost exclusively until their mid to late teens at Rome. Subsequently, women in their late teens and twenties tend to be commemorated by husbands. Saller (1994: 32) suggests that this patterning within the epigraphic data points to a change in the life course, which identifies the age of marriage and the renegotiation of commemoration defined by marriage. Hence the funerary inscriptions inform us indirectly about the age of marriage, rather than being data for life expectancy. These inscriptions subtly encapsulate the stages of life and its association with kin and spouses, in combination with statements of chronological age.

The Romans conducted censuses of the population of the empire. The data taken town by town, region by region, province by province, were available to be perused by individual scholars. Pliny the Elder, in discussing human longevity, uses these data. He finds in the AD 73 census for the region of the Po plain (Region 8 of Italy) that fifty-four people had said they were a hundred years old, fourteen that they were a hundred and ten years old, two had announced that they were a hundred and twenty-five, eight were maintaining that they were in their hundred and thirties and three were adamant that they were one hundred and forty years old (HN7.162–3). These statements should not be seen as fact, but as classic cases of age exaggeration in census returns that are common today in the figures for the over eighty-year-olds. When broken down into the towns where these people lived, we can say that in many towns of the region there were usually one or two people who maintained they had already lived to a great age; exceptionally so in Veleia there was a concentration of eleven such individuals. The question remains, how long could a human being have lived in the Roman world? Modern life spans have a potential of being one hundred and fifteen years (Medina 1996: 10), but circumstances tend to reduce that life span via, for example, heart failure. In antiquity, people could in theory have lived for a similar length of time and Pliny is at pains to make this clear, with numerous examples of long-lived males and females in their nineties and hundreds (HN7.153–67). Galen, also, sees the maximum at one hundred and seventeen years (Remediis Parabilibus 3.14.56K). This implies that the life span in modern twentieth-century humans and those living two thousand years ago is not necessarily so different. Where there is a difference is in the way a life span could be terminated at an earlier date. Today in Britain and the USA, we view the major threats to our own longevity as cancer, heart disease, AIDS, car accidents, etc. For those living in antiquity the focus would have been on a different variety of threats: famine and malnutrition, epidemics, sanitation related diseases and warfare (Parkin 1992: 93). The effect of these can be seen in the calculation of infant mortality in Rome compared to the USA today: in modern

America the infant mortality rate is about ten per thousand, whereas in ancient Rome it is calculated at roughly three hundred per thousand. In other words in Rome infant mortality is thirty times that in the West today. Those living in ancient Rome could have lived into their hundreds as we can today: what was different was the risk to life, particularly in childhood. Hence, we would describe the population of the Roman world as one associated with a high death rate and a high birth rate.

Demography

A cultural approach to the life course needs to take account of how a society is structured by its demographic make up. In the late twentieth century in Western Europe and North America, there has been a significant increase in the proportion of the population over sixty years of age. This has had some impact on our cultural expectation of old age and has caused retirement at age sixty or sixty-five to be put into question. In the Roman world, the demographic structure into which an individual was born raised basic questions such as: how old were that person's parents; were their grandparents alive; did he have or will he have had brothers and sisters? Equally, when were the major changes going to occur through that person's life in terms of the life course: marriage, death, and the birth of offspring? These questions cannot be directly addressed via the evidence from the ancient world – after all, no ancient writer says: 'generally the age of marriage is such and such in my home town'. Instead, we need to rely on cultural statements and interpret these statements in the light of the study of demography and the statistical simulation of population structures. This will not provide absolute data in itself, but will model the population trends that were likely to have resulted from the information we have.

The study of demography has since the 1950s been informed by what are called 'Model Life Tables'. These vary according to the region, level of development, nature of life threatening diseases, and other variables in the modern world. To establish which of these tables would fit the ancient world, demographers looked to papyri found in Roman Egypt that are census returns recording the age of the population (Parkin 1992: 19–27 for discussion). The sample of 532 ages is not a large one but provides us with a guide to the nature of the age structure of the population. It found that the average age of this group of people was 26.6 years and few were over the age of fifty. If taken with some standard biological assumptions, in particular that in childhood an individual's immune system is underdeveloped and the possibility of death is much higher, we can postulate the closest fit for Roman empire's life table is with that of a developing country in the mid–late twentieth century. A model life table for the Roman empire from which it is possible to view the possibility of survival into old age was established (Parkin 1992: 91–136 for discussion of this topic). Figure 1.1 shows the probability of an individual

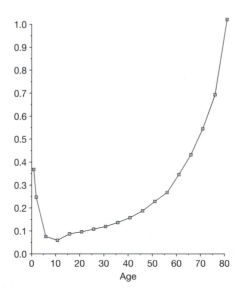

Figure 1.1 The probability of dying in the Roman Empire. This graph plots out the likelihood of not surviving between different ages across the life course. Note that death is most likely for the very young and this likelihood returns after the age of sixty (after Parkin 1992 Plate 4).

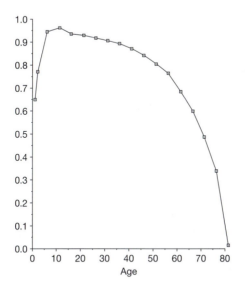

Figure 1.2 The probability of survival in the Roman Empire. This graph plots out the likelihood of surviving between different ages across the life course. Note that there is a stability to the survival rates after infancy that continues into a person's fifties (after Parkin 1992 Plate 5).

dying in antiquity over their maximum life span. For children and the over fifties, the risk from death is modelled as particularly acute. The data can be expressed as a prediction of survival through the maximum human life span – this is shown as Figure 1.2. In this case we can see again that the pattern of survival is most likely in the adult years before the effects of biological degeneration occur. What these graphs show is that at birth survival into adulthood was unlikely, with many children dying within their first year of life. As the child approached adulthood, the expectation of living into his or her forties or fifties becomes more realistic. The factor of death in early childhood for roughly one third of those being born caused the average life expectancy of the population as a whole to be lowered to around twenty-five to thirty years. This masks the fact that those who survived childhood could have lived into what we today regard as old age and have experienced a similar longevity. Demographically at Rome, many children were born and died in childhood but, if we were able to visit ancient Rome, we would be shocked by the sheer number of children. These factors are reduced to the bald statement that the average age of life was twenty-five to thirty-three years, but this effectively masks the variation of experience from the child dying at birth to the old person in his or her eighties or nineties.

Another demographic consideration is the shape of the Roman family and a person's kinship universe. These have been simulated by Richard Saller using a computer programme devised by the Cambridge Group for the History of Population and Social Structure. This procedure produces a model of a stable population based upon a set of probabilities within demographic parameters (Saller 1994: 43–73). Critical to the modelling of the Roman kinship universe is the age of female and male marriage – for the average female this was seen to have been by age twenty and for average males age thirty. In contrast, the elite married rather earlier and a separate calculation was made with reference to their marriage ages at an earlier point. The tables (Appendix A) allow us to read off the probable shape of a person's kinship universe through the life course. However, this presents the probability of a person having both parents alive or the likely ages of their in laws, thus in no way is this absolute data. What the tables do is to provide us with an idea of the overall pattern of the kinship universe.

The implications can be seen when we examine the effect of different ages of marriage of females and males within the senatorial elite. If they were to marry at the expected ages of fifteen and twenty-five, the differential in marriage age through the generations would create an interconnection between men and women of different age groups (for full discussion see Chapters 6 and 7). The father of the bride would have been about forty-seven years old whereas the mother would have been roughly thirty-eight; the groom's parents would have been about fifty-six in the case of the father and forty-seven in the case of the mother. This created a male linkage between the groom and his father (25 and 56 years old respectively) and the father of the bride, aged about forty-seven, an intermediate age between father and son. The son gained access to a person at the peak of the life course at the time when his father was about to bow out of public life aged sixty. Another result of the age differential between females and males was that there was a strong possibility of a large number of women outliving their first husbands (the reader is referred to Appendix A for further information).

Chronological age

The ages at death of individuals are found on a total of 55,000 inscriptions (Shaw 1991: 67) on tombstones even down to the number of years, months and days that a person had lived. The question remains: why were these individuals recorded in this particular way? Here we need to discuss briefly the pattern of commemoration found in the inscriptions. One subject that has been discussed extensively within the last thirty years or so from the time of Hopkins' (1966) observation is that the ages given on inscriptions did not reflect the demographic pattern of the Roman empire but instead the pattern of commemoration. Ages of death are recorded for men and women of all social classes whether born free or enslaved, whether a slave at death or a citizen, whether a soldier or a civilian (all figures are drawn from Shaw 1991). About 30 per cent of all these inscriptions from the city of Rome commemorate the age at death of children. Both free and slave populations are recorded in a similar manner. When broken down into gender groups, it becomes clear that in Rome there was a preference to commemorate the age at death of males over females (Shaw 1991: 69). This is the type of gendered commemoration that we expect within Roman society; it points to a greater importance in the use of chronological age in connection with male over female children.

The use of chronological age in inscriptions indicates a need to record the exact ages of individuals. Although at times far from accurate, these ages point to the desire to utilise a system of exactitude with the potential for the sophisticated recording of a person's age (on accuracy see Duncan-Jones 1977). However, the level of inaccuracy can inform us about who was using chronological age and what it may have been used for. The pattern of inaccuracy would appear to have been directly affected by the status and gender of the person. High levels of inaccuracy were found for all groups in Italy with the exception of the local town councillors (Duncan-Jones 1977: Table 2). The fact that a minimum age for office was applied in the majority of cases may have caused the age of all councillors to be recorded officially – for example from Canusium a list of councillors and their ages survive (CIL9.338; Mouritsen 1998). Attempts have been made to reconstruct the demography of the elite from this data, but it is undercut by the fact that we do not know at what age the members became town councillors (Parkin 1992: 137–8; contra Duncan-Jones 1990). It is notable that other epigraphic evidence reports the early entry to the town council (e.g. *CIL*10.846 N. Popidius Celsinus to the council of Pompeii at the age of six). What is clear though is that the age of officials serving a city was displayed in public. Hence, we would expect a reduction in the level of age rounding in the funerary epigraphy. Age rounding has been seen as more acute in female commemoration and was greater in the inscriptions recording slaves and freed slaves than for those of citizens (Duncan-Jones 1977). Evidently exactitude was not achieved, but there is an emphasis on exact chronological age – however inaccurate that might actually be. The pattern of age-rounding across the empire shows a higher level of inaccuracy than reported ages in censuses this century in countries such as Turkey in 1945 (Duncan-Jones 1977: 345–6). Hence, we may be looking at a different approach to chronological age than that utilised in our own time. Nevertheless, the ability to know your age or your offspring's age (if inaccurately) and to display it was still important, as the evidence has shown.

So far, we have identified a pattern within the commemorative inscriptions that points to a greater use of chronological age in relationship to male children and greater accuracy in the recording of the ages of the elite generally. This might simply reflect a wider use of chronological age generally by males or a greater retrospective recording of male life spans epigraphically. The prediction of chronological age was also utilised in the calculation of tax to be paid on bequests in the form of an annual return on property. The bequest had to conform to the *Lex Falcidia* that ensured that no more than three quarters of a testator's estate was left as a legacy to anyone apart from the principal heir. To do this, Roman lawyers needed to calculate what life expectancy could be (*Dig.*35.2.68 pr). This was defined by the following formula: any person under twenty years old was to receive maintenance for a further thirty years: a person between twenty and twenty-five – twenty-eight years' maintenance; a person between twenty five and thirty – twenty-five years' maintenance; a person between thirty and thirty-five – twenty-two years' maintenance; a person between thirty-five and forty – twenty years' maintenance; a person between forty and fifty – as many years' maintenance as there are left to sixty; a person between fifty and fifty-five – nine years' maintenance; a person between fifty-five and sixty – seven years' maintenance; and anyone over sixty – five years' maintenance. This formula, given by Ulpian, has a sophistication to it that has caused some scholars to see it as evidence of demographic awareness and a reflection of Rome's actual population structure. Such assumptions have effectively been demolished by Parkin (1992: 27–41; compare Saller 1994: 13–5). However, what the evidence does point to is the utilisation of chronological age that is divided into bands of five and ten years. In other words, the typical units of age-rounding found in inscriptions. To utilise the calculation, all you needed to know was into which band the person fell (except in the case of forty to fifty year olds). The lack of exactitude may have

12

suited the use of age, as can be seen in the reported census returns or statements of age in funerary epigraphy.

Ulpian's formula is also a measurement of the life course that begins with a wide band from birth to twenty followed by a series of smaller bands through adulthood and finally a general band for all those over sixty, with little expectancy of life beyond that age. This is a cultural perception of human ageing in relationship to chronological age that emphasises a separation of adulthood from the dependency of childhood and old age. In practice lawyers tended to make the calculation on the basis of those under thirty with expectation of receipt for a further thirty years and those over thirty with receipt of use until they were sixty. The distinction between the two groups reflects a limited period of use up to a maximum of thirty years in all cases. A figure which seems a little arbitrary, but actually was based on three stages of life – childhood and youth, adulthood, and old age.

Chronology may measure a person's age, allow for a calibration of the stages of life and locate the points of change within the life course. Underlying this, whatever predictive value we may find in the legal evidence, are the basic cultural expectations of human growth and ageing. These in many ways override considerations of chronological age. It seems as though the mathematical measurement of someone's exact age (often inaccurately) might be related back to concepts of a person's future that were bound up with astrological prediction. The time of birth was crucial for any such prediction (e.g. Suet.*Aug*.5, 94.12). The publication of Augustus' horoscope had a crucial role in the legitimation of his new rule at the end of the first century BC (Barton 1994: 40–7). The appearance of age on epitaphs expressed in terms of years, months, days and even hours, alerts us to the significance of the hour as well as the day of birth. An individual's ability to recall this information accurately would vary according to status and gender, as we have seen. What is apparent from all the ancient evidence is that many simply did not report their own age or the age of others accurately, but that does not mean there was not a concept of chronological age at Rome.

Human growth

Many authors writing on the subject of the Roman family (e.g. Treggiari 1991a: 40) have assumed that biological development at Rome was the same as a modern twentieth-century Western European pattern. For example, the age of menarche is assumed to have been at about thirteen or fourteen at Rome, along the lines of the growth curves of modern Western populations (see critique by Hopkins 1965). However, this should be challenged on the grounds that physical anthropologists have found a variation in the age of menarche and fertility in modern populations. The lowest fertility identified in the late twentieth century is that of the !Kung hunter gatherers (Howell 1979; for comparison the Canadian Hutterites have the highest known rate of fertility: Hostetler 1974; Bennett 1967). It was found amongst the !Kung that menstruation did not occur when body weight became reduced after giving birth (Howell 1979: 90–92; Huffman 1978; Morgan 1990: 106–17). Similarly, nutrition and fat retention have been shown to be key factors in the development of fertility and the age of menarche in adolescent females in the West (Frisch and McArthur 1974; Nardi 1981). In another study, Eveleth (1979) found a variation of menarche from just over twelve years for females in Istanbul to between fifteen and sixteen for Transkei Bantu hunter gatherers. The study by Eveleth also identified a significant variation of the age of menarche according to wealth, and found that it occurred earlier in urban as opposed to rural situations. This would suggest that residents in cities have easier access to food generally and food relief in times of food crisis or famine, which would have promoted faster human growth and biological development within urban populations generally. A key factor emerges from these studies for that of the Roman life course: biological development varies according to a person's socio-economic situation, hence we should not regard either human growth or the life course as a standard biological experience. Many variations in growth and biological development may be related to nutrition and disease in childhood (on nutrition see Garnsey 1999: 43–61). The greater security in terms of access to food and immunity to disease would have prevented the disruption of growth in childhood.

However, where we position the experience of human growth and its variety at Rome is open to debate. Human growth and biological development varies and need not be the same for different historical times and situations. Short (1976) has used statistical data from the nineteenth century to highlight the changes in chronological age in relationship to biological development. The reduction of the age of menarche in Norway, from seventeen-and-a half to thirteen-and-a half between 1840 and 1950, is a classic example of biological change through time (Short 1976: 6; May 1978). More controversial perhaps are his observations on male growth. He cites evidence for the age at which males reached maximum height in Britain as twenty-six in 1926, whereas fifty years later a male reached maximum height by seventeen. Certainly, evidence from the anthropometric surveys from the late nineteenth-century in Britain points to a later completion of growth than the current population experiences. The pattern found in the surveys fits that of other human growth trends with the important difference that the period of growth is extended beyond the age of eighteen. In some cases the Anthropometric Committee found that growth continued until at least twenty-one, but concluded that it was complete in all cases by twenty-five. There was also a vast variation in the rates of growth according to access to nutrition, and psychological conditions of childhood. These factors caused a working class male child at the age of fourteen to be seven inches shorter and nearly twenty five pounds lighter than a child of the same age from the aristocracy (Galton *et al.* 1883: 296; compare Roberts 1876). In effect, physical growth and appearance in terms of height varied according to factors other than chronological age. Biological development later in the life course can also vary. Frisch (1978) demonstrates the variation in the chronological age of menopause; for example, in nineteenth-century Manchester this occurred at age forty-five to fifty, an age at which Hutterite women today are still giving birth to children. The implications of such variation of human growth, biological development, and ageing according to a person's socio-economic position in society suggest that the variation in the distribution of wealth should be subtly reflected in the overall physique of a human population. The variation across society might suggest that biological development, rather than chronological age, may be of greater significance to the structure of a society's demographic pattern and cultural perception of ageing.

There is no anthropometric data from the Roman period of a similar type to that of the nineteenth century in Britain. However, there is evidence that is indicative of a different rate of biological growth at Rome alongside a variation in the life course according to gender. The nearest thing we have to an anthropometric survey is the excavation of a late Roman cemetery at Poundbury (Molleson 1993). The analysis of the 1600 skeletons from the site demonstrated that growth in both females and males occurred some two years later than in modern European populations, and also stressed that teenage death in females may have occurred due to early pregnancy and death in childbirth (Molleson 1993: 180). Such a patterning within this large body of skeletal evidence points to both early marriage for women and a slower rate of growth for both men and women. This pattern gives credence to Galen's view (17.2.791; 792) that male puberty began at fourteen and ended at twenty-five (a text discussed by Eyben 1972). This view of human development fits the Roman cultural assumption that character could be determined through the observation of the body (see Gleason 1990, 1995), and a further assumption that in terms of mental capacity a person was not capable prior to the completion of their physical growth. More importantly, what we conclude from this discussion of human growth is that it varies, according to access to resources, with a result that the elite literally grew up faster: a factor which would have reinforced their social status relative to others from outside the elite.

Cultural explanations

The stages of the life course for females and males were constructed very differently. The female life course seldom appears in the literature that characterises the different stages. In part, this reflects the total dominance of male authors within the surviving body of literary sources. The stages of the male life course ultimately rested on Aristotle's division of man as a youth, an adult and an old man (*Rhet*.2.12–4; Chandler 1948; see Garland 1990 on life course in Classical Greece) and the discussion of the type of voice and speech in rhetoric. What is seen, though, is a series of changes, which by analogy were compared to those of plants (Sen.*Ep*.121.15–17). Just as a plant began life as a soft and moist shoot, and later developed through maturity to produce grain that was hard and dry, a person was seen to have matured in the same manner. Biological development and human socialisation could be utilised to characterise these stages. An infant was distinguished from older children initially by a lack of teeth and an inability to utter words. In the next stage, the boy or *puer* was able to speak and socialise with other children. He grew older and reached the next stage, that of the youth associated with an inability to grow a beard. Once a beard had grown the youth became a man before reaching the final stage, that of the old man, made clear through the degeneration of fitness and health (Horace *Ars Poetica* 156–8). The other side of these stages was the development of character associated with these visible biological changes. Horace saw the child as subject to rapid mood swings and simply not in control of either character or mind. For him, the youth, physically training on the Campus Martius and enjoying hunting on horseback, was mentally soft and could have been bent to evil. The youth had no control over his expenditure and, although he had strong desires, he would often change his mind. The adult in contrast was a man who aimed to be consistent, sought wealth and friendship and was enslaved to his ambitions. The life course ends with the old man, mentally and physically slowed by age, and only capable of condemning the actions of the young (Horace *Ars Poetica* 156–8).

However, there were alternatives to these general observations of development that attempted to relate these fundamental cultural concepts to the measurement of chronological age rather than physical and mental maturity. The linkage made in these cases was directly related to that of the Roman census, the source of information about the age of the population and a means for the categorisation of the population according to age. Varro (*ap. Censor* 14), writing at the end of the first century BC, provides a definition of five different stages each associated with a fifteen year time span: *puerita* until fifteen; *adulscentia* from fifteen until thirty; *juventus* from thirty to forty-five; *seniores* from forty-five to sixty; and *senectus* from sixty until death. The link with the census is also apparent in Livy (1.43) in the division between the *seniores* over forty-six years who defended the city of Rome and the *juniores* who went out to fight in battles. This mathematical division blurs the distinction of beardless youth and adult by extending the period of *adulscentia* to thirty, and creates a threefold distinction in the adult population. There was more than one way of accounting for the stages of life and these accounts develop to include new intellectual developments such as the importance of mathematics. This is made clear by Ptolemy's account (4.10.203–7; for discussion see Eyben 1972; Néraudau 1984) of the life course made in the second century AD with a division into seven stages associated with seven astrological signs. Until four the child, as we have seen, is moist and soft, growing quickly, and mentally changeable under the rule of the moon. Then from four up to fourteen, Mercury takes over, a period in which the child was seen to become articulate, to learn, to develop a personality and to learn the first physical exercises. Puberty marked the change to the sign of Venus and the frenzied, uncontrolled sexuality of an eight year period until the age of twenty-two that also saw the person as capable of only ingenuous errors of judgement. The middle stage of life, from twenty-two until forty-one, was under the Sun with control and mastery of actions, and a desire for glory, reputation and position. The fifth stage, from forty-one to fifty-six, was commanded by Mars. The passage of time was now apparent as the man was past his prime, and a severity and misery of life became expected. After fifty-six, a renunciation of labour, exposure to danger, and turmoil under Jupiter was seen to produce the aged advisor to others who carefully considered his thoughts. After man's sixty-eighth year, the rest of life was run by Saturn: the body cooled and gradually declined.

Although Ptolemy developed an astrological and chronological dimension to the stages of the life course, the explanation and characteristics of the individual stages were not so different from those of Varro and Horace already discussed, which ultimately follow on from Aristotle's division of life into the three stages – youth, adult and old – in his discussion of rhetoric (*Rhet.*2.12–14). Thus, although there was consideration given to chronological age and the addition of astrological derivation for the stages themselves, the cultural expectations of behaviour and explanation of that behaviour in relationship to age remained fairly constant and did not radically change. Ultimately, it continued to be based on a division between the behaviour of the adult from that of the child and the old man. The intersection of these stages with chronological age provides a calibration of the cultural perspective of a person's stage of life. As we have seen on tombstones, chronological age was in use at Rome and was considered as a means of definition of a person in the census. The technical writers, including Varro and Ptolemy, developed the intersection of the life course and chronological age to new mathematical and, by association, astrological heights. Whether these were shared by the rest of the population is unclear, but it is evident that they drew on the cultural view of the life course in the construction of their calibrated models based on mathematics and astrology.

The cultural view of age or a person's stage of life influenced the way in which they were viewed at Rome. A person's behaviour is fitted around a set of preconceived patterns. For example, Suetonius' biography of the emperor Nero is highly stylistic. Nero, after he murdered his mother in the year in which he first shaved his beard, performed all the vices of a youth out of control: drinking, assaulting individuals at night and lacking control of his sexuality (see Eyben 1993 for further discussion). In a similar way, in our source material, the emperor Claudius has withered from being a personality to an old man commanded by his slaves and freedmen (see Parkin 1997,

1999). What we see in these two examples is an explanatory framework that stylised the actions of individuals (see Laurence 2000). This works in a similar way to the idea that men and women were characterised by a set of values or expected behaviour according to their gender, which need not be wholly conformed to (Edwards 1993: 63–97; Fischler 1994). However, age and gender should be understood in conjunction to allow us to focus on the individual as male or female at a certain age and to understand their behaviour at that point in the life course within these parameters. The emphasis on the interrelationship of age and gender in terms of agency or individual empowerment needs to be recognised (Laurence 1997). Individuals held different positions within the social structure according to age as well as gender. This is not an unusual phenomenon, but one that the literature on ancient sexuality has not come to recognise or pay attention to (compare Rossi 1985). The division male:female that presents a dominance of the male over female at Rome in terms of power is to our mind simplistic. There is evidence within the ancient source material for a more complicated interrelationship between older females and younger males, which is particularly prominent in the early Roman empire. Similarly, the power of younger females to influence and control their older husbands needs to be highlighted as well. The differential in the age of female and male first marriage (about 14 and 25 respectively) created a situation in which the relationship between different sexes lacked symmetry in age. This factor causes the interrelation of age with gender to be seen as critical to the understanding of the social relations of both the Roman family and, at a wider level, between families via marriage (see Chapters 6 and 7). The explanation or creation of behaviour according to someone's age is clearly ideological, but it was a mode of thought that was utilised in practice at Rome. More difficult to recover is whether individuals consciously adapted their behaviour to fit the cultural model. It is clear, though, that we find this mode of representation not just in texts but also in a number of monuments, for example the arch at Benevento and the Ara Pacis in Rome (Currie 1996; Laurence 2000). These various examples all illustrate the way in which age as much as gender played an important role in the creation of the individual at Rome.

Our major interest in this book is the cultural construction of the life course and social ageing at Rome. The book begins with an examination of the household in Chapter 2. This was the structure into which children were born and it continued to play a part in structuring the lives of female and male individuals throughout their lives. It is the focus of emotion and provided an initial social world from which a person was socialized gradually into the wider environment of the city. We move from this initial discussion to that of the key stages of life that transformed a newborn child into an adult. Chapter 3 examines the social world and the socialization of the infant and child within the familial structure of the household and the person's kin relations. Chapters 4 and 5 focus on the transitions to adulthood and the processes by which female and male genders were defined at the end of child-hood. These public rites of passage created adults and integrated the child into the world of citizenship or marriage according to their gender. Moving on from the transition to adulthood, we discuss the place of marriage within the life course (Chapter 6) and the role of marriage in the extension of kinship relations (Chapter 7). This major transition altered the lives of individuals so that they became wives and husbands with a view to becoming mothers and fathers. Chapter 8 examines the role of age in the political structures of the republic and empire. In doing so, we identify a fundamental change in the attitude to age and youth following the rise to power of Octavian at the age of nineteen. The unusualness of his age marked him out as different from others, unlike later imitators including Caligula and Nero. Our interest then moves to the old and the experience of old age – a time when the individual was defined as different from the adult in their prime. The penultimate chapter examines the commemoration of a person at the end of their life and the creation of memorials of their identity. This shifts away from the indi-vidual towards the way in which the Romans remembered past lives and created narratives about the past, in other words history itself. Finally, we offer by way of conclusion thoughts on the significance of the life course at Rome for the study of ancient history, archaeology and gerontology.

2

THE LOCATION OF THE
LIFE COURSE

The household

The household was considered by Cicero (*Off*.1.53–5) to have been the bedrock on which Roman society was built. The experience of life was conducted with reference to the home to a far greater extent than to that of the politics of the city in the forum. The forum was an adult male space that had less relevance to women, children and the elderly. The house, in contrast, was the central location for all participants whether young or old, male or female. Some confusion can arise in the discussion of both the house and family, because there is no direct equivalent of these English words in the Latin language of antiquity. The Latin word *familia* covers a range of meanings far wider that that of the close conjugal unit or wider kin group. In legal terms the *familia* was all those under the power of a *paterfamilias*. This could include his wife and would certainly include his children and household slaves (Ulpian, *Dig*.50.16.195). The word the Romans used to most nearly equate to a western sense of family was *domus*, which was also used to mean the physical fabric of the house (Saller 1984, 1999). In this chapter our use of the term household refers to the *domus*, both as a physical location and as a definition of the group that inhabits it. We must always be cognisant of the constant presence of slaves within the household as providers of services and silent witnesses to the lives of those within the house. Confusion can also arise over the way we see the head of the household or *paterfamilias* in relationship to both the property of the household and his family. It has recently been shown (Saller 1999) that the Latin term *paterfamilias* was most often used to refer to an estate owner and could even be used as a legal term to define that owner, whether male or female. However, in the works of many modern scholars, the term is utilised to indicate head of a family or simply as the father of sons.

In this chapter, we wish to set out the centrality of the structure of the household to an understanding of the life course. It was a constant throughout the life of a person: as a child, they grew up within its structure, as adults they left their childhood home, but might return, in the case of daughters, upon divorce; at marriage, a new household was created with the groom conducting his new wife into their new home where, having raised their own children,

Plate 2.1 View across the *atrium* of a house in Herculaneum showing the *impluvium* in the centre and the door into the street beyond it.

they might grow old. Hence, the house was the physical setting for much of the time that constituted a person's existence. However, it needs to be stressed at the outset that the personnel within the household may have changed through the life course due to death and divorce (see Chapters 6 and 10).

Central to all lives at Rome was the household structure and the emotion attached to the location of one's birth, childhood and adult life and, as we will argue, the nature of a house constructed and reflected the identity of its occupants. Houses also encapsulated a family's memory or history over the previous generations. Cicero (*Leg.*2.3) viewed his family home in Arpinum as a place that was changing alongside the family's fortunes. His grandfather had lived simply in surroundings that did not possess the architectural sophistication of his own time in the middle of the first century BC. It was his father who had developed the property in keeping with changes in architectural fashion and a need to establish suitable surroundings for himself as a local magnate. The house itself, although defined as a cultural object with a similar structure across Rome and the Italian peninsula, when seen individually was subject to change, elaboration, partition and re-sale. Equally, it should be remembered that the rich in Roman Italy did not simply own one house, they could have many. For example, Cicero regarded his birth place in Arpinum as home, but also owned houses in Rome, Tusculum and Pompeii. Whether his son and daughter grew up in any one of these houses, they would have experienced a very similar household structure that was

Plate 2.2 Door to a house. This painting from the Naples Museum shows an image of the door to the house with a woman looking out into the street. Nothing can be seen of the house inside.

generic to the organisation of the Roman family. However, it needs to be understood that the form of the Roman house had become more elaborate over Cicero's life course. Indeed, we might suggest that building work and its associated noise was a common experience for those growing up in Rome during the first centuries BC and AD.

The house was the place in which children and wives observed the public world of their father or husband. The glimpse of the formal meetings at the morning *salutatio* between this figure and his friends and clients gave them a glimpse of the outer world of politics, business and the forum. It was here that a child learnt the notations of status and rank, alongside manners and deference to others. The transitions from girl to woman and boy to man were marked by ceremonies within the house and before the household gods. The house and its gods looked on as its inhabitants grew up (Foss 1997) and could be seen to care for the lives of its charges. They, in their turn, revered these gods and embellished the house. The changes of life times were marked on the house's fabric as families grew or gained (or lost) wealth. Its personnel changed with the introduction of outsiders via marriage. The new wife walked into her husband's house and maybe tripped over his children by a previous marriage or was received with hostility by his mother. The possibility of disruption, dysfunction and domestic argument should not be ignored or forgotten when observing the domestic environment of past societies. The Roman home was a place of change and fluidity in terms of occupants, size, decoration, and fortune, but above all a focus of emotion, value and identity (Treggiari 1999).

Viewing the house: creating identity

The pattern of change from houses simply as a place for living to a new form of domestic architecture that sought to impress can be dated to the early first century BC. Livius Drusus, a tribune in 81BC, is recorded as having a discussion with an architect over the design of his house (Vell.Pat.2.14.3). The architect offered to create a house that would have been private and out of the public view. This did not please the owner, who insisted that the design should make his property visible to all. Others were building with this in mind as well – causing the houses of the famous senatorial families in Rome to become objects for the public to gaze at and admire (Cic.*Off.*1.139). However, the best houses of the early first century BC were only a generation later not considered to be within the top one hundred properties (Plin.*HN.*36.110). This can be seen as a change that resulted from a greater emphasis on competitive building of domestic properties, that had caused the original grand houses to be eclipsed. The houses of Rome were changing within the lifetime of a citizen born in that city. These properties of the wealthy in particular, but also the residences of the rest of the population of the city, were a reflection and representation of the inhabitants' status and importance. For most viewers of a residence in Rome, there were a series of signs that revealed the nature of that household. A large palace was appropriate for a successful senator with many clients and *amici* calling on him, but the visitors had to be present to justify the need for such a large property. If a large house appeared deserted or empty, it would show the owner up as attempting to impress the world via his house rather than his own merit (Vitr.6.5.1–2; Cic.*Off.*1.139). Equally, an ostentatious house could have been seen as a sign of unnecessary luxury and of the degenerate lifestyle of its owner. For instance, for a wealthy freed slave to acquire such a property as a signifier of success would have been seen as an attempt to gain acceptability on his part; but, as Petronius cleverly shows us in the *Satyricon*, the house would reveal a level of ostentation that would highlight the display of the owner's wealth rather than his acceptance by the freeborn elite. The key here, as with other indicators of a person's status or personality, was to get it right, and there were many ways to get it wrong. Significantly, for Petronius' audience, it was the freed slave who was emulating what he saw as the ways of the elite and failing to understand the nuances of the language of domesticity. In contrast, those who had spent their childhood as free people within a Roman house had learnt the subtleties of taste from their parents and by observation of visitors to their domestic realm. In learning the code of domesticity, an adult could judge the nature of a person just from a glimpse of the house with its open front door and doorkeeper.

The house and its household were on display and seen by outsiders (Juv.*Sat.*14.59–71). This has caused part of the Roman house, its doorway and atrium or entrance hall, to be seen by modern scholars as public, whereas the rest of the house was a place into which guests caught glimpses, were invited on occasion, or excluded from altogether (see Wallace-Hadrill 1994, 1997). Within sight, but maybe not taking centre stage, in the atrium were the wife and children of the male head of the household. The visitors would also have been seen by the children speaking to their father and the home would have been a context for them to view the actions of their father as a potential source of learning and socialisation. Visitors, arriving later in the day to call on the *matrona* of the house, have a particular role in the socialisation and definition of gender for the daughters of the household.

Age and gender: experiencing domesticity

The house was not simply a vehicle for the display of the personality of its male head, but housed his wife, children and a range of domestic slaves as well. To see the Roman house only in terms of the politics and status of the male adult restricts our vision of the domestic environment. The intersection of the politics of display and the needs of the inhabitants of the household affected their lives and would have developed over a child's lifetime. This was more apparent in the life course of the male child once the *toga virilis* (toga signifying adulthood) had been taken up, and the child had become a young male adult (see Chapter 5). The female child did not experience this side of the politics of the house, because by the time she was in what we call her teens she would be introduced into a new household through marriage (Catul.61.151–80; see Chapter 4). As an adult her control over the domestic environment was limited in terms of the choice of which house or how the house might be arranged, because architecture and the home were provided either by her father, her guardian or her husband throughout her life. Only after marriage and the assertion of a greater degree of independence by women in middle to later middle age can we envisage a greater assertion of her ideas and will in this sphere (see Chapter 6). Males in contrast gained control of their domestic arrangements by their late teens and certainly by the time they were married in their twenties. Architecture was an interest for such men (Nepos *Atticus* 13) and was pursued in adulthood, supposedly to the ruin of many inheritances (Juv.14.86–95).

The archaeology of Pompeii, Herculaneum and other sites in Italy has revealed the structure of Roman houses. They are considerably smaller and less sophisticated than those of the senatorial elite at Rome, but nevertheless illustrate the overall arrangement of domestic environments. The largest house in Pompeii, the house of the Faun, shows us the overall structure of a series of courtyards with rooms distributed around them to create a number of parts to the house that were utilised at different times and for different purposes (Figure 2.1). There is no evidence here for upper floors, since these were not preserved by the eruption of Vesuvius in AD 79 – however they have been shown to have existed in antiquity. The house conforms to a format of two *atria* with a peristyle behind them, which ultimately led to a large monumental garden/peristyle. Dickmann (1997) has demonstrated that the addition of the peristyle to the atrium house created a need for a wider frontage adjacent to the atrium, hence we find in a number of houses with peristyle courtyards the feature of a double atrium towards the front of the

Plate 2.3 View of house in Herculaneum from the street.

house. In order to view or represent the intersection of the family during the day within this space, it is necessary to represent creatively the possible activities that took place within houses similar to that of the House of the Faun. This involves the creation of an ideal *familia* for the household from literary sources. This is done as a heuristic device to illustrate the interaction within Roman houses rather than those that actually took place within the House of the Faun, which now are probably unrecoverable due to the loss of archaeological evidence on and since its excavation. This house anchors the temporal structure of the Roman *familia* within an actual Roman space. To recover the experience of a household structure of slavery, reference will be made to the list of slave occupations found in the *columbarium* (family tomb) of the Statilii at Rome (Joshel 1992: Table 3.2). Hence, although a fiction in some ways, it is an alternative representation to a purely literary approach that does not reconnect the time and space of the Roman house, which survive discretely in

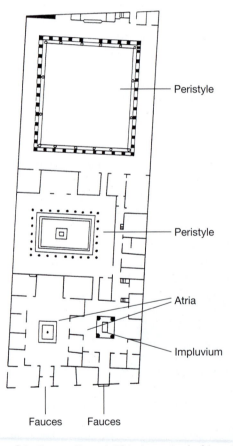

Figure 2.1 Plan of the House of the Faun at Pompei. This shows the double atria, two impluvia and the two peristyle gardens of one of the most extensive houses in Pompei.

texts, and archaeological evidence (see George 1997 on location of slavery within the domestic context).

The time of day affected the way the house was used by its *familia*. Before dawn, the noise of the town awakening would have been heard as clients shuffled to the houses of their patrons for the dawn *salutatio* or ritual start to the day (Hor.*Ep.*2.1.104). Within the house itself, the head of the household was awake in his *cubiculum* (bedroom) and preparing to meet his clients. The slaves cleaned or covered over with sand or saw-dust mud and dog excrement in the atrium prior to the arrival of the guests (Juv.*Sat.*14.59–71). The door-keeper would have been in position ready to open the door to the corridor (*fauces*) that led into the atrium where the clients would be received. At dawn the first clients arrived, close friends were let into the master's *cubiculum* (bedroom) whilst he was dressed by his slave and his beard shaved and hair dressed by another slave. Constantly, there was exchange of questions and answers between the patron and his clients at the same time as signals of superiority and deference that established a client's value or worth with regard to the patron. For the first two hours of the day, this interchange of information, favours and business took place in the house and was noted presumably by a slave secretary (Mart.*Ep.*4.8), before the whole group of clients left the house for the forum with their patron alongside his body-guards and other attendants. As they did so the house changed and again became a place of domesticity.

The question is what happened within the house once the male head of the house had departed since he was not only the head of the household, but, in legal terms, defined the place of his wife, children and slaves within Roman society. The household is without this defining person or agent, the object of interest for literary and legal sources, for much of the day. It is here that we need to rebuild the domestic environment of the family in the absence of the legal definition provided by a male head of the household. The dependence on a particular legalistic view of the social unit or household masks other forms of social activity that took place at that location. It was here that the lives of children and women were acted out, in contrast to that of the male adult away from the house in the public arena of business and politics. How should we view the house now that its head is no longer there?

The house needs to be regarded as more than a place to receive clients in. It has been shown that goods were delivered to the atrium (Atkinson 1914) and this area was also a place for the storage of goods. For example, amphorae were washed in the *impluvium* at the centre of this part of the house (see Figure 2.1). Indeed, rather than the empty house we see today in Pompeii we would have seen goods stored even in places we associate with display, for example the peristyle courtyards of the House of the Faun (Berry 1997). We can imagine goods being delivered throughout the day, but wonder about how they were purchased – were they sold on the doorstep or brought from a shop and by whom? Or were these goods brought to the house from the owner's estates further afield? How were female and male properties linked by marriage but seen as separable in law managed? These questions may not have specific answers in our literary texts, but need to be raised and considered.

The child's view of the house in which he or she grew up is intriguing yet elusive. We can find evidence for children playing in the *atria* of the Roman house (Virg.*Aen.*7.379; Lucr.4.401–4) suggesting that this space was not exclusive to the male head of the household at the *salutatio* or maybe that one atrium in houses with two *atria,* such as the House of the Faun, was utilised for reception and another for other purposes. This has important implications for the intersection between children and adults through the life course. Some modern authors present an image of the infant at birth as discarded by free-born mother and father to a wet nurse and then a *pedagogus* (tutor), with no further interaction between parents and child accounted for (see Chapter 3). If we view the child in the atrium, alongside her or his mother who was not confined to any part of the house (Nepos *Praef.*6–8), we have a situation in which mother and children were in close proximity. However, slaves in the house of the Statilii performed roles as nurses and attendants to children and would seem to have been ever present in a child's world and within close proximity (Joshel 1992: 74–5) – so that the mother's role in child rearing itself may have been limited (Garnsey 1991). The maxim 'The grief of a nurse comes next to that of a mother' summarises the intersection of mother and slave/free childminder in antiquity (Gardner and Wiedemann 1991: 47; for discussion see Chapter 3 below). What is unclear is where in the house these interrelationships were constructed. However, there is no reason why child care should be excluded from any part of the house, including the atrium.

Alongside the domestic setting of childhood, slaves would have worked in some rooms in the house to fulfill their occupational titles. For example, in the household of the Statilii, there were social organisers, financial agents, administrators, secretaries and copyists following up the exchanges made during the *salutatio* or acting on information brought from the forum by runners and messengers. The household was as much a business as it was a domestic or political arena (Parkins 1997). These were the people who kept the accounts of the business of the *paterfamilias*, not just within the household itself but also those matters relating to his or her estates that may have included the birth of slaves, agricultural production, training of draught animals, punishment of slaves, money spent, fires at other properties and the actions of freed slaves of the *paterfamilias* (Petr.*Sat.*53). The work day for these slaves lasted from dawn until dusk with an hour's break at midday (Laurence 1994: 132).

The wife of the male head of the house had a prominence once her husband had left the house. She, it is assumed, supervised arrangements within the household, for instance of the social organisers, entertainers, gardeners and others within the house of the Statilii. She may have ostentatiously woven cloth in the public part or central area of the house, so that all visitors could view her morality or the reflected morality of her husband in her behaviour (Liv.1.57.9; Tibull.1.3.83–9), perhaps accompanied by her daughters in this activity. She was attended wherever she went in the house by the various room attendants assigned to each of its parts (Joshel 1992: 74–5). It is not impossible that the wife and her household slaves used a separate part of the house from that of her husband. The appearance of double *atria* houses in Pompeii such as the House of the Faun suggests this possibility, and it is also evident in the imperial palace at Rome that members of that family had separate houses and households of slaves on the Palatine hill, even when related by marriage. During the day, visiting the baths with her attendants and masseuse, or another part of the city in a litter, involved another set of slaves devoted specifically for these purposes, as can be seen from the evidence for the organisation of slaves in the house of the Statilii.

The head of the household's public business in the forum was usually completed by midday, whence he went to the baths followed by his clients (Mart.3.36; 10.70). At the baths he met members of his household including bath attendants to guard his clothes, masseurs, and other slaves from his household. Petronius' fictional account, the *Satyricon* (26 following), of Trimalchio's bathing and return to his house for dinner is instructive for seeing how the household slaves interacted with their master and invited guests to the house. Trimalchio was observed first at the baths exercising with a ball attended by youthful long haired slaves and two eunuchs. He then went into the baths, first the hot room and then the cold room, followed by a scrape down by three masseurs. Having completed the procedures of bathing, he was carried in a litter back to his house with slaves clearing the way for the litter in front. His guests for dinner followed behind. On arrival, the guests found that their host was no longer in view. They moved past a doorman and encountered a slave who attended the atrium of the house – who explained the significance of the wall paintings when asked. Having examined the atrium, the guests moved through to the *triclinium* or dining room. Here they discovered a *dispensator* or steward attending to the household accounts – there was a calendar set up on which the master's dinner appointments were marked. The *triclinium* was then quickly converted from steward's office into a dining room. The guests sat down, at which point the slave attendants multiplied; only later does Trimalchio enter. It is notable that at dinner his wife was present. However, the house had returned to its former state, one that included the presence of the male head of the household. It is significant that during his absence the steward had moved into the dining room to run the household's accounts, illustrating how the rooms of the Roman house could have changed in function according to the time of the day. Similarly, the atrium was a place of reception for guests in the early hours of the day and later for dinner guests, but in between this room was utilised for play by children, domestic labour by women and the reception of goods – all observed by the steward from the adjacent *triclinium*. Whilst the *paterfamilias* was out, labour did not cease in the house. Cooks and provisioners prepared food to be consumed on his return, so that the food would have been ready at the right moment to impress his guests. After dinner, the readers and entertainers were employed in recitations that they had learnt and practiced during the day. Finally, in the dark the guests leave and the house becomes silent, yet is still attended by its slaves.

Not every day was like this. Many days in the Roman calendar forbade business in the forum, and there were days when the head of the house did not need to attend to such public business. Instead, he may have remained at home at work with the *dispensator* or simply at leisure. These days would have included a greater interaction with his wife, children and members of the household, and provide a contrast with the normative structure.

Sex and privacy

An element that is seldom discussed within a spatial context is sexual activity within the household itself. Much of the modern literature on Roman sexuality has highlighted the adult male or husband's numerous sexual partners apart from his wife (e.g. Parker 1998: 54–5 on 'the normal male'), because legally sex with any female who was neither freeborn nor married was not limited for a male (Williams 1999: 15–19). In contrast, in Roman law his wife's only sexual partner should have been her husband. This creates an illusion in which it is assumed that married males had sex with numerous partners, including the household slaves. However, the design and nature of the Roman house, alongside the visibility of the free born members of the household within the community, may have placed a limitation on sexual activity (note criticism of those who break this taboo e.g. Plu.*Sul*.35–6). Unlike the modern world, the house and one's family were the subject of public scrutiny. Activity within the household was on view and the home was far from what we would call private – even though the Romans would call it secret. Only one part of the Roman's home world remained exclusive and to our mind private – the *cubiculum* of either the husband or wife. It has been shown by Riggsby (1997: 50) in a detailed study of the use of the Latin word *cubiculum* that this was an expectation of the community itself, but the one exception to this general norm was sex within the *cubiculum*. Seneca (*Ep*.83.20; Riggsby 1997: 37) is critical of the lustful man who cannot wait until he is in the *cubiculum* to have sex. Once within that room, in contrast to the other rooms of the house, there was privacy and an absence of slaves (Riggsby 1997). This was the room in which sexual encounters occurred, so, for example, a wife's entry into her husband's *cubiculum* publicly marked the consummation of the marriage (Riggsby 1997: 37). The fact that the wife and her husband had separate *cubicula* established the possibility, however, of adultery and of sex with others within the household both by the wife and the husband (Riggsby 1997: 38). Equally, for the visitor or young male adult within the household, sex with slaves is portrayed as occurring within their *cubiculum* (Apul.*Met.*2.15–6). These were places of privacy and secrecy that could cause a husband, absent for much of the day, to wonder about the relationships between his own wife and children and the slaves within his household (Juv.*Sat.*3.109–15). The *cubiculum* as a place of rest and of privacy could have been utilised during the day, but anyone entering that room would have been observed by the slaves and others within the household. Hence although sex itself was private, the occurrence of sex was observed by the household. This would suggest that a wife could have been aware of her husband's sexual activity with others, but equally the household could have obscured what occurred within his *cubiculum*.

Adultery, or at least allegations of adultery, are relatively common in classical literature (Treggiari 1991a: 507–8 gives a list) and would appear to have occurred within the household of one or other partner. Maybe the most famous unproven case is that of Julius Caesar's wife Pompeia and the young Publius Clodius. This case reveals the nature of the household and the suspicion and observation of his wife. According to Plutarch, the house was large but Pompeia was under close observation by Caesar's mother Aurelia (Plu.*Caes.*9–10). Hence, even though Clodius and Pompeia sought to meet in private within the large house, they were prevented from so doing by the strict observation of Aurelia and presumably of slaves within the household. Such close observation and scrutiny led to the audacious plan by Pompeia and Clodius to meet during the festival of the Bona Dea held at Caesar's house and attended exclusively by women. Clodius, a beardless youth, was let into the house dressed as a flute girl. However, his voice gave him away as a man and he was chased from the house (Plu.*Caes.*9–10; Suet.*Jul.*6; Cic.*Att.*1.12). Subsequently, Clodius was charged with sacrilege and Pompeia was divorced because 'Caesar's wife should be above suspicion'. The extreme nature of the measures taken by Clodius and Pompeia to meet reveals the level of observation that a house permitted of an individual member.

Household and life course

The household did not remain static throughout a person's life. It was changed through marriage, birth, divorce and death of its members. Julius Caesar's well documented life provides a model, if not a typical one, of the changes that could occur. Prior to wearing the *toga virilis*, he had been betrothed to Cossutia, who was from a very wealthy equestrian family (Suet.*Jul.*1). However, when his father died and he took up the *toga virilis*, he broke this off and married Cornelia daughter of Cinna (who had held the consulship four times). This marriage resulted in the birth of his daughter Julia, who presumably was part of his household until her marriage with Pompey in 59 BC (Suet.*Jul.*20–21). His wife died in 69 BC (Suet.*Jul.*6; Plu.*Caes.*5) and he married Pompeia, the daughter of Quintus Pompeius and granddaughter of Sulla. The tension between his mother and the new wife is clear; and we could expect tension between stepmother and daughter as well. (This type of tension can, at any rate, be seen between Cicero's virgin bride Publilia and his daughter Tullia (Plu.*Cic.*41), who was in her early thirties.) The divorce of Pompeia in 61 BC left the household without a wife and in any case Caesar was in Spain. Presumably, the house was mothballed or continued to be run by his mother Aurelia. On his return, he was betrothed to the daughter of Servilius Caepio, but married Calpurnia the daughter of Lucius Piso in 59 BC (Suet.*Jul.*21). At about the same time, Julia married Pompey. This arrangement removed the daughter from the household by marriage and introduced a new wife into the household structure simultaneously. Calpurnia remained Caesar's wife until his death in 44 BC (Suet.*Jul.*81). The wife in the household was, as we have seen, under observation to prevent the possibility or even the suspicion of adultery. The latter reflected on the husband and was seen as a cause for divorce.

In contrast, the male adulterer was a figure celebrated (Suet.*Jul.*51) and the seduction of other men's wives may have been a means of moral attack on their integrity (Suet.*Jul.*50; Plu.*Caes.*14; *Pomp.*47). Female adultery, at least during the Republic, resulted in the loss of *dignitas* to the wife's husband. This creates a link between the private world of the house or *cubiculum* and the public persona of the *paterfamilias*. Adultery was not simply a private affair, but had an effect in the political realm as well – the house that appeared to all in the city to be admired was shamed by the actions of a wife. As a result, the means to remedy the situation was to remove the wife from the house by divorce – an action approved of by others and seen to re-establish a reputation (Cic.*Att.*1.12). Not surprisingly, the widow or single woman in charge of a house and without a husband was viewed with suspicion (Cic.*Cael.*48–9; see Chapter 6). The later Augustan marriage and adultery laws regulated the effects of adultery and ensured that adultery resulted in divorce or the re-establishment of honour within the household. Equally the law may have curtailed the extent to which this form of shame or dishonour could have been utilised and exploited by political enemies. This would have legally protected Augustus' public *familia*, but in fact did little to prevent his humiliation in 2 BC on the discovery of the adultery of his daughter Julia. Under the marriage laws, women under the age of fifty were expected to remarry after a brief period of mourning. This would have curtailed the possibilities of households run by independent widows (such as Clodia; Cic.*Cael.*48–9). In effect, the laws regulated the politics of shame in an attempt to eradicate or at least regulate the outcome of sex outside marriage or with a freeborn person.

The experience of the household changes through the life course and varies according to gender. Childhood within the house of a *paterfamilias* featured the exclusion from certain parts of the house at certain times according to the adult activities taking place in those rooms or spaces. The male youth prior to marriage was involved in the adult activities associated with the *salutatio*, the reception of guests and dining. He may also have had sex with slaves within the house itself (Catul.61.127–31). That relationship was curtailed upon marriage to a woman from another house. Indeed, at marriage or even before the youth may have moved out of the parental home to set up a new household. In contrast, the female child upon maturity left the house to join a new household as wife. As we have seen in the case of Julius Caesar, that household could contain potentially hostile members of the husband's family – mothers or children. Those just married were subject to change via the birth of children, death of a wife in childbirth or adultery and its associated divorce. The latter two aspects reveal the household as a structure that was evolving through the life course and far from static. It should also be pointed out that the house itself may have physically changed or the entire *familia* may have relocated to another house purchased or inherited. The remarriage of the head of the household created a new structure for the children of the previous marriage. There is also the possibility of further marriage. The divorced wives left the house behind and the children with it. These children would reside within the house until, if female, in their early teens or, if male, in their twenties. Once they had left the home of their father, the house would gradually change as the *paterfamilias* reached the age of sixty and relinquished the more public side of life. The house received less visitors and eventually the male head of the household died, frequently leaving his wife to live as widow within it.

The schema links the house to the age and ageing of its male *paterfamilias*, but it should be remembered that there were other trajectories of ageing that were also present. The household slaves were becoming steadily older, or could have been freed according to the will of the *paterfamilias*. Some slaves were born and died within the same house, others were brought and introduced into the existing structure. The *columbaria* of the Roman elite families record the deaths of their slaves and commemorate their presence in the household. The ageing of slaves and their deaths suggests there was a need to replace them with others. However, the identity of these slaves and freedmen was tied into the concept of the *familia* or household belonging to the *paterfamilias*. His personality or actions determined the nature or age of the household. After all, it belonged to him. His wife, in committing adultery, brought shame to him. The house ideally reflected his personality and honour, just as its inhabitants did whether slaves, children or his wife.

3

THE BEGINNING OF LIFE

Infancy and childhood

The Roman view of childhood was complex: on the one hand Roman parents abandoned unwanted children while on the other they saw their offspring as vulnerable and in need of protection. An overarching picture emerges from the sources of the child as an unformed being that required shaping for adult life. This shaping involved all aspects of the experience of childhood, from the physical moulding of the body to socialisation and education for entry into the adult world. Within this spectrum adults perceived children both as savages in need of civilising and simultaneously as individuals with the virtues and qualities of grown-ups. Romans were no less ambivalent and inconsistent in their views of children than present day society and a single author can show both detachment and sentimentality towards children in their work. The corollary of the desire to mould is the desire to control. The notion of control is fundamental to understanding the Roman idea of childhood. It was a time when control and guidance by adults was considered essential, a time when the child was in the power of adults. This is underlined by the fact that children are often associated in the Roman mind with other groups who lack the ability of self-control: women, slaves, the insane, barbarians. Romans writing about children assumed ideals of the over-riding power of the father and of the state; this informed all their opinions and is the point from which to measure perceived moments of indulgence and sentimentality.

The difficulty in studying childhood in the past is that our view is always mediated by the adult world. The child's experience of its own world is absent. There is a dangerous tendency always to compare family behaviour in the past to that of the present, with the implicit assumption that temporal progress creates an improved situation to that of previous eras. Within any given community today a multiplicity of attitudes towards children and child-rearing exist; these are dependent on the cultural, social and economic background and environment of parents and their own social expectations. Childcare in the West today is highly varied, ranging from the highly child-centred to gross abuse. It is also a matter of political and social debate. The range of care within a single family may differ from child to child as the family members and environment fluctuates. The difficulty with examining

34

Roman childhood is that we have a very un-nuanced view of it. Despite the fact that we have a number of diverse sources from which to construct a picture of Roman childhood, it is nigh impossible to create any coherent view. Whether the source is legal, medical, literary or iconographic, it was produced by the dominant adult male elite who were not necessarily directly involved in day to day child rearing, but were instrumental in making the decisions that affected a child's life. Inevitably the children we know most about are those of the elite. However, even with this group it is difficult to trace them from the cradle to puberty. We can, however, highlight those times in their lives where they received most attention from adults, although these adults might not necessarily be their parents; for children of lower status and slaves we can infer certain practices but little more. (See Bradley 1991: 103–24; Rawson 1966; Wiedemann 1989: 154–56.)

It has become customary to begin any text on childhood with a mention of Philippe Ariès, and for authors to position themselves with regard to his influential work, *Centuries of Childhood* (1962). The main thesis of this work is that childhood is a relatively modern invention and the separateness of childhood as a stage of life is not evident in the West, or France in this particular case, until the eighteenth century (discussed by Burton 1989; Wilson 1980; Dixon 1991; Cunningham 1995: 7–18; Garnsey 1991). For those who accepted the Ariès view, the study of childhood at Rome came to be associated with the idea that the Romans were indifferent to their children. In addition, by taking a literal view of the rights of *patria potestas* (power of the father) in conjunction with the prevalence of practices such as abandonment, wet-nursing and swaddling, children were considered to be routinely physically, sexually and emotionally abused by parents and carers generally indifferent to childcare or their children (e.g. DeMause 1974). It is not the intention of this chapter to address these arguments in depth as many recent studies have really laid them to rest. The 'indifference' debate can only be sustained if one takes a very one-sided view of the evidence, ignores its cultural and socio-economic context and makes comparison with a modern western ideal of parenting to highlight the perceived irresponsibility of the Roman social system (cf. Harris 1994; Rawson 1991, Garnsey 1991; Dixon 1991, 1992). Childhood was undeniably perceived by the Romans as a separate stage of the life course and associated with particular rituals, codes of behaviour, personnel and emotions. Adults expected certain types of behaviour of children and children were raised and moulded to suit the status in life to which they were born.

Definition

The definition of what it meant to be a child in the Roman world is not simple, although it is tempting to be simplistic about it (e.g. DeMause 1974). Chronologically it was the period between birth and puberty, legally defined as twelve for a girl and fourteen for a boy (Gaius *Inst.* 1.196). However this time-span was based on social custom and tradition rather than chronology or biology (see Chapter 1). In Roman law all offspring, no matter what their age, were in the power of their father until his death, or legal 'emancipation'. i.e. a father might release a child from his power for a particular reason, for instance to allow him to accept an inheritance. This meant that in the eyes of the law a man of say, thirty-five, with a living father, was, unless 'emancipated', still a child in terms of financial dealings, receipt of inheritances, etc. Demography and social custom mitigated against this, but in the eyes of the law a Roman male was not independent until the death of his father. A woman would be *sui iuris* (legally independent) on the death of her father (or husband, see Chapter 6) but this nominal legal independence was curtailed by the existence of *tutela mulieris* (guardianship of women; see Gardner 1986: 5–29). Legal texts reveal the anxieties of adults about the place and role of children in society so, while they may reveal in passing commonly held attitudes about the physical and mental capabilities of children, their prime concern was with the transmission of status, property and inheritance. The law addressed both those in power and those who were independent, that is those who were freeborn but fatherless. For those who were outside of paternal control a series of guardians were appointed whose duties and responsibilities varied according to the age of their charge. Fatherless children under seven were considered too young to deal with any matters pertaining to property or business and were assigned a guardian to deal with these matters for them. The guardian would be named by the father in his will, or fall to the nearest male agnates, or, if those mechanisms failed, a tutor may have been appointed by the urban praetor. As the child grew he or she would be allowed to assume responsibility in stages: between the ages of seven and fourteen he would have been allowed some role in the decision making process but this still required the consent of a guardian to act. Once the child reached puberty the guardian was required to give an account of his management of property and any business transactions undertaken. At this stage the system changed depending on gender: for boys a *curator* was appointed to deal with business matters until they reached the age of twenty-five; for girls a *tutor mulieris* was appointed (for full discussion see Saller 1994: 181–202). As far as legal definitions were concerned women were considered children all their lives because of their innate light-mindedness and general weakness. They could not have *potestas* (power) over their children, or legally act as guardians (Gaius *Inst.* 1.104) and were generally considered to need guidance in legal matters, like their children (see Dixon 1984b; 1992: Gardner 1986; 105–6). Legal texts viewed childhood as a period of incapacity which could last until the age of twenty-five for men, but could be extended if they had a living father, and for females could last a lifetime.

The Latin language does not in itself explain the complexities of childhood at Rome. Several words are used to describe children at various stages of life. One of the most significant facts is that there is no Latin word that would translate as 'baby' (Dixon 1992: 104; Manson 1983; Néraudau 1984). Legal texts use the term *infans*, literally 'not speaking', for those under seven. For older children a variety of terms come into use, and the precise meaning can only be ascertained by context. Most common in the legal texts are terms like *liberi*, which implies free born legitimate offspring, and terms such as *progeni* and *filii* (offspring and sons and daughters) – all of which could apply to children of any age. For young children, as opposed to youths, the term *pueri* was common usage, and covered both male and female children. The implications and derivation of *pueri* are both instructive and ambiguous in trying to ascertain attitudes to children. *Puer* has the sense of pre-pubertal in that it defines boys who are not yet capable of reproduction or of fighting for the state. Additionally it also has a connotation of ritual purity (Néraudau 1984: 49). It is also the term that is used to address slaves, and while for free born boys it was a stage that they outgrew, slaves would still be 'boys' into their old age. This double meaning of the word has led some authors to argue that sons were regarded in much the same way as slaves within the household and indeed that slaves may have proved to be more emotionally rewarding to masters than their own offspring (Néraudau 1984: Veyne 1987, and contra. Saller 1994: 137–53). The feminine version of *puer* began as *puera* but was quickly overtaken by the diminutive *puella* by the first century BC. The use of *puella* seems to cover both young girls (ages seven to twelve) and also young women between puberty and motherhood (Néraudau 1984: 52). It was also used to describe the young girls who took part in religious rituals and were still unmarried, i.e. virgins. Conversely, in poetry it became a term of affection that described a married lover (Wiedemann 1989: 33).

This somewhat legal lexicon appears relatively impersonal and unemotional. To find a more sentimental and emotive view of children and childish characteristics it is necessary to look at poetry and epigraphy. Diminutives were common – *parvulus* for a baby (Catul.61.209; Vergil *Aeneid* 4.328), as were terms such as *pupus/a,* doll (Suet. *Gaius* 13; *CIL* VI, 27556). For language that enjoys children for their own sake we need to look at personal letters (see below).

Infancy

Childhood appears to have several stages for the Romans. The period before the age of seven, *infantia,* was marked by a series of rituals and behavioural expectations. It was defined legally by the coming of the seventh birthday, associated with the physical loss of milk teeth (Pliny, *HN* 7.16), and socially by the commencement of participation in public and private cult. For boys it coincided with the start of education outside of the family, and the movement away from the domestic and into the public environment (Néraudau 1984: 55).

Plate 3.1 Tellus relief from the Ara Pacis. This idealised image of fertility includes two young naked infants alongside their mother. In reality, few infants of elite parentage would have been breast fed.

Rituals and traditions associated with pregnancy, childbirth and childhood suggest that children were wanted by parents (see Plate 3.1), and that the dangers of the first years of life were recognised. They also suggest a difference in attitudes to male and female children, which illustrates the significance of assumed gender distinctiveness in Roman life. It was a commonly held belief that gender differences were established from the moment of conception. According to some medical experts a male foetus would have been produced on the right side of the uterus and a female on the left. This was due to a belief in the theory of oppositional relationships common in Greek philosophy, which aligned the male with the right/hot/rational and the female with the left/emotional/cold/etc (see King 1998: 32–4; Galen K.4.172–3; 174.6ff). Galen, following Hippocrates and Aristotle, then translated this into his ideas of physiology: a male foetus was the result of strong seed from the right testes of the father, embedded in the right side of the womb and vice versa for a female child. Cultural assumptions about gender roles and relations informed understandings of biology and physiology. Galen understood a female child as one somehow mutilated, i.e. not a perfect male specimen. However, he thought the reason for this inferior body was because of the female role in the process of generation, thus placing a female firmly into her central social role as producer of heirs (Galen K.4.161.13–164.1; see Chapter 6).

A child that reached full term still had to undergo the dangers of child-birth and the first few days of life. The perils of the neonate are demonstrated by the number of protective deities: Diespater for the birth; Mena and Lucina for women menstruating and childbirth; Opis for placing the child on the earth; Vaticanus for the first cry; Levana to lift him from the ground; Cunina to guard the cradle; Rumina for breastfeeding and many more. This list, derived from Varro, is taken from Augustine, in the fifth century AD, who is decrying the pagan need for a multiplicity of deities (*De civitate dei* 4.11). While we may, or may not, share Augustine's derogatory overtones, this list reflects anxiety about a dangerous process and the need for the protection of the child and mother.

Rituals that accompanied early life also recognised change and develop-ment over time, with each successive step towards the full adult world. The child first had to be accepted by the father into the family, which was not automatic. This ritual, known as '*tollere liberos*', was performed after the midwife had checked the child for any physical deformities (Soranus *Gyn.*10). The father then literally lifted the child from the ground and with this gesture accepted the child into the *familia* and its inheritance networks (Suet. *Nero* 6; Belmont 1973; Dixon 1992: 101; Néraudau 1984; Veyne 1987: 9; Thomas 1986: 198 suggests that the process may not have applied for female children). Presumably these rituals would have been more elaborate in a household that had status and property to transmit and they are discussed in ancient source material in terms that stress paternal power. These factors may obscure the involvement of other family members in the decision either to rear or to expose a child. It is clear that the Romans, along with most other pre-modern societies, practised exposure of unwanted children, however abandonment must not be equated with infanticide. Exposed children were often raised by others, and while the practice is not the concern of this chapter, the life course of the exposed child was very much the stuff of ancient drama and novels, and had an important place within Roman culture (for discussion see Engels 1980; Boswell 1988; Harris 1982, 1994).

The next festival took place very soon after the birth, on the eighth day for a girl and ninth for a boy (Macrobius *Sat.*1.16.36). The gender distinction was seen to depend on the idea that females matured more rapidly than males, and according to Plutarch was also associated with an arithmetical preference that associated the number nine as the first square of the first odd number (odd numbers being considered generative so more suited to the male), whereas eight is the cube of the first even number (*QR*102) – though one wonders how many Romans knew that. The festival was a purification rite, a *dies lustricus* which was accompanied by non-blood sacrifice, a party for the family with gifts. The child was named on this occasion (Suet. *Nero* 6). Naming also highlights gender differentiation. On the eighth day after her birth a girl would receive her name, usually a feminine version of her father's *nomen*, for example, Marcus Tullius Cicero's daughter was named Tullia, and

Plate 3.2 Ara Pacis: distinguishing adults and children. The friezes from the Ara Pacis provide, in a single mode of representation, the language of adult-child and male-female distinctions. Male Roman children wear a *bulla*, the female child on the right does not. Male children wear the same clothes as adult males, female children wear the same dress as their adult equivalents. The child on the far left wears barbarian costume and may represent a child hostage being brought up in Rome.

his friend Atticus' daughter was named Attica. If she had any sisters there would be a high chance that they would share the same name. Her brother, on the other hand, would receive the full *trianomina* on the ninth day after his birth. A boy would be given the *nomen* and *cognomen* of his father and a *praenomen* that would differentiate him from his brothers. Naming reinforced the blood relationship between father and child and stressed the family line: Appius Claudius Pulcher (*cos.* 79 BC) had five children; his sons were Appius Claudius Pulcher and Publius Claudius (changed to Clodius) Pulcher; his three daughters Clodia, Clodia and Clodia (Syme 1986: Table 1). On this occasion children were also given the sign of freebirth, the *bulla* – a protective pendant (see Plate 3.2). We have visual evidence of the *bulla* for boys but no evidence of it for girls; it is unclear whether they wore them or not. The *bulla* and the *toga praetexta* (toga with a purple stripe, also worn by senators) were meant to give children some protection when they were outside the family home or in contact with people beyond their kin group, though upper class children would rarely have done these things alone. It was a sign, like the protective rituals and deities, that children were seen as vulnerable and in need of protection (Plutarch *QR*101). While the *toga praetexta* was apparently meant to be worn by both boys and girls, it is rarely seen on little girls in sculpture. Female children were less distinguished in dress and adornment as they tended to appear in similar garb to that of the adult woman (see Plate 3.2). All females, whatever their age, were considered vulnerable and in need of protection.

The same concern with protection for young children is present in medical texts on the care of infants, particularly that of Soranus. In the *Gynaecology* he gives very comprehensive advice on how to choose a midwife, how to make a mother comfortable during childbirth, and how to care for the newborn. While some of the advice given for both mother and child might have accidentally increased the high infant and post-natal mortality of mothers, it was given as the best advice. In following it parents and nurses might have hastened a child's death, but this was through ignorance, not ill will. The Roman practice of using wet-nurses, prevalent among all classes but the very poor (who were probably the nurses), has been instrumental in the negative construction of Roman attitudes to children (DeMause 1974; Bradley 1986; contra Garnsey 1991). The Romans themselves were ambivalent about the practice in the sense that although it was widely used, male writers were critical of Roman women, particularly those from the elite, 'abandoning' their offspring for the sake of their figures (Aul.Gel.*NA* 12.1). It was also a common belief that children imbibed morals with breastmilk; so by using slaves, especially Greek slaves, to feed their children, Roman mothers risked the moral contagion of slavery and foreign decadence passing to their young (Tac.*Dial.*29.1). Wet-nursing may have been common for a number of reasons, not all of them to do with vanity. It would have been necessary if a mother died in childbirth, or if she needed to return to work immediately after the birth, or if she wished to conceive again very soon. It may also have been considered best practice in some contexts. Soranus expressed the opinion that all things being equal, maternal milk was best for an infant as 'it was natural to be fed by the mother after birth, as it was before it', and because it encouraged the bonding process between mother and child. However, even he recognised the tension between medical advice and social convention and finished by saying that if anything prevented maternal feeding then the best wet-nurse must be employed and mothers should not be made prematurely old by daily feeding (*Gyn.*2.18).

Soranus was obviously addressing the elite as presumably poorer women did not have such options available to them. Paradoxically Soranus' advice, given with the best intentions, might have created a problem for both mother and child. He advised against giving the baby colostrum and that the mother should wait a period of twenty days before starting to breast feed. He thought colostrum too thick, and not good for a child's digestion. This would mean that the child missed out on the vital antibodies we now know are contained in colostrum, which may have protected him or her from some of the early diseases of childhood. It would also make the arrival of the milk more difficult as it is stimulated by the suckling and make the mother uncomfortable and liable to infection herself through engorged breasts (Garnsey 1999: 107). When it came to weaning the advice was to give infants a semi-liquid cereal based diet, with mixtures of honey and water or wine and softened bread (Soranus *Gyn.* 2.46).

According to Soranus once a child had been recognised as fit to be raised and the umbilical cord was severed (*Gyn.*2.10–11), it should then be cleansed first by a finely ground salt and oil rub, followed by a warm bath with special attention paid to the eyes, nose and mouth. Soranus rejected the customs of other cultures who bathed babies in cold water to test for weakness, or used wine or urine for the purpose (*Gyn.*2.12). Once the baby had been bathed the swaddling process began. Iconographic evidence suggests that swaddling was widespread and thought to have a beneficial effect on children. Its purpose seems to have been twofold, to control the child and to mould the body to the desired shape (*Gyn.*2.14; 42). Again Soranus started by rejecting the swaddling techniques of other cultures that he deemed cruel, particularly the 'Thessalonian' which bound the child to a hollowed out log (*Gyn.*2.14). He gave precise instructions on the process of swaddling with stress on the care and handling of the infant – the nurse must be gentle, the swaddling bands clean, soft and seamless. The infant is swaddled limb by limb, with the binding of the upper body done with even pressure for boys and tightly around the breast for girls, while the pelvic area was left loose, 'for in women this form is more becoming' (Gyn.2.15). Feet were bound so that they were broad at the end and narrow in the middle and knees straightened to avoid bandy legs. The whole body was then bound together with the arms trapped at the babies' sides, to avoid scratching. The head was bound separately.

Swaddling was not the only process the child underwent in its very early days. Regular warm baths were advised along with massage to further shape the body. The massage of the infant is described in some detail and begins with being held up by the ankles to straighten the spine (*Gyn.*2.32). After that each limb is manipulated while being rubbed gently with oil. The physical moulding includes flattening out the hollows of the knees, hollowing out the region around the buttocks (for comeliness), and the gentle massaging of the cranium so the head is neither too long, or pointed. Even the nose is shaped, by pinching if it is too flat and stretching if it is too aquiline. Boys whose foreskin was retracted had it gently lengthened to the 'natural good shape' (*Gyn.*2.34). Freedom from swaddling was treated in the same careful manner and occurred sometime between the fortieth and sixtieth day after birth (*Gyn.*2.42).

Release came gradually to the infant, a limb at a time over a number of days, for instance the right hand was always freed first to encourage right-handedness. Soranus was nothing if not pragmatic; at the end of all his painstaking advice he says that if a child is made sore by swaddling it should be removed (*Gyn.*2.42). The need to care for the child continued after its initial swaddled period of life to ensure that it grew to be a well-formed human being. In context, the action of swaddling should also be seen as a concern for their child in adult life to be a respected and fully formed person (Suet. *Claud.*3). The normative conventions of Roman society dictated the outcome – an adult whose limbs and mind were moulded in childhood.

As children grew so attention was paid to their health, although early death would have come to at least 50 per cent of those under ten who survived the first year (Garnsey 1991: 51–2). The details that survive are not as rich as Soranus on the care of the recently born. Pliny offers a series of remedies for childhood ailments which, although they may look outrageous to the modern reader, reflect an anxiety about the dangers that the young faced. Teething could be helped by rubbing sheep's brain on the gums or by the wearing of an amulet that contained the sandy grits found in the horns of snails, or a viper's brain tied on with a piece of its skin. Another amulet, this time for curing a baby's cough, was made by tying the dung of a raven with wool (*HN*30.135–7).

Socialisation

Socialisation, the process whereby an individual learns the social mores and body language required of his or her social status, began at the moment of birth with the physical moulding of the body in swaddling. The personnel associated with a child's early life were recognised as important in the early formation of behaviour and morals. The Roman child came into contact with a large number of adults who were influential in his or her life and responsible for their care. Interestingly, peer pressure at this stage seems to be lacking in our picture of Roman childhood; even stories of sibling relationships in childhood, as opposed to later in the life course, are very few despite the pervading myth of Romulus and Remus (see Bannon 1997; Hallett 1984). Until the age of puberty socialisation took place within the household, although parents of upper-class Roman children were not usually involved in the day-to-day chores of childcare. Tasks such as nappy changing, feeding, playing or sleepless nights were devolved to a series of carers, often of slave or freed status. Cato the Elder, the paradigmatic old Roman who insisted his wife feed her own children and rushed home from the forum to be present at the child's bath, is presented as both the ideal and the exception. He himself took over his sons' education and wrote a 'History' in large letters to help his son to read; he also took him swimming and taught him to box and ride (Plutarch, *Cato the Elder* 20. 4–7). Cato also thought his son should not be disciplined by a slave or owe his education to someone of servile status. The use of servile carers posed a dilemma for Romans other than Cato but it seems to have been an intellectual debate that did not impinge greatly on social practice. While later Romans might applaud the virtues of Cato they also recognised the realities of Roman life. Quintilian, for instance, offered advice on choosing a nurse:

... of course she should without doubt be chosen on the basis of good moral character, but still make sure that she speaks correctly as well. The child will hear his nurse first, and will learn to speak by imitating her words: and by nature we remember best those things which we learned when our minds were youngest.

Elements of Oratory 1.1. 4–5.

Roman authors were keen on the theory of raising children, even if they had no direct personal experience in the practice of it. In the context of an essay on self-control and anger Seneca expressed the following:

It is extremely important that children should be brought up properly from the start, although training them is no easy matter. Although we should not restrict the development of their personality, they must not be allowed to have tantrums... Freedom that is unrestricted results in a character that is unbearable; total restriction leads to a servile character. A child will be encouraged to gain self-confidence by being praised; on the other hand too much praise makes him over-confident and irascible. We should follow the mean in bringing up children: sometimes the child must be held back, sometimes encouraged. He should not be humiliated or subjected to servile treatment. He must not be allowed to cry and ask for rewards, nor should such behaviour gain him anything; rewards should be given only if he has been good, or promises to be good. When he is competing with others of the same age, he should neither be allowed to give up or to lose his temper... if he wins a game or does something remarkable, he should be praised, but not to excess: for excessive pleasure leads to over-confidence, and over-confidence to pride. Children should be left some free time, but that should not be allowed to turn to idleness; a child must not be allowed to get used to living an inactive and easy life... If a child has always been given everything he asked for, if his anxious mother always comforted him when he cried, if his childminder always let him do what he wanted, then he will never be able to cope with anything unpleasant in life.

(*De Ira* 2.21. 1–6)

Whatever the ideals of child-rearing in Rome, the realities are harder to grasp. Children could have expected to be raised by a collection of people: parents, grandparents, step-parents as well as nurses, pedagogues, teachers and general household slaves. Evidence suggests that children developed close relationships with carers and that these relationships sometimes lasted into adult life. Relationships between nurses and charges, whether female or male, seem to last long into adulthood. In Livy's tale of Verginia, often told to support the idea that girls as well as boys attended school outside the home, it was the nurse accompanying the girl who raised the alarm at her abduction (Livy 3.44.4–7). Here the nurse had taken on the role of chaperone in the girl's outings to the forum. Pliny recognised the importance of the relationship of the young Minicia Marcella to her nurse and attendants. She died before reaching the age of fourteen and was said to love her nurse, pedagogue and attendants (*Ep.*5.16.3) and he himself provided for his own nurse in her old age with the gift of a farm (*Ep.*6.3). Fronto complained about nurses who resented their charges' move into adolescence as they lost their close connection and influence over them (*Ep.*2.124; Bradley 1991: 25–6). At the end of Nero's life it was his nurse who helped to bury his body. The nurse was both a companion and conduit of socialisation for children (Suetonius *Nero* 50). Bradley's studies (1991) have shown that enduring relationships existed with nurses alongside that of parents and other carers. There are inscriptions from nurses to children and from children to their nurses that illustrate a respect if not a direct expression of affection (Bradley 1991: 13–36 provides a full list and discussion of the evidence).

Other carers a child was closely associated with were male pedagogues. Like nurses these men could be of servile or freed status and were in charge of both boys and girls (Bradley 1991: 39–76). They served two main functions in the child's life: that of the minder who superseded the nurse as the child grew and, less often, as teacher (*educator*, see Bradley 1991: 51). Pedagogues tend to be written about in a similar way to nurses: they should speak well, teach charges to walk correctly, sit properly, how to wear their clothes and how to eat (Plut.*Mor.*439F–440A; Sen.*Ep.*94.8; Bradley 1991: 52–4). Once a child left the confines of the *domus* (home) the pedagogue acted as a chaperone, particularly on the way to school. Like nurses, pedagogues seem to have been remembered fondly, though their closeness to children meant they had a certain amount of power, which they could abuse. Martial complained that his pedagogue, Charidemus, who was his constant companion while a *puer*, was still trying to control him in his youth when he was drinking, greasing his hair and pursuing girls. Martial claims that Charidemus thought he could still beat him (*Ep.*11.39). Valerius Maximus tells the story of a girl seduced by her pedagogue. Her father, under the right of *patria potestas*, which gave him the power of life and death over all those in his *familia*, killed both his daughter and her lover (Val. Max.6.1.3). As with nurses, inscriptions suggest that relationships with pedagogues were long lasting and more positive despite a period of possible tension during adolescence (Bradley 1991: 54–5). A short extract from Cicero suggests that despite social differences the pedagogue and nurse had an intimacy with the child that was influential but should remain part of childhood and not be extended into later life:

> In general, decisions about friendships should not be made until we have developed maturity of age and strength of mind.... Otherwise our nurses and our pedagogues, on the principle that they have known us longest, will claim the largest share of our affections. They must not, of course, be

neglected, but they must be regarded in a different manner from how we regard the friends we have made as adults.

(*De Amicitia* 20.74)

We know very little about the lives and activities of small children before they ventured into the public sphere at about age seven. There are passing mentions of childish behaviour by male authors (Fronto *Letters to his Friends* 1.12, Horace *Sat.*2.3) but the daily lives of small children were not the stuff of literature. It is hard even to track a space for children within the household. There is a tendency to assume that because children built up close relationships with carers of slave or freed status that they spent their time in servile areas of the house, but there is little evidence to support this. Roman houses do not seem to have areas that are specific to children (see Chapter 2) and they seem to have roamed freely within the domestic environment, curtailed more by the social occasion than any physical barriers.

Viewing the child

The written evidence provides us with a guide to how the adult world viewed that of their children. It mirrors the author's own childhood and is a reflection of their own development and position within the life course. At the same time, we also find authors reflecting on the growth of a child's mental faculties and character – noting the adult-like qualities of a specific child. Here, we find the authors once again looking forward to a time in the future when the child had become an adult and had passed through this part of the life course.

When adult writers refer to childhood games it is often with nostalgia for their own lives or from the point of view of watching a charming episode. Minucius Felix explains the game of ducks and drakes as he watches a group of boys skimming pebbles into the sea from the beach outside Ostia (*Octavius* 3. 5–6). Horace and Seneca both refer to building sandcastles (Hor.*Sat.*2.3; Sen.*Const.*2.2). Sport of all kinds seems to feature in the lives of boys. Cato taught his son to swim and to fight (Plut.*Cato* 20), Pliny talks about boys fishing and swimming (*Ep.*9.33). Poets make much of young boys' fascination with spinning tops (Tibullus 1.5.3–4; Virg.*Aen.*7.378–383). While all these actions are open to idealisation by adults they are also useful as indicators of what was expected of and allowed to children. There is also evidence of games with hoops, balls, of leapfrog and blind man's bluff, as well as guessing games, all typical of the earliest stage of life the world over. In terms of gendered toys there does seem to be evidence that girls played with dolls and boys played at being soldiers, though we have no evidence that it did not also happen the other way around. Dolls made of terracotta or ivory have been found. As Wiedemann notes, these are not baby dolls but rather young women, though not perhaps the Roman Barbie, with the implication that

46

Plate 3.3 Representation of childhood games that emulate the adult world of soldiering.

girls are being encouraged to identify themselves as wives rather than as mothers (1989: 149–50; Janssen 1996: 239; Martin-Kilcher 2000: 63–77; Rawson 1991: 19–20). Adults writing about children's games also stress their educational aspects. Quintilian thought riddles sharpened the intellect (*Inst.*1.3.11). Jerome, writing in the fourth century but undoubtedly influenced by Quintilian, suggests ivory bricks with letters of the alphabet (*Ep.*107, 128; Petersen 1994; 34–5). In Horace we see the future adult in the behaviour of the child at play:

> Since the time when I saw you, Aulus, carrying your knuckle-bones and
> nuts about in a loose toga, giving and gambling them away – and you,
> Tiberius, anxiously counting them and hiding them in holes, I have greatly
> feared that madness of different kinds might plague you.
>
> (*Sat.*2.3.171)

One of this dying man's sons had grown up to be too free with his money and the other too mean.

Adult writers also referred to children in sentimental ways. Fronto described the behaviour of his namesake grandson to the toddler's father. Despite the adult self-interest apparent, Fronto's letter illustrates behaviour typical of a young child. Little Fronto's favourite word is 'Da!' (Give me!) and his grandfather hands him suitably educational 'toys' of writing paper and tablets, but he also describes the child's attempt to eat grapes, 'licking and kissing them

47

Plate 3.4 Young girl portrayed holding a bird, a common motif in Roman statuary.

with his lips or biting it with his gums'. This child also loves young chicks, pigeons and sparrows. This association of children with young animals is a common motif in both art and literature (see Plate 3.4; Fronto, *Letters to his Friends* 1.12; Wiedemann 1989: 98).

At the same time as acknowledging that certain behaviour might be typical of children, male writers also praised them for being like adults or at least having adult-like qualities. It is a topos of ancient biography that children who grow up to be powerful adults were often the leaders in games they played as children, thus predicting their future positions. Poor Rufrius Crispus played at being an emperor and a king, but Nero was his stepfather and this proved to have been a bad idea: he ended up drowned by his own slaves (Suet.*Nero* 35.5; see also Wiedemann 1989: 49–83 on imperial children). A similar motif was that of *puer senex* which endowed children with mature qualities. Pliny wrote of Minucia Marcella who died before the age of fourteen, just before her wedding day:

> [She] combined the wisdom of age and dignity of womanhood with the sweetness and modesty of youth and innocence. She would cling to her father's neck, and embrace us, his friends, with modest affection. She loved her nurse, her attendants and her teachers, each one for the service given her; she applied herself intelligently to her books and was moderate and restrained in her play. She bore her last illness with patient resignation and, indeed with courage; she obeyed her doctors' orders.
>
> (Pliny *Ep.*5.16. 2–4)

When Plutarch described his recently deceased two-year-old daughter he mentions a sensitivity unusual in one so young: 'she had herself, moreover a surprising gift of mildness and good temper, and her way of responding to friendship and of bestowing favours gave us pleasure and afforded an insight into her kindness' (*Consolatio ad uxorem* 608C-D). This tendency to see the qualities of the adult in the behaviour of the child is typical, as shown by the father in Horace who could tell the future vices and virtues of his sons in the way they played with nuts as children. Carp (1980) has shown that while authors such as Pliny and Seneca use this motif, it is not the only model of childhood in their work. They too recognise behaviour that is particular to children, and that they cannot always be expected to behave like adults. This notion of presenting children as adult-like is instrumental in the notion that Romans only valued children as potential adults, but this fails to take into account that there also exists a sense that children do behave in a certain way and that they should be indulged. At times all adults around children have the occasional wishful thought that the sooner they behave like adults the better!

A key area for our understanding of childhood activities is found in the scenes on children's sarcophagi dating to the second and third centuries AD.

Plate 3.5 Detail of child's sarcophagus (Louvre) showing boys practising athletics. Although a common motif not exclusive to children, notice the plumpness and only incipient musculature of their bodies.

The iconography shows children in a number of different settings at play. Huskinson (1996: 16–17) has analysed several examples that show children at play and interacting with one another – pushing, hair-pulling and fighting. The scenes often show both boys and girls playing together in the same scene but in separate groups and architectural details may suggest that the boys play outside while the girls are inside. These figures are identifiably child-like with plump faces and limbs (Plate 3.5). Children in these images are presented in a relaxed fashion, they are not the bulla-wearing, togate children of the earlier Ara Pacis (see Plate 3.2). However, we would stress that this change probably has more to do with the mode of stylistic representation and context rather than a change in attitude to the child over the first two or three centuries AD (see Huskinson 1997 for discussion, Rawson 1997 provides a chronological overview of the representation of children). On the sarcophagi, they wear tunics with cap sleeves and their hair styles are unsophisticated (Huskinson 1996: 88). They are not presented as small adults but rather, as Huskinson argues, as beings as yet unready for the adult world. Similarly, the representation of children in biographical programmes on sarcophagi illustrates that certain moments in a child's life can become symbolic for the progression from babyhood to puberty/adulthood. These narrative sculptures appear to simulate a chronological narrative of the male child's life. It begins with infancy represented by being held by mother or nurse, or the first bath, moves on to an early childhood marked by the child

Plate 3.6 Sarcophagus of Cornelius Statius (Louvre). A biographical sarcophagus that gives a 'narrative' rendition of the child's short life. On the left he is shown as a baby, suckled by his mother with his father watching on. Next he is depicted being held by his father. In the centre he is riding a tiny chariot pulled by a ram and finally, reciting to his father. Such scenes reflect not only an idealised version of the child's life but also the child as small adult stressing his lost potential as soldier and orator.

pushing some form of ancient baby-walker or riding in a small chariot pulled by a ram or some other small animal (cf. Hor.*Sat.*2.3. 247–8). The transition to youth is marked with attending school or a scene where the boy recites to his father (Plate 3.6). The scenes of play and childhood transition are marked by a sentimentality and loss of the child through death – yet another indicator that the experience of childhood need not be associated with parental indifference. However, these scenes are presented in terms of the adult life course, in that the child's prematurely terminated life is shown as an adult one cut short, not for its own value. The child's potentiality as an adult is mourned (Kampen 1981: 54–5) see chapter 10.

Beyond the family

In the later stages of childhood, contact with the world outside the home became greater; this most often came in the form of some sort of formal education. One of the duties of the father was to educate his children and in the ideal world a child may have had the uninterrupted attention of a father like Cato, but more often than not a tutor was engaged, or children attended school in the town. Education, inside and outside the home, was available to both boys and girls, though literary references allude almost exclusively to boys and their schoolteachers, with the exception of some brief references (Livy and Verginia, see above; or Mart.*Ep.*9.68). Children were sent first to an elementary school run by a *magister* or *litterator* who taught basic reading writing and arithmetic (on long division see Hor.*Ep.*2.3.325–30). Learning consisted mostly of memorising huge tracts of Roman legends, laws and epic poetry by rote. Since there was no regulation of teachers and anyone could have set himself up as one, and their pay and status were not very high (Juv.*Sat.*7.215–243), the standard of education was somewhat erratic.

The child learnt not only lessons at school but also self-control of his body language and desires, and to deal with both pleasure and pain with equanimity. If a child overstepped the mark they might have expected to be beaten by any of the adults in charge of them. Cicero said if boys misbehaved they might expect both sharp words and beating from mothers and teachers (*Tusc.*3.640) and Quintilian's comment that a youth would have felt insulted by a whipping given after childhood (*Inst.*1.3.14) implies that beatings in childhood were acceptable (Saller 1994: 147). The adult nostalgia for childhood games was matched by a horrific recollection of their school teachers and beatings that they inflicted (see Saller 1994: 150 for examples of this topos). The use of verbal reproof as well as simply beating the child is well attested in the literature. This was clearly expressed by Plutarch (*De Lib. Ed.*12), who argued that beating was not suitable for the free born and that such children should be reasoned with rather than taught their lesson with blows. Horace (*Sat.*1.4) praised his father for teaching him by example rather than violence. Teaching by example is the didactic concept behind Valerius Maximus' collection of *Memorable Doings and Sayings*.

While their brothers were having a taste of life outside the domestic environment, girls would have been learning the skills and behavioural norms that would transform them into good wives and mothers. Many upper class girls were educated in literature and philosophy as well as more traditional skills such as weaving and organising a household, but there is very little direct evidence for this (see Chapter 4; Hemelrijk 1999).

The child and the life course

Children were desired by Roman families and once born and accepted were raised with care and attention. The difficulty for modern interpreters is the cultural/social context into which children were born and the social expectations assumed of them. The crux of the 'indifference debate' lies in two assumptions – that children born in a time of high infant mortality were not invested in emotionally by their parents and that a society which practised exposure had little time for young children and only valued them once they had achieved adulthood. Our argument is that the one need not preclude the other. Economic and demographic reasons need not determine or exclude emotional attachment to children (Weidemann 1989; Garnsey 1991). The child was seen as the future of the family, just as their ancestors were their past. Children were to be nurtured or physically shaped in infancy and once speaking were to be trained for life in the adult world and the transition into that world. Hence, children were to be protected from that world, yet needed to be converted from mute things, as different as barbarians, into mature citizens or wives. Women continued to need the protection from others in a similar manner to that of the male in childhood. This points not only to the marginalisation of both children and women, but also to an aspect of childhood that is not made explicit by the source material: the development of gender distinctions between, for example, brothers and sisters. The lead-up to the transfer to adulthood is not discussed, although the initial biological changes to female and male bodies were present and observed (see Chapter 1).

Childhood was, and still is, a time in the life course when the individual was very much in the control and power of others. For a parent a child was one of their greatest assets and it was necessary that they develop into a well behaved and dutiful adult, so behaviour was carefully watched. The child's lack of power over both the physical and mental was highlighted in a slave society. Free children grew up within a system where an oppressed group was a constant and visible presence; in which there was an endemic undercurrent of the threat and fear of violence. We have seen that there are similarities in the way that slaves and children were marginalised in the adult-citizen-centred world of Rome and the question of control and self-control are fundamental to this. It is only at this stage of life that free-born individuals could legitimately suffer corporal punishment, even the theoretically paradoxical position of the free suffering a beating at the hands of a slave. When Seneca (*De Ira* 2.21.1–6) stressed the balance necessary in bringing up children he recognised the difficulties for Roman parents; the child should not be 'humiliated or subject to servile treatment' but neither must it be indulged or allowed to grow overconfident, or rewarded unless it was deserved. The child had to learn the behaviour appropriate to their social standing and gender; failure to do so, in the Roman mindset, could have resulted in idleness, depravity, and an adult life wasted. It also reflected on the parents (see Chapter 6). Childhood formed the personality that would experience the adult world over the rest of the life course.

4

TRANSITION TO ADULTHOOD 1

Female

Throughout the early period of the female life course, there was an ever present male decision maker – a woman's father, husband, brother or son. Seldom was a woman independent of a male who decided, or at the least influenced, her actions. The transition from a childhood of total dependence on her parents into an adult world associated with marriage marked a change in identity. She became a wife, living in a different household, maybe even a different town, and her social personality also changed – she was no longer a child. In this chapter we turn our attention to this change and its associated anxieties and dramas. The process of change, however, is seen through the prism of male writing and attitudes that privileged the elite male. The dominant voice in the expression of the female life course is that of the *paterfamilias* or her father. This is a problem in terms of information; we will not discover the feelings of a young girl about to embark on her first marriage and transition into adult life. The information we have is constructed with reference to the adult male's experience and perception of his daughter, sister, mother or wife. Only rarely do we get glimpses of the female experience of her own life. We are dealing with the methodological problem of studying a gender that is known only through the writings of another gender (see Joshel 1992: 3–24 for a lucid discussion of this problem). The prism through which we glimpse women consists of idealised images and stereotypical 'bad' women, that usually served a first purpose other than telling us anything about the women concerned (see Fischler 1994; Laurence 1997). However, these images are often framed or constructed with reference to the ideological image of the female at Rome that reveals the structure within which the experience of the transition to adulthood was made.

The female life course consisted of a number of more or less distinct stages – acceptance by father, childhood, betrothal, marriage, childbirth and motherhood, followed in all likelihood by bereavement and/or divorce and/or remarriage. Where her brother may have made the transition to adulthood in a series of gradual stages and growing worldly experience, a girl made it on the day of her wedding (see Chapter 6). Prior to this day most of a girl's education would have been focused on preparing her for marriage. For a girl

Plate 4.1 Muse depicted as young girl.

it was *the* major change in her life, it meant a move to a new residence, to a new network of social relations, and the undertaking of new social and domestic responsibilities, not to mention a sexual relationship and its consequences. The emphasis in Roman society generally on female virginity (Beard 1980, 1995) and specifically at first marriage (e.g. Val.Max.2.1.3) highlights a cultural need for early marriage. Ideally once married motherhood would follow, one transition – from child to wife – leading seamlessly to another – that of parent.

Female adolescence

There is a period of the female life course that is rarely mentioned in the literary texts, that is the time from the separation from their elder brothers and half-brothers who might now have legitimate roles outside the home, to the time of first marriage. Traditional thinking, based on close reading of legal texts, held that Roman girls were commonly married in their early teens, an age that coincided with the age of menarche (Hopkins 1965). This conveniently linked biological and chronological age with social custom, and cut out any need for a female equivalent of '*iuventus*' (youth). A *puella* (girl) appeared to transform rapidly and imperceptibly into a *virgo* (virgin), and then to a *uxor* (wife), the prenuptial ceremonies being seen as the female equivalent to the donning of the *toga virilis*. More recent studies (Saller 1994: 37; Shaw 1987) have pushed back the age of first marriage for most Roman girls, with the exception of the elite, to the late teens and early twenties, thus leaving a part of the female life course unaccounted for.

There is, in fact, sparse evidence for Roman attitudes to girls of this age group (see Fischler, forthcoming). For boys the period of *iuventus* (youth) was defined, there was an expectation of youthful excess, a freedom of the city and all its pleasures, a licence for lack of control and sexual indulgence (see Chapter 5). For girls no such equivalence existed; the control over them that was evident in earlier childhood was all the more strictly enforced once the physical signs of puberty became apparent. We cannot assume that the age of menarche in Roman times was comparable to that of the modern western population (see Chapter 1). Indeed, it seems likely that it often usually occurred later than thirteen, the current western age of menarche. What we can say is that the physical changes that come about in puberty start earlier in girls than in boys and that the Romans were aware that once these changes started adulthood was approaching, though perhaps not as fast as they thought. Girls and boys reach puberty at different rates; while boys are potentially fertile from the earliest sign of physical change, girls develop almost all of the secondary sex characteristics before menstruation and regular ovulation set in. The earliest sign of physical change in a girl is the development of the breast bud; the ability to bear children can take several years to become established (Lancaster 1985: 15–17).

Ancient medical writers and philosophers had various theories as to how puberty came about, and while these were often at odds with one another about the mechanics of the process, the general overarching view that the female body was in some way inferior to the male was constant. (cf. Hippocrates *Morb.Mul.*1.1 Aristotle *G*728a; Galen *de Usu. Part.*6.II.296, 299; Macrobius *Saturnalia* 7.6.16–7; 7.7.2–12, arguing on whether females are naturally hot or cold, and incidentally claiming 'that women reach puberty quickly is due not to the excessive heat but to the greater weakness of their nature, just as inferior fruits ripen more quickly but the hardy more slowly' (7.7.11)). While the Romans might not have recognised the full sexual ramifications of the physiological change of puberty, they were at pains to control it in terms of behaviour. The various medical reasons for the onset of puberty (see King 1998: 71–8) were both a reflection of and creators of the prevailing perception of the 'natural' gendered social hierarchy. It was assumed that girls as well as boys developed a desire for sexual relations with the onset of puberty (Soranus *Gyn.*1.33) and here the different meaning of marriage for girls becomes apparent. For a freeborn girl the only arena for sexual relations was marriage and it was essential that her virginity be closely guarded until her first marriage. Chastity was one of her main assets as a marriageable commodity and had to be ensured (cf. Beard 1980, 1995).

The onset of puberty resulted in changes in the life style of young women and should be seen as the period of transition from girl to virgin. Chaperoning had occurred throughout a child's life, but may have become more intensive during this phase of the female life course. It was also thought that a young woman's sexuality could be controlled by a strict regimen of diet and judicious exercise:

> When they are older and growth has all but stopped, and when young girls out of modesty no longer want to play childish games to the full, then one must give much more continuous attention to their regimen, regulate and moderate their intake of food, and not let them touch meat at all, or other foods that are very nourishing.
>
> (Rufus of Ephesus quoted in Oribasius, *Liber Incertus* 18.10, cited in Garnsey 1999: 101)

Although Rufus may have been unaware of the relationship between fat and fertility (Lancaster 1985: 18–9), he suggested that food intake should be kept low and that wine should be avoided (Garnsey 1999: 102). He was concerned to persuade others not to marry their daughters off at a very early age for the good of their health and their fertility. Soranus (*Gyn.*1.34) presents a similar case and suggests that women should not marry prior to the age of fifteen, when they are fit for conception. Given the ancient view that all women had little control over their sexuality, a regimen of control was necessary alongside surveillance and the control of visitors between the onset of menarche and marriage. The biological changes need not be apparent to other members of the *familia* or visitors to the *domus*, but the regimen, itself, would have identified to others the change from girl to virgin.

Betrothal

In terms of socialisation it is probably safe to assume that young women learnt their responsibilities and behavioural norms from close association with female members of their families, most usually mothers and aunts. A girl's formal education may have continued throughout this period. If the household had a private tutor it seems likely that daughters as well as sons would have benefited from studies in grammar, literature and perhaps Greek and the study of music and philosophy. There is little evidence for the education of girls during this stage of their life but if we consider the accomplishments of older women, we must assume that they learnt their skills at an earlier stage in the life course. Cornelia, mother of the Gracchi, Terentia, Augustus's daughter Julia, and Pliny's wife Calpurnia were all praised for their intellectual talents; and those who ran their own affairs were also presumably numerate. The later a girl was married the longer this stage of her education might have lasted. (Hemelrijk 1999: 17–57). Such talents, if carefully regulated, could have enhanced a girl's chance in the marriage market. Betrothal at an early age would further have focused everyone's mind on the girl's future role as wife. For example, Atticus was looking for a husband for his only daughter Attica by the time she was six (Cic.*Att.*13.21a.4); this would suggest that socialisation of girls for marriage began at a very early age. Throughout Attica's childhood, her future as a wife was known to her. She was in effect informed of her transition to adulthood and prepared for that transformation from an early age. Marriage ended childhood, but was looked forward to through a search for a marriage partner well in advance of the actual marriage and was expressed as an intention as a betrothal. Marriage served many purposes in the Roman world but its primary aim was for the procreation of children. Among the upper classes it also created social and political links. For both these reasons marriage was arranged by the two families with their respective fathers or guardians taking the leading role in the negotiations (Treggiari 1991a: 134–38).

The actual search for a suitable partner also involved female family and friends (e.g. Plu.*Pomp.*9.4.; *T.G.*4.2; Plin.*Ep.*1.14; for discussion see Dixon 1988: 62–3; Treggiari 1991a: 127–38). Social interaction between female relatives and female friends would have provided a network of information about which males were available, their families and also the negotiations between the heads of families. These informal female networks may have been capable of influencing the choice and negotiation itself (see App.*B.C.*4.32–4; Laurence 1997: 131–6 on female networks of power). Romance, while not unknown, was not seen in any way as a criterion for marriage choice on the part of men and when it did occur was considered both irresponsible and foolish (e.g. Plu.*Sul*.35.3 on Sulla's passion for Valeria). We would expect a *paterfamilias* to view romantic love as expressed by his daughter as a medical symptom of puberty and best ignored. Affection, or at least, *concordia*, was an expectation of married life but by no means a prerequisite. Since parents were concerned to marry their daughters off quickly, in part due to an anxiety that they may cease to be virgins, and not marrying was not really an option (with the exception of having your daughter accepted as a Vestal), they were under pressure to find and select a suitor for their daughters. While it was the legal duty of a *paterfamilias* to find a partner for his child the process actually involved a range of family and friends and involved the female side of the kin group.

Rank and wealth were key criteria throughout Roman antiquity with a view to the creation of marital links between families that were similar. In addition to legal and economic considerations it was expected that the groom be of good character, good looking and in good health. These attributes were considered fair exchange for the bride's chastity, modesty and domestic abilities. Pliny, writing in *c.* AD 97, recommends Minicius Acilianus as a husband for a friend's niece (*Ep.*1.14). Acilianus is suggested first because of his respect for Pliny, but also his good character and his family – he can claim, by association, the virtues of humility and honesty from his father, propriety from his maternal grandmother and wisdom and integrity from his paternal uncle. Acilianus has also already achieved the office of praetor so will not be a burden on his father-in-law in terms of having to support an election campaign. He is also good looking with natural nobility, a fair exchange for the bride's virginity in Pliny's view. Finally Pliny mentions his wealth, although he disingenuously claims this will be last on the friend's list, but must be considered in relation to children and inheritance. Here we see the mixture of pragmatism and philosophy that makes the examination of Roman marriage so complex. While this marriage looks on the surface as the union of two people to their advantage, it was also the linking of two families, and, if it was a successful match, also enhanced the relationship of the Mauricus brothers, the father and uncle of the bride, to Pliny. Status, rank and wealth are, in reality, of equal importance to character but it was not acceptable to express this. The unnamed niece of Junius Mauricus does not look like she is being given much say in the matter, and obviously very young girls probably had very little voice at home. For a first marriage the bride herself might have little input.

The bride's role in undertaking marriage was to understand the nature of the contract with her husband. This seems dubious in cases in which betrothal occurred at a young age before a girl was ten years old (*Dig.*23.1.4; 17, on reasons for allowing a longer betrothal), and there are many examples, not least among the Julio-Claudians, of children being promised from infancy. As we have seen, Atticus was actively looking for a husband for

Attica from when she was at least six – she married Agrippa, a man old enough to be her father, in 37 BC, aged about fourteen. The daughter of this marriage, Vipsania Agrippina, was herself betrothed to Tiberius when she was only one, and he seven (Nepos *Att*.19.2; Treggiari 1991a: 109). At first marriages, girls might be as young as twelve, but even in their late teens girls were still very much subordinate to parents, with very limited life experience. Their opinion, if it was sought, might have had bearing, dependent entirely on a parent's whim, but a good *paterfamilias* did not marry his daughter off against her will. Marriage required the consent of both parties and their *paterfamiliae*. While Augustus might forbid a father to prevent the marriage of a daughter by denying a dowry (*Dig*. 23.1.7.1; 2.19; Treggiari 1991a: 146–7), a young girl was clearly under pressure to marry her family's choice of spouse. However, during the negotiations, the opinion and ideally the approval of the female side of the family would have been sought. These female relatives may have been instrumental in persuading the young girl that a given partner was acceptable. These female opinion formers are not present in many of our sources written by men or dominated by the legal writers collected by Justinian into the *Digest of Roman Law*, but may have had considerable influence with the *paterfamilias* from inside the family itself. The public face of an arranged marriage was an agreement between families, but would also be accompanied by agreement within the family as well.

Once the negotiations were concluded, the betrothal might be celebrated by a party and gift exchange – the male *sponsus* might have offered his betrothed a ring. The girl's father usually hosted these celebrations, using the opportunity to advertise a new alliance (Cic.*Quint*.2.6.2). The party was not part of the formal or legal process but it was clearly quite common to hold one – Pliny complains that this is the sort of social engagement that takes up his time when in Rome (*Ep*.1.9). The public recognition of the promised marriage was for the girl a step in her life course, and presumably a personal recognition of her future role as wife and mother.

Wedding rituals

Marriage, when it did come, could have been hedged about with ceremony and ritual but none of this was necessary for the marriage to be legitimate. This in itself shows the disparity in the value of rituals in the male and female life course. This, the event that marked the departure of a daughter from the family home and changed her status forever, could happen with very little ceremony, and even without the presence of the male partner (*Dig*.23.2.5; 6). A man might be considered married *in absentia*, although the same was not true of a woman, who must at least, in reality or symbolically, be led to the husband's house.

We know of prenuptial ceremonies only from passing comments in poets' and antiquarian works so it is difficult to know how prevalent they were, and how much of a marker they were in a girl's life. However, by looking at the known events of the marriage ceremony, we may understand the role of marriage for the female life course. For a boy the public sign that he had reached puberty was the laying aside of the *toga praetexta* and the donning of the *toga virilis*. It is thought that girls may have performed a similar ritual to this on the night before the wedding but the evidence is scanty. There is a passing line in Propertius: 'Soon when her *toga praetexta* yielded to the marriage torches' (4.11.33). This is certainly symbolic – we have seen that young girls are rarely depicted in the toga – but the implication that childhood things are laid aside is typical of rites of passage to adulthood (see also Arnobius *Adversus nationes* 2.67: the *puella's togula* was dedicated to Fortuna; Lactantius, *Div. Inst.* 2.4.13 on dedicating toys to Venus). Pliny (*Ep.*5.16) describes the characteristics of a thirteen year old bride to be: the wisdom (*prudentia*) of age, the *gravitas* of a matron, alongside the sweetness (*suavitas*) of a girl and the coyness (*verecundia*) of a virgin. The mixture of characteristics seen by Pliny in this young woman illustrates the nature of the transition from Roman girl to Roman matron with the former laid aside along with the *toga praetexta* and other symbols of childhood. That this is as much as we know of a ritual for girls analogous to a boy's assumption of the *toga virilis* and the transition to citizenship is a reflection of the male construction of the sources (Sebesta 1994: 47; see Fischler, forthcoming; Weidemann 1989: 92–3, 114; see Chapter 5).

The transition was not complete once a girl had given up her *toga praetexta*. Dress marked the final transition from *virgo* to *uxor*. As with female rituals, information is gleaned from antiquarian writers and it is unclear how precisely any of the rituals were followed. The night before her wedding, her final night as a virgin, the bride wore a *tunica recta* (so called because woven on an upright loom, Festus 342.L; 364.21 L) and a yellow hairnet, both woven by herself as proof of her matronly virtues (Sebesta 1994: 48; La Follette, 1994: 54–5). The bride slept in these clothes and for the wedding itself tied the tunic with a belt specially woven from ewe's wool to symbolise fertility, and tied with a special knot (*nodus Herculaneus*). The knot was thought to be difficult to undo and symbolised both fertility, by reference to Hercules' seventy children, and chastity, as it was undone by her new husband on the wedding night. It represented not only the binding together of husband and wife but also the binding of her chastity and fertility to her husband (Festus 55L; Sebesta 1994: 48; 1998: 111). The bride's hair was also dressed in a special way known as the *sex crines* (six tresses, see Plate 4.2) but it is unclear exactly what this was (see La Follette 1994: 56–60). It was also, according to tradition, parted with a spear, but the symbolic meaning of this practice was unknown by the second century AD (Plut.*QR* 87; Festus 55.3L). She also wore a garland of flowers around her head (Festus 56.1L) that she had picked herself. As a young girl her head and hair would have been uncovered when she went out (see Plate 3.2, the

Plate 4.2 Head of Vestal illustrating the *sex crines*, the somewhat obscure hairstyle that a bride shared with the priestesses.

figure on the far right), but with the wedding begins the stage of life when covering the head was considered correct behaviour. The bridal veil, the *flammeum*, covered head, face and most of her body. This rich yellow veil was thought to protect her as she travelled from the house of her father to that of her husband (Festus 174.20L; La Follette 1994: 55; Treggiari 1991a: 163).

In the same way that the original meaning of the rituals and details of bridal dress were not clear even to the Romans, the details of the wedding ceremony were in some ways equally archaic. We need not assume that all weddings encompassed all these symbols, since a wedding ceremony was not in itself necessary to make a marriage legitimate but often part of the ostentatious upper class Roman life. For the bride the wedding started in her father's house. Both houses would be decorated with garlands and wreaths (Catul.64.293). The bride would dress surrounded by female relatives, taking this last moment to offer advice (Apul.*Met.*4.26, cited in Treggiari 1991a:163). Sacrifices were performed. The bride's parents or other close relations handed the bride over to the groom and their hands were joined by the *pronuba*, a once-married woman or *univira* (Catul.62.60ff; Treggiari 1991a: 164). The joining of hands was a traditional sign of faith, used also at business deals. It is the traditional iconography of the married couple in Roman art (see Plate 4.3) (Walter 1979). Equally important at the ceremony was the witnessing of the contracts. Dotal arrangements were formalised and arrangements made for payment of the dowry, which could have been in stages if necessary (Treggiari 1991a: 165–6).

Plate 4.3 Dextrarum Iunctio: a married couple in the centre in the traditional gesture of marriage — the joining of right hands. Behind and between them stands the *pronuba*, the once-married woman who joined their hands together as part of the wedding ceremony.

The next part of the formal ceremony was the *deductio in domum mariti*. This procession of the bride to her new home, the groom having gone ahead, was a formal recognition of the marriage. The bride traditionally left her mother with reluctance (Claudian *Car. Min.*25.124–5) and was led through the streets by torchlight by three boys with living parents. One to carry a special torch, the *spina alba*, lit from the bride's hearth, the others to hold her hands. Someone else carried a distaff and spindle, again signifying the bride's new domestic role (Treggiari 1991a: 166). They were accompanied by a crowd of guests and cries of *'Fortuna'* or *'Talassio!'* (Catul.61.56, 64; Plut.*QR* 31.), as well as obscene songs (Catul.61.120, 122). On arrival at her new home the bride anointed the doorway with oil and woollen filets and was lifted over the threshold by her attendants. The groom offered her fire and water, a part of the ritual that was considered important. Fire and water symbolised the two fundamental elements of life and of the Roman home. The symbolic wording for banishment denied a man fire and water (Plut.*QR* 31, 29; Pliny *HN*28.142; 29.30; Treggiari 1991a: 168). All these symbols associated with the transition from girl living in her father's house to that of a matron and wife living in her husband's house highlight the centrality of marriage to a woman's life. Significantly, as we have noted, the whole event can take place without the presence of the groom, who is not required to be personally present for the marriage to be valid. This is indicative of the fact that a large component of the adult male population was involved in military service and could have been absent on the day of a marriage. The fact that a marriage could continue without the presence of the male partner might suggest that marriage did not have the same level of significance in the male life course. However, we would not argue that this caused men to view marriage as trivial.

The final stage of the ritual for the bride should have been the sexual initiation of the wedding night. Not surprisingly, this was shrouded in the sorts of obscene tales that accompany such events in most cultures. In Rome, the idea that it involved violence on the part of the male and timidity on the part of the new wife was current, which when taken literally as a descriptive text has led to a misrepresentation of the evidence in some modern scholarship (e.g. Veyne 1987: 34–5). It is difficult, however, to sift through the primarily poetic sources to understand quite what the norm was during this first night, no doubt because the event took place within the privacy of the *cubiculum* (see Chapter 2). A decorated *lectus genialis* (bridal bed) was prepared in the atrium of the couple's house but it is doubtful that this was the bed actually used by the couple (Treggiari 1994: 168–9).

Young females and the life course

The period of a young girl's life before marriage is rarely accounted for in ancient texts. However, as marriage was the normal expectation and aim of life for the daughter of a member of the propertied classes her preparation for the event is significant. As the marriage of a daughter was very important in the life of her parents, particularly her father (see Chapters 6 and 7), it was in their interests to see that she appeared in the best possible light. To this end a young girl's life could be quite rigorously monitored, but this need not necessarily have been oppressive or unhappy. We must assume that for the most part young girls bought into the social norms of their time and while they might approach marriage with some trepidation, they expected it to be part of their future as much as their parents did. Whether it happened as young as fourteen or as old as eighteen, the wedding day transformed a girl forever: she would never return to her former position in the social hierarchy; though she did not stop being a daughter, she was now a *matrona* with the responsibilities of a husband and a household. The pre-marriage stage of a girl's life could vary in time span but once the wedding had occurred the girl became part of the adult world.

5

TRANSITION TO ADULTHOOD 2

Male

The question at what point a boy becomes a man is an area of debate not just within our own modern societies, but one that preoccupied others in the past, including those within the Roman empire. Aligned to this question was another: how did a child become a man? Distinctions of gender are important here; for females the transition from childhood to adulthood was via marriage (a topic we covered in Chapter 4). For men, the transition was not made quickly but was a drawn out process from the age of fifteen or sixteen until their marriage at the age of about twenty-five. In a society that could believe that the survival of the state depended on the morality and sexual restraint of its citizens (Val. Max.4.3), this period of male transition, often known simply as *iuventas* or *adulescentia* (youth) could be seen as a time in which these forms of morality and restraint were formed, but at the same time were totally beyond the control of the individual. The terms *iuventu* and *adulescent* define the young adults as not yet fully grown and equally as no longer children. In fact, this group are defined as in a state of transition or liminality that is regarded by adult writers as fundamentally dangerous not only to the individual, but also to the state itself. It demonstrates that within Roman thinking a male child could not suddenly have been turned into a responsible adult citizen via a ritual that celebrated that change, unlike his sister who simply entered the adult world upon marriage (see Chapter 4). The mind and character of a youth was in need of nurture by an older man (e.g. Cic.*Att.*14.13a, 14.13b in the case of a son of Clodius). However, a youth was still capable of being inactive, slighting a bride to be and living with a prostitute (Val.Max.3.5: again the case is Clodius' son) with the result that his life could degenerate into gluttony and ultimately death from over-eating. Hence, care was needed during this period of transition to nurture a morally upright citizen. However, at the same time, youth was seen as a phase in which the male was an adult citizen, but subject to impulses that were not those of an adult and were instead exclusively associated with the liminal phase known simply as youth. In a way, youth was perceived as an illness that lasted until a man's twenties, when he recovered and married, could take up public office and was trusted by his fellow citizens and the state. Given this view of youth

Plate 5.1 Young boy with *bulla* and wearing *toga praetexta*, indicative of his status as child citizen.

as a stage of life the transition from childhood to adult citizenship for males was more complex and enshrined with a certain anxiety expressed in the writings of older men (Eyben 1993 for discussion of the activities of youths).

The rite of passage: from boys to men

The change from the status of child to man was marked by the change in dress from a *toga praetexta* with a purple stripe to the plain white *toga virilis* that all adult males wore. The age at which this change took place varied, but tended to occur by a male's seventeenth birthday – the age from which men could have been enlisted for military service (Gell.*NA*.10.28). For many, the day chosen for this change to take place was at the festival of Liber on seventeenth March. However, the *toga virilis* could have been taken up at other dates (Warde Fowler 1908: 56 for examples). The change in dress marked a coming of age and a transition from boy to youth, just as the god Liber was represented as both boy and youth according to Ovid (*Fasti* 3.771–90). The decision that a son was ready to become enrolled as a citizen was taken by a father or guardian, hence the chronological age at which an individual became officially recognised as a man could vary. The actual festival of Liber and the ceremonial associated with it are relatively well known (Ovid *Fasti* 3.771–90). The son dedicated his childhood *bulla* to the gods of the household and then having put on his new *toga virilis*, he left the house with his father for the forum. From the time of Augustus, the ceremonial of transition occurred in the Forum of Augustus (Dio 55.10). Here the setting is significant. The son was standing in front of the temple of Mars the Avenger, vowed by Octavian at the battle of Philippi to celebrate the vengeance he had sought for the murder of his adopted father Julius Caesar (Suet.*Aug.*29). Hence, for the young man, filial duty to his father was stressed. Equally, other features of the forum are significant. Augustus' statue as Father of his country stood in the centre of the forum as a prominent reference point for the youth wearing the toga of citizenship for the first time. In addition, the statues of the famous men from the past who had celebrated triumphs were looking on. The inscriptions beneath the statues detailed the magistracies they had held and the triumphs they had celebrated over Rome's enemies (Zanker 1988: 210–12). These were to be *exempla* of behaviour and aspirations for the young to follow. Equally, the temple of Mars, in Augustus' new geography of Rome, was the place from which warfare was decided upon and was the place from which Mars unleashed warfare on Rome's enemies (Ovid *Fasti* 5.533ff). In taking up the *toga virilis*, the boy had become an adult citizen and part of citizenship was to fight in wars for the *res publica* (society). If warfare was let loose by Mars, it was Rome's citizens, including the young, who would have been fighting Rome's enemies within the tradition of those *exempla* present in the forum from the past (note also that the procession of the *Argeii* occurred on this day [Ovid *Fasti* 3.792–808]).

The setting itself is significant for other reasons, not least of which is duty not just to the state but also to one's family. We have already mentioned the role of Augustus as avenger for his father's murder in 44 BC. Other poignant reminders of filial duty were present. Aeneas was represented as the leader of the Trojans – he brought them to Italy – and the son of Venus. He is often seen in wall painting and on coinage as a man leading his son Ascanius, whilst at the same time carrying his father Anchises. The absence of a wife is significant here: for the viewer she is unimportant, what is significant were the three generations of male relatives and their legitimacy. Aeneas is dutiful to his father and leads his dependent son, but the mother of that child has no role in the myth of the Trojan flight to Italy and hence is omitted. We might say that in the context of the Forum of Augustus, a role for motherhood is suppressed. However, we should note that a statue of Cornelia, the mother of the Gracchi, was set up in the Forum (Plin.*HN*34.31; *CIL*6.31610). The choice is significant. She was celebrated as an ideal wife, mother, and widow. She devoted her attention to her sons after the death of her husband and refused to remarry. For those young men whose fathers had died by this point of transition in the life course (about 33 per cent, see Appendix 1), duty to their mother as the surviving relative was important. This feature included a role for women and duty to mothers as well as fathers for the sons of the family (Tac.*Dial.*28). That duty, in the case of the Gracchi, was to serve the state and become examples to future generations that were proudly discussed by their mothers as well as their fathers, even after a violent death in the political turmoil of the late republic. Hence, the expectations of the young were to serve the state not just for the sake of the state but also for the sake of their families. These features were highlighted in the decoration and structure of the place at which the public ceremony of transition was held.

The day was completed with feasting and the festival of Liber (the Italian god of fertility), which would have included a greater celebration of the addition of a new adult male to Rome's citizen body on the part of the son's family. Moreover, presents and dinner invitations were given by those who had donned the *toga virilis* to friends and friends of their family (*ILS* 1083). This practice could have been extended to not only *amici*, but also clients and even strangers (Plin.*Ep*.10.116). It was an occasion to launch the new adult member of the family into the public sphere and was said to have been the occasion on which they assumed their own individual identity by using their *praenomen* (Varro *Auctor de praenominibus* 3.6; Funaioli 1907: 331; Gardner and Wiedemann 1991: 109). Pliny (*Ep*.10.116) makes it clear that this occasion ranked alongside those of marriage, entering public office or dedicating a building. It marked the beginning of the young man's public life, but also the continuation of the family within public life for the father and grandfathers. It was the occasion that created a citizen for the state; hence it occurred in public in front of the gods of the state, as well as those of the household and the family.

Although the transition in the setting of the Forum of Augustus was an arena of *exempla* that stressed the duty of the young man to parents, ancestors and the state, there was also a stress on the freedom associated with citizenship (Ovid *Fasti* 3.771–2). This is a clear distinction from the dependency of childhood protected in public by the presence of both a *bulla* and a *toga praetexta*. The latter made older children distinguishable from youths in the plain white toga. A transition that Persius (*Sat.*5.30–38) viewed as a childhood protected from trouble by the nature of the purple band on the toga to a youth led astray by friends to investigate the whole city, including the Subura. This was a place associated with prostitutes (Mart.*Ep.*6.66, 9.37, 10.45) and female barbers (2.17). The latter did not solely concern themselves with shaving of facial hair (Cic.*Tusc.*5.58; Plaut.*Truc.*400–410; Val.Max.3.2.15), and were also associated with sex and/or prostitution (*CIL*6.6368). This region of Rome was also the place in which violent incidents were perpetrated by youths after dark (Liv.3.13.2). It is the place in Rome that was the location for activities that were associated with youths throughout antiquity – drinking and violence, alongside the presence of brothels and prostitutes as catalogued by Eyben (1993). The *toga virilis* created or was associated with a difference in behaviour; unlike the child or *praetextatus*, the youth was seen as capable of penetrative sex (Suet.*Cal.*24). There is a clear expectation that the period after the transition out of childhood would have been a period of youthful excess that was seen as a response to the lifting of the restrictions associated with childhood (Sen.*Contr.*2.6.11). There is equally a conception of the youth as a person who had no control over their sexuality or was possessed or controlled by their lusts (Plutarch *On Listening to Lectures* 1.37). These were to be overcome and controlled by the end of the period of transition to full adulthood – in short the youth was faced with a choice between a path of vice or a path of virtue (Cic.*Off.*1.118). However, the strongest imagery of youth from antiquity is of a young man who was aggressive and impulsive, alongside an uncontrolled sexuality.

The characterisation of youth

Writers who attempt to account for the life course in antiquity are at pains to portray the characteristics of youth as fundamentally different from those of an adult male citizen. Ptolemy (4.10.203–7) suggests that the eight years between the ages of fourteen and twenty-two were a time when a kind of frenzy overtook a man that resulted in a desire for any form of sexual gratification and a blindness of judgement. The sentiment was also expressed by both Aristotle (*Rhet.*2.12–14) and Horace (*Ars Poet.*156–8). Aristotle seems to have been the source for most Roman thought on the nature of youth and saw these young men as forming a strong bond between each other and likely to follow a noble course of action, rather than one which they may have considered carefully or have calculated the outcome. Typically, in rhetoric and

Plate 5.2 Memorial showing three brothers: note the difference in ages shown in this sculpture.

historical writing, it is youths who took part in conspiracies – because their minds could easily be turned by the older man at its head. The Catilinarian Conspiracy in 63 BC is a case in point (for an account of this event, see Rawson 1975: 60–88 or Stockton 1971: 110–42). Catiline, according to Sallust (*Cat.*5), was a man of both physical and mental qualities including an ability to endure cold, hunger or a lack of sleep – all areas which youths in military training were beginning to experience for the first time. He is said (Sall.*Cat.*14; also Plu.*Cic.*10) to have sought out the youths of the city of Rome and brought them round to his cause. This was achieved by appealing to their uncontrollable youthful passions for access to prostitutes or the purchase of hunting dogs or horses (*Cat.*14). For Sallust, this was all a by-product of the greed created by Rome's wealth, young men were placed into jeopardy by the presence of such riches and disregarded their modesty and chastity, and were instead utterly reckless (*Cat.*12). With the influence of an older man, such as Catiline, these young minds were directed towards crime (*Cat.*16).

The concept that the youths were innocent and compliant is also present in the rhetoric of Cicero: some were corrupted to the cause even before they took up the *toga virilis* (*Cat.*2.4); Catiline offered satisfaction to their lust or even the murder of their parents (*Cat.*2.8). The danger for the state, as Cicero saw it (*Cat.*2.23), was the creation of an effeminate group of youths reeking of perfume, banqueting all night, gambling, drinking and whoring – yet at the same time capable of poisonings and murder. Catiline did not simply have an attractive personality, his cause and the abolition of debts were attractive ideals that attempted to better the lot of the people; in contrast, Cicero's opposition to the recent agrarian law proposed by Rullus could have been seen as conservatism or a laissez-faire socio-economic mentality (note also that Cicero had his own youthful thugs: Cic.*Cat.*3.5–6). For Sallust (*Cat.*38), the actions of tribunes, who proposed bills to aid the masses, in opposition to the senate, could be explained with reference primarily to their age. Here, thinking of Clodius in 58 BC, Sallust may be underestimating his age (probably over thirty). However, it is notable that the prominent tribunes of the plebs, who pursued measures for the people, could have been perceived as idealists, rather than men making calculated political judgements (Tiberius Gracchus is a case in point, see Plu.*TG*). It was not seen as the fault of young men that they were led astray by Catiline and other older men, but they were a constant danger to the state all the same. They were impressionable and Cicero was later to defend one of them, Caelius Rufus, in court against the allegation that he had taken part in the Catilinarian Conspiracy on the grounds that he was too young to know better (see *Pro Caelio* for the text). The explanation is clear: conspiracies could take hold if an enigmatic leader could gain support of the sons of the elite at an age when they were men, wore the *toga virilis*, but were not yet in control of their bodies or their minds. Youths were easily led to violence, aggression, idealism, hatred, love, and excess (Arist.*Rhet.*2.12). The very nature of youth was not the danger for Rome, but its conjunction with the wealth and luxury of Rome (Sall.*Cat.*12). After all, the characteristics of youth were universal and only a phase to be passed through on the way to the creation of an adult citizen. However, all youths required the guidance of an older man who would shape the young man's character towards the things that Roman society held dear.

Cicero and Caelius Rufus

Aristotle's views on the subject of youth and its characteristics can be found to underpin Cicero's discussion in the *Pro Caelio* of the actions of Caelius Rufus from the time he put on the *toga virilis* until he was taken to court in 56 BC. It is also possible from this speech to reconstruct the life course in youth of a single individual. Caelius had been born in 82 BC and had been educated by his father until he began the period of youth. At that stage, his education was put into the hands of Marcus Cicero and Marcus Crassus – older men, in Cicero's case by twenty-four years, who would look after and advise the young man. They would also ensure that in this early period of youth, strongly associated with sexual vulnerability, Caelius did not see anyone without either his father, Cicero or Crassus acting as his chaperone. It is clear that by the age of about nineteen this phase had ended and that Caelius was free to meet people as he wished. He had spent time on the staff of Quintus Pompeius, the governor of Africa from 62–59 BC; we are uncertain as to the length of time but can be sure that he was in his twenties. On his return to Rome, at the age of twenty-three, he prosecuted the ex-consul C. Antonius for extortion success-fully and continued to attend the courts and the forum until he was twenty-six. Hence, publicly he was prominent. He would also have been seen running as a *lupercus* at the festival of the Lupercalia (see below pp. 74–5 for discussion) and his beauty and good looks had attracted attention that had led to gossip. The substance of this gossip, according to Cicero, was the proxim-ity of his rented house on the Palatine to that of the notorious Clodia. He lived there, rather than at his father's house, to gain access to the forum and to the houses of the eminent men of Rome on the Palatine. This is a marked contrast to the period of early youth, in which Caelius was chaperoned; now in his twenties he was seen as an adult. However, like all youths, he was subject to the nature of that phase of life:

> When he has listened to the voice of pleasure and given some time to love
> affairs and these empty desires of youth, let him at length turn to the inter-
> ests of a more domestic life, to the activities of the forum and public life.
>
> (Cic.*Cael.*42)

This is a marked contrast to the Romans' views on their daughters' sexuality, which was controlled by either early marriage or *regimen*. In men, youthful lust was tolerated as long as it did not damage the community. Hence, sex with prostitutes and slaves was seen as a means of controlling the dangers of over-sexed youths within society. Another feature of youth that would be grown out of in due course was their flamboyance, glamour and, above all, burning ambition. These, as Cicero says, would mellow with age, as will the love affairs once a man is older, when his *domus*, the city's forum and public affairs in general play a greater role. What is clear from Cicero's defence of Caelius Rufus is that youth was seen as having more than one part: to begin with these new men were vulnerable, later they were flamboyant, and finally they were simply men.

Hairy youths

The phase of transition through youth was marked physically with the growth of body and facial hair. Youths did not shave until they had grown their first full beard. Hence, the downy growth was associated with the period of adolescence (Amm.Marc.14.11.28) that marked out the unshaven young adults from the rest of the adult population. Indeed, the *inberbus iuvenis* or beardless youth was associated by Horace with the joys of horses and hounds, the exercises of the Campus; the absence of a tutor; and equally the lack of control of money, soft still and easily moulded to evil, and finally full of spirit and strong desires (Hor.*Ars Poet*.156–78; for example Cicero associ-ated foolhardy political ventures with the passions of youthful exuberance.

*Att.*1.14.5, 1.16.11; *Cat.*22; *Dom.*37). The growth of a beard marked out the transition; those with the beginnings of a beard could have been seen as the first stage, others with shaggy faces were at the end of the period of transition. In other words, these young men were still incapable of being a citizen or acting responsibly. This was a problem for Octavian, who did not shave his first beard until 39 BC when he would have been twenty-three (Dio 48.34.3; compare the inscription from a cemetery on the Via Salaria *NSc* 1900: 578, see Chapter 8 on Octavian). To gain acceptance for his youthful looks, he associated himself with Apollo – a god who was *inberbus* (Cic.*Nat.Deorum*1.83, 3.84; Val.Max.1.1.ext.3). The youthful action of Octavian was played upon in the *Res Gestae* (1) towards the end of Augustus' life, but between 44 and 39 BC his youth was not seen as an advantage. It is significant that after his first beard was shaved, Octavian kept his chin smooth (Dio 48.34.3), maybe to ensure the continuation of an association with the unbearded Apollo.

The actual cutting of the first beard was seen to mark the end of a period of misdeeds and a further change into a more adult period of life (Juv.*Sat.*8.166). Shaving could occur at the public festival known as the Iuvenalia (Ovid *Trist.*4.10.58; Juv.*Sat.*3.186–9), or at another public occasion. It was a key moment of transition that would seem to occur in the early twenties (Dio 48.34.3; *Pal.Anth.*6.161; Suet.*Cal.*24; *Ner.*12; *NSc* 1900: 578) and was marked with the sacrifice of bullocks and the dedication of the first beard to a deity (Petr.*Sat.*28; Suet.*Ner.*12.4). From this time onwards, the person was viewed in a different way. Regular shaving, drinking and sex were associated together by some authors (Mart.*Ep.*11.39). The male body during the growth of the first beard was associated with other changes as well: through exercise in the Campus Martius muscle tone developed, alongside the growth of body hair (Ovid *Ars Am.*1.505–20). The latter presented a dilemma about whether to remove it by singeing, depilation or plucking (for methodology see Kilmer 1982: Julius Caesar, whose sexuality was put into question in his late teens because of his association with the court of Nicomedes, was criticised in later life for having his hair plucked – Suet.*Jul.*2, 45).

The hairy body was seen as desirable because it was warlike and masculine, whereas those who removed hair from their legs, torso and buttocks were viewed as effeminate but beautiful (Juv.*Sat.*2.9–13, 8.114, 9.13–5; Mart.*Ep.*2.62, 2.29, 6.56, 10.65). This aspect of the body was revealed to all in the baths, and the place was associated with voyeuristic activity with a focus on the smooth buttocks of young men, as well as being the place for the removal of body hair in general (Toner 1995: 55–7). The youth, as opposed to the child, went to bathe without the accompaniment of a tutor. In the same way as the youth was led to prostitution in the Subura, so he went to the baths in the same manner and was the object of desire for other men. His attractiveness was in some ways defined by the absence of body hair; once that hair had grown, he was no longer desirable and had moved on to join those gazing on the youths as opposed to those who were the object of that gaze. The growth of hair on the body and the face defined early youth in the Roman world (see Williams 1999 for discussion of sexuality). This was seen both in public in the forum and in the Campus, but also in the baths.

The transition associated with the growth of a beard in a man's early twenties is confirmed and further revealed with reference to the festival of the Lupercalia. The procedure of the festival is well known: the *luperci*, composed of youths and the leading magistrates, met at the cave known as the Lupercal where Romulus and Remus were said to have been suckled by the she-wolf (Warde Fowler 1908: 310–21 for source material). There they sacrificed goats and a dog. The bloody sacrificial knife was then wiped on the foreheads of the two leading youths and wiped away with wool dipped in goats milk. The youths then laughed and dressed in the goatskins, then they feasted. After eating, the naked *luperci* ran through the city, striking women with thongs made from the skin of the sacrificial goats (*februa*). Explanations of these actions vary (Beard, North and Price 1998: 47), but only the one that is significant for the life course need concern us. Ovid (*Fasti* 2: 267–470) provides an explanation with reference to the life course of the city in myth. He suggests that following the Rape of the Sabine Women, there were no pregnancies, the reason being that a fertility rite did not exist at Rome. This fact was brought to the mythical Romans' attention by Juno Lucina by the phrase: 'Let the sacred he-goat go into the Italian matrons', which an Etruscan augur carried out by striking the women with thongs of goatskin; within ten lunar months the women became pregnant. In other words, as Herbert-Brown (1994: 58) points out, the Lupercalia was a celebration of an incident that created the birth of the first generation of Romans. The fact that youths were involved, whom Augustus insisted should not be *inberbes* (the unbearded; Suet.*Aug.*31), suggests that these were the young men at the end of youth. These youths needed to display their fertility by running naked. Their hairiness or beard was a sign of their masculine ability to cause women to become fertile by striking them in a mode reminiscent of the action that took place, when Rome needed to conceive its first generation of children, in myth. At the same time, we should recognise the violence of the festival that is directed towards women by the *luperci*. The whipping was far from symbolic as Hopkins (1991: 479–84) has shown. In funerary sculpture, the *luperci* were represented as muscular and half naked with a whip that could inflict serious wounds (Veyne 1960) and literally carried off women to be whipped. The violence returns us again to the Rape of the Sabine women in mythology, which often described the Sabine women metaphorically as a flock of sheep attacked by the young Roman wolves (Beard 1999; Ov.*Am.*1.101–34). In the festival of the Lupercalia, we might read the dash of the whip carrying *luperci* amongst the wives of Rome as a retelling of the incident – women were carried off and then whipped by the *luperci,* just as the Sabine women were carried away at the festival of the Consualia and then later whipped (the imagery is comparable in sculpture – Veyne 1960 and Kampen 1991). Like the mythological rape, the run of the *luperci* marks a change – the completion of their life as a youth and at the same time their running or scampering chase of women represents their uncontrollable sexual desires as a youth. Also, for the whipped women, their life course is also changed via the beating; fertility could have been seen to have been promoted and motherhood to have become a possibility.

Violence and youth

Within the structure of the Roman state prior to the first century BC, there was an expectation that all adult males take part in military service. The number of campaigns varied from sixteen years as a member of the infantry to ten years in the cavalry (Polyb.6.19). The army itself and a soldier's equipment varied according to their age. The young men described by Livy (8.8) as the flower of the *pubescentes* fought as *velites* or skirmishers (Polyb.6.22). They were armed with three foot shields, javelins and a sword (Liv.38.21.13) and were employed for the most part with the guarding of the stockade of the army camp (Polyb.6.35; 10.15). However, the swift young men were often utilised to fight elephants in the wars with Carthage (Liv.21.55.11) or at the start of battle were deployed in front of the main body of *hastati* (Polyb.6.23) made of older citizens. In fact, the deployment on the battlefield created a division whereby the young were always placed in front of the older and more experienced citizens. The tension and pressure on the young to perform in the face of the enemy was increased by the fact that the older men stood behind them watching their exploits and in a way assessing their potential (Val.Max.3.1.6b). Stories of the brave youth abound in Roman history (e.g. Plu.*Aemil*.21–7). Battle and the observation of the actions of young men was a key means to gain *gloria* (Cic.*Off*.2.45) in front of those who were older. It was a means to create the citizen warrior for the rest of that person's life and began at the point when the *toga virilis* was adopted ceremonially at Rome. Not only were the young men or *velites* involved in guarding the camp and the battle itself, it was these young men who murdered the enemy wounded (Liv.38.21.13) or engaged in the burning of villages and the sacking of cities. The violence of Roman warfare was not confined to the battle field (see Goldsworthy 1996), but included the assault, mutilation and death of the aged, women, youths and children as well as the men who fought against Rome's legions (see Ziolkowski 1995 for examples).

Later in the empire, youths were seen as the ideal recruits to the army. Reasons given for this were that they were at the beginning of puberty and hence would have become accustomed to being given orders easily (Veget.1.4), unlike a grown man who was fully formed. Also Vegetius (1.4) is keen to point out that the exercises (e.g. running or jumping) associated with military service needed to be acquired before the body slowed with age. Those who recruited soldiers looked for certain features, many of which were associated with the physiognomy of the masculine male – lively eyes, head erect, broad chest, muscular shoulders, strong arms, long fingers, a small belly, thin buttocks, sinewy feet and calves. In other words a trained body that was superior to that of the average citizen (Juv.*Sat*.16.7). The association between puberty and first service in the army throughout Roman antiquity demonstrates another side of the transition from childhood – the youth fought and killed – by the end of this period he was an experienced soldier or fighter and had graduated from the youngest group originally associated with speed in battle to skirmish with an enemy to the main body of soldiers or *hastati*, who decided the outcome of many battles. Progressively as the man became older he began his battle further away from the enemy, until he ceased to be expected to fight at the age of sixty.

The end of youth

The characterisation or expectation of the young man as incapable of public action was legally recognised by the *Lex Plaetoria* and the *Lex Villia Annalis*. These laws prevented youths from taking an active part in business or holding public office prior to the age of twenty-five or even thirty. This was the end marker of a young man's period of transition to adulthood (Eyben 1993: 8–9). An attitude summarised by Dio Cassius (52.20) in Maecenas' speech to Augustus:

> As for the matter of eligibility of office, we should put men on the roll of knights (*equites*) when they are eighteen years old, for at that age their physical soundness and their mental fitness can best be discerned; but we should not enrol them in the senate until they are twenty-five years old. For is it not disgraceful, and indeed hazardous, to entrust the public business to men younger than this, when we do not commit our private affairs to any one before this age? After they have served as quaestors and aediles or tribunes, let them be praetors when they reach the age of thirty.

The age of entry into the senate reported here is twenty-five, but we do find in the municipal laws an entry age into a magistracy in the local town councils was given as thirty (*Tabula Heraclenensis* 89–97) with the qualification that the individual had served either three campaigns on horseback with a legion or six campaigns on foot with a legion. In other words, the law defined a youth as a person incapable of adult thinking but capable of fighting and other adult activities. The years between eighteen and twenty-five are yet another transitional period in the journey towards adult status (see also Chapter 10 on funerary commemoration of the young).

It is also in their mid twenties that men tended to get married for the first time. There was little choice in the matter. Not to marry was to be subject to severe criticism (Val.Max.2.9.1) and penalties under the Augustan marriage laws. The change was marked by the setting up of a *domus* of their own into which they would bring their wife. Unlike female first marriage, the role of their father or *paterfamilias* was not as great – particularly if we recognise that demographically less than 50 per cent of sons in their mid twenties had a living father (see Appendix 1). This did not mean that they acted alone in the marriage negotiations, other older men were often involved (Plin.*Ep.*1.14). We have already seen how Caelius Rufus was advised by Cicero and Marcus Crassus in Rome (men in their early fifties in 56 BC), whilst his aged father lived away from the political arena. In the absence of a living father, it would have been these men who would have been the brokers in the arrangement of a man's marriage. Demographically, these fifty year olds were of an age where they were likely to have daughters at marriage age (older than fourteen) and were also intimately involved in the politics of the time. Hence they could utilise their influence on men, such as Caelius Rufus, to make marriages that were politically and financially advantageous to themselves.

Although politics influenced the choice of a wife other factors were involved as well (see Chapters 7 and 8). Roman society put a particular value on marriage to a *virgo* or virgin and an ideal of marriage to one person for life; we often see inscriptions referring to women married to one man (they were referred to as *univira*, see Williams 1958: 23–4; Treggiari 1991a: 232–5). The reasons for this were twofold: firstly, because the purpose of marriage was the reproduction of legitimate children, certainty could only be assured if the bride was a virgin; and second, Roman men found the post-pubescent young male or female the most attractive objects of sexual desire (see discussion in Williams 1999 on male sexuality). One set of thoughts, identified by Treggiari (1991a: 106–7), suggests that Roman men thought that young virgins had a precocious sexuality but went through a pretence of masking this with a veil of innocence. This view fits with the thinking of medical writers on the subject of female puberty (see Chapter 4). However, Treggiari (1991a: 106–7) has also found in the literature evidence for a degree of trauma for the young bride on her wedding night as well. What is clear though is that Roman men at their first marriage expected their young bride to be a virgin and found this in itself to be an object of sexual excitement (see Kelly and Leslie 1999; Kelly 2000 for discussion). In subsequent marriages, the possibility of finding a virgin bride was less likely with remarriage to a widow or divorcee. The ideals of a virgin bride and marriage to one person for life were later appropriated by Christian writers to create an ideal of monogamy and sexual experience with a single partner (Cooper 1996: 97–104; Williams 1958: 23–4). Marriage, for the Roman male, marked the end of a phase when they had had no responsibilities, had been free to sleep with anyone as long as they did not break the law, and had experienced the violence of military training. Tacitus' account (*Agr.*4–6) of his father-in-law's youth is a classic example of how a phase of life came to an end. Agricola had been spared the temptations of youth in Massilia (Marseilles), although he had become interested in philosophy to an extent that was seen to have been unhealthy. This was something Tacitus (*Agr.*4) thought he simply grew out of with age. He was a military tribune in Britain in his early twenties during the Boudiccan revolt and returned to Rome to marry, and was elected Quaestor by the age of twenty-four or twenty-five. Military service, marriage and the quaestorship confirmed the final stages of transition marked by the growth and shaving of a beard. The youth was now a responsible citizen proven in the army, fertile, a suitable marriage partner and capable of holding office. A marked contrast to the child who had for the first time put on the *toga virilis* and entered into military training on the Campus Martius, with little knowledge or control of his sexuality and incapable of responsibility. Youth as a category marked this transition, but included both those at the beginning of this phase as well as those older and visibly different making the transition to marriage, responsibility for his own business negotiations, holding their first magistracy and entry into public responsibility.

6

THE PLACE OF MARRIAGE IN THE LIFE COURSE

Roman marriage is a topic that has been the subject of extensive discussion, culminating in the encyclopaedic treatment by Susan Treggiari (1991a). It is not our intention to represent this material again. Instead, we wish to examine the variety of meanings and social conventions associated with marriage in Rome according to the age of the participants. Marriage created a new form of identity for both the woman and the man, but this identity was subject to variation according to the age of the participants and whether those participants had been married before or had children from an earlier marriage. Our evidence for such marriages is partial and we may only find in our sources an indication of the potential variety of meanings of marriage. What is made clear by this evidence is that marriage was a key experience for nearly all adults, but the nature of marriage and its characterisation by others varied according to the age of the participants. In these cases, their age affected their expected behaviour within marriage and ultimately their character or what we might call today their psychological profile, or personality.

On marriage the husband's life might continue much as before, with the exception that now other men's wives could visit his home with no danger to their reputation. His wife's life, especially if this was a first marriage, was irrevocably transformed. The Roman matrona's life was characterised by ambiguity: the ideal wife as expressed on epitaphs was beautiful, chaste, devoted to her husband, a good mother, pious, modest, stay-at-home, accomplished at wool-working and thrifty (e.g. *CIL*1. 1007; 6, 29580, 34268; 8, 11294; 9, 1913; Gardner and Wiedemann 1991: 53–4); as a member of the upper classes a wife was endowed with a certain amount of authority, the lived experience of her life was at odds with this ideal image. As *materfamilias* her responsibilities could include running the household, organising childcare, attending and providing social functions with and for her husband, particularly in respect of female guests, and maintaining social links with her own family (see Chapters 2 and 7); if legally independent she could be managing her own estates and incomes (Saller 1999). While the two images were not necessarily mutually exclusive, it is clear that at times the demands of social class could conflict with the prescribed norms of female behaviour. Only a cursory glance at the ancient sources illustrates the existence of abundant examples of powerful and able women who could maintain households and were seen to be involved in many of the activities associated with their husbands.

Marriage and motherhood were undoubtedly the fast track to status for a woman of the Roman upper classes and they were processes thought to be appropriate to a certain stage of the life course. Ideally marriage should have taken place at a time when the bride was ready to produce heirs. As we have shown, from the point of view of the female life course, first marriages at least were controlled and arranged by the older generation (see Chapter 4). This control may have been reduced but did not cease when a woman married. A bride may have left childhood behind her on the day of her wedding but she did not cease to be a daughter. Legally recognised marriage (*iustum matrimonium*) could only exist if the couple fulfilled certain criteria: they should be citizens with the right of *conubium* i.e. they should not be within prohibited kinship groups, must be willing and of a suitable age. Such a marriage produced legitimate offspring who took the name and status of their father; they were born Roman citizens in the power of their *paterfamilias*. In the period we are considering, *iustum matrimonium* took two forms. In both of these the wife remained a daughter in some form. In the older version, one that had almost gone out of fashion by the late Republic, known as marriage with *manus* (legal power of husband over his wife), the wife left the *potestas* (power) of her father and entered that of her husband, or his father. She entered the inheritance networks of her new family, inheriting as a daughter from her husband, that is, she bore the same legal relationship to her husband as their children and her husband replaced her father as guardian and protector. Any property the wife might own prior to such a marriage or acquire during it passed to her husband. To say a wife in *manus* related to a husband like a daughter is to obscure the social reality of the marriage relationship. Her legal status placed her in a position similar to that of a daughter but as a wife she was clearly differentiated socially and emotionally (for a fuller explantion of these terms see Treggiari 1991a: 15–32).

The more common form by the first century BC, marriage without *manus*, meant that while the wife lived with her husband, she remained in the power of her father and in the inheritance network of her natal family and outside that of her new in-laws. On the death of her father she became legally independent (*sui iuris*). Another effect of this form of union was that a mother was not in the same legal *familia* as her children (for fuller explanation see Treggiari 1991a: 32–6). Legal niceties here do not necessarily reflect social realities – a mother's loyalty was expected to be towards her children. However, as we shall see below and in Chapter 7, in such unions a wife was often torn between loyalty to her husband and her natal family (see Dixon 1988, 1992; Hallett 1984). Marriage highlights the fact that individuals play several roles within the family simultaneously: the woman is wife, daughter and mother at the same time – not to mention aunt, sister, etc. In the course of her married life a woman's loyalties pulled in many directions at once.

Looking at first marriages where we can establish at least the approximate age of the partners, the norm was for an older man to marry a younger woman. The age differential varied according to a number of factors. Most of our examples are either from the Imperial family or from the aristocratic elite, whose women tended to marry at an earlier age than the norm for the rest of society (Saller 1994: 25–66 for discussion of this and demographic factors). For example, Augustus' daughter Julia was married twice before she was eighteen. Her first husband, Marcellus, was only three years older than her, but her second, Agrippa, was a contemporary of her father. Marriage did not necessarily involve a husband of a similar age to that of the teenage bride. Pliny's marriage at forty, to the fifteen-year-old Calpurnia, was more acceptable to his family and friends because he was still childless, despite two previous marriages (*Ep.*4.1; 4.19; 6.4; 7.5; 8.10, 8.11; 10.120, 10.121). By marrying such a young girl he was giving himself a good chance of begetting heirs; whilst her own family were seeking heirs as well (*Ep.*8.10, 11). His view of her affection for him is made clear in a letter. It is not youth or his body, but his *gloria* or status which was attractive, and she would seem to have expressed an interest in his speeches and public actions that he undertook – at least Pliny presented such an image (*Ep.*4.19: see below). For a young bride at first marriage, partners would have varied according to their age. Although all young brides, at say the age of seventeen, were at the same age and same position in the life course, their social world and outlook varied according to the age of their husband (see Chapter 7). The nature of a woman's first marriage varied according to the age, stage in their life course and status of their husband. The identity of their husband changed their own status and maybe differentiated them from their peers married to other men either younger or older than their own husband or from a different social group or geographical location. However, common to all marriages was the pressure from both the husband and the bride's families for children.

Age and asymmetrical marriages

Marriage at an early age might have enhanced the 'virtue' of submission and sense of subordination a young girl might have felt towards her husband, and increased his sense of superiority, dominance and paternalism, but we must remember that such an image was the product of the husband's mind. Pliny's third marriage to the fifteen-year-old Calpurnia was presented by him as a perfect match:

> My wife is highly intelligent and a careful housewife, and her devotion to
> me is a sure indication of her virtue. In addition this love has given her an
> interest in literature: she keeps copies of my works, to read again and again

and even learn by heart. She is so anxious when she knows that I am going to plead in court, and so happy when all is over! (she arranges to be kept informed of the sort of reception and applause I receive, and what verdict I win in the case). If I am giving a reading she sits behind a curtain nearby and greedily drinks in every word of appreciation. She has even set my verses to music and sings them, to the accompaniment of her lyre, with no musician to teach her but the best of masters, love.

(*Ep.*4.19.2–4)

Calpurnia fits the image of the ideal bride as epitomised on epitaphs. This ideal wife and marriage reflected favourably on Pliny himself; by implication he was an ideal husband and good upright citizen. The transference of virtue by association was continued as a compliment to the addressee, Calpurnia Hispulla, his wife's paternal aunt who raised her to be a paragon of virtue. Calpurnia's opinion is not recorded; these letters tell us little of her experience of being Pliny's wife, besides the activities with which she passed her time (Shelton 1990). Such activities – writing, reading and music – illustrate how the socialisation and education of a young bride could continue under the guidance of her husband. Pliny's position makes him the 'natural' teacher of his bride, a role he admired in his friend Pompeius Saturninus (*Ep.*1.16.6; Hemelrijk 1999: 32; cf Plut.*Mor.*145b-146).

In second or subsequent marriages, where the age gap between the couple was often reduced, the wife may have felt more confident of her position. We have glimpses into the interior of a marriage of a couple in which the wife is, unusually, older than her husband – Quintus Cicero and Pomponia, sister of Cicero's friend Atticus. Atticus and his sister were close in age (Nepos, *Atticus*17.1) but she does not seem to have married Quintus until she was at least forty, a remarkably late age, so it is unlikely this is a first marriage. The glimpses we have of Quintus and Pomponia are filtered through the letters of her brother and brother-in-law and are not particularly complimentary to Pomponia. Both partners are criticised by their respective brothers for not behaving as husband and wife should towards each other but the details are often unclear (*Att.*1.2; 2.2; 17). In 50 BC a letter from Cicero to Atticus demonstrated how the marital discord exposed itself: the brothers and their families and entourage had stopped at a villa for lunch:

> When we arrived, Quintus said in the kindest nice way, 'Pomponia, will you ask the women in, and I'll get the boys.' Both what he said and his intention and manner were perfectly pleasant, at least it seemed so to me...She answered in our hearing 'I am a guest here myself'. That I imagine, was because Statius [Quintus' slave] had gone ahead to see to our luncheon. Quintus said to me: 'There! This is the sort of thing I have to put up with every day'. You'll say 'What was there in that, pray?' A good deal. I myself was quite shocked. Her words and manner were gratuitously rude.

Plate 6.1 Married couple and their children from the Via Tiburtina cemeteries. This grave marker set up by Vettia Hospita to her deceased husband Lucius Vettius Alexander also includes images of the couple's children, a son and a daughter. Note the difference in ages represented here. The man is represented with a furrowed brow and receding hairline, whereas the woman is somewhat younger. The children appear only as miniature persons in the spaces around the central scene.

> I concealed my feelings, painful as they were, and we all took our places at table except the lady. Quintus, however, had some food sent to her, which she refused. In a word, I felt my brother could not have been more fore-bearing nor your sister ruder... early the following day he [Quintus] told me that Pomponia had refused to spend the night with him and that her attitude when she said good-bye was just as I had seen it. Well, you may tell her to her face that in my judgement her manners that day left some-thing to be desired. (*Att.*5.1, 3–5; trans. Shackleton-Bailey)

Concordia, the ideal of marital harmony, was obviously lacking between Pomponia and Quintus, but note that Cicero refrained from saying anything directly but left reprimands up to her brother, while supporting his own flesh and blood, thus illustrating the continued influence of the wife's natal family. Other letters do show how close knit the families were with Terentia and Pomponia often visiting each other (Bradley 1991: 188); marriage integrated the two kin groups further (see Chapter 7). In Pomponia's defence, her husband had spent the best part of the previous ten years away from Rome on official duties and was about to go away again and take their son with him this time (Gratwick 1984: 34). Life for a *matrona* without a husband present could have been more restricted than life with a despised one, if a woman was to retain her good reputation. The marriage did finally end in divorce, after about twenty-five years.

The power of mothers

The primary reason for marriage was the production of legitimate heirs: once this was achieved, the marriage would have been considered a success. Parents were expected to share responsibility for their children and likewise to share equally in the reflected glory of a child's success as an adult (see Chapter 3 on children). It is almost axiomatic in Roman history that children who achieved highly had at least one good parent, and that good parents produced good children. For both husband and wife the birth of the first child marked another stage in the life course, the transformation from wedded couple to parents. Even if the child may not have been directly in her father's power, as parents, the husband and wife were responsible for the raising of their shared child. For the mother this was a significant step as it proved her fertility and justified her place in the marriage and in the marriage market, should she have reason to re-enter it. Becoming a mother also highlighted a woman's ambiguous position within the conjugal group: outside it by virtue of her legal status, inside it by virtue of her reproductive role. Her children were considered primarily as assets to their agnate family; her wealth was considered separately to her husband's but was expected to pass to their mutual children (on the legal gymnastics to avoid this being absorbed by the *paterfamilias* in the event of a mother's early death see *Dig.*38.17, *sc Tertullianum, sc Orphitianum*; Gardner 1986: 146–54).

Motherhood altered the status of women from that of a bride or wife to a person with direct influence over their offspring. Their status with respect to their husband increased as well. It is this stage of the female life course that produces the 'bad girls' of Roman history. We can see this graphically with reference to the younger Agrippina. As young wife of Claudius and mother of Nero she is an archetypal powerful woman who is characterised as having control over her husband and her son – until he commits the ultimate crime of murdering her (see Suet.*Claud; Nero*; Tac.*Ann.*13–14 for Agrippina's influence). It is mothers in their late twenties and early to mid thirties who constitute the 'bad girls' of Roman history: Sempronia, Clodia, Julia, Messalina, Agrippina, to mention an obvious few, and we might include foreign queens such as Cleopatra alongside these Roman matrons. All had been married, had children and had been widowed. They had fulfilled their role to the state and their husbands through the production of children. This factor enhanced their status as paradigms of Roman motherhood, but at the same time they also constituted a threat to male power (on Clodia see Chapter 7). If married again, where was their loyalty – with their children or with their husband and his children from an earlier marriage? These questions were played out in the succession of Nero, the son of Agrippina, over Claudius' son Britannicus via his previous marriage to Messalina (Griffin 1984: 23–33). Those women at this age who did not remarry and were *sui iuris* had total control of their property and lives. They cannot be categorised as submissive wives like Pliny's Calpurnia. Instead, they possessed freedom and status in their own right, as well as the possibility of influencing their adult sons to gain access to a world of male power (Laurence 1997).

These 'problem' women are as socially constructed as the ideal matrona of epigraphic evidence, as Fischler (1994) pointed out, they have all the right attributes but use them in all the wrong ways. They become inversions of the traditional Roman matrons. We can see this from Sallust's description of Sempronia (*Cat.*25) compared with that of Calpurnia given by Pliny (see above):

> Among these women was Sempronia, who had often committed many crimes of masculine daring. In birth and beauty, in her husband also and children, she was abundantly favoured by fortune; well read in literature of Greece and Rome, able to play the lyre and dance more skilfully than an honest woman need… But there was nothing which she held so cheap as modesty and chastity; you could not easily say whether she was less sparing of her money or her honour; her desires were so ardent that she sought men more often than she was sought by them.

Here, we see the power, education or good fortune of a married mother undercut by the attribution of male personality traits. The characteristics of a young bride have been transformed after pregnancy and birth into a power that can only be subverted by the characterisation of the woman as transgressive of gender boundaries. This transition from innocent bride into the deviant mother was not a reality, but a further means of male rhetoric to attack or maintain an ideological submissiveness of wives. The threat of the powerful mother in their thirties may have caused many men to prefer to marry a young girl even if the man was in his sixties (see Chapter 7).

Ending a marriage

The consequences of ending a marriage, whether by death or divorce, were far reaching. They effected the individual husband and wife, their children and their property. Remarriage created new families, with many parents finding a new role as step-parent. Divorced or widowed, those of marriageable age were expected to remarry. The emphasis within marriage on the production of children did not just come from the families of the couple, but was also implemented by the state. At the five yearly census, the husband had to state clearly on oath that his marriage was for the procreation of children (Treggiari 1994: 57–8). It was the need to fulfil this oath that resulted in the first divorce of a woman for infertility in 230 BC by Spurius Carvilius (Dion.Hal.2.25.6–7; Plu.*Mor.*267C; Gell.*NA*.4.3.2; Val.Max.2.1.4; Treggiari 1994: 442; cf *Laud.Tur.*2.45). For the young bride, we can see the implications of such a divorce if it was stated that she was sterile. In a society that viewed the purpose of marriage, and the reason for the existence of women, in terms that primarily emphasised reproduction, for a woman to have been infertile was to markedly reduce her status. The period of time over which sterility was measured would appear to have been five years (Sen.*Contr.*2.5, *Decl.Min.*251, note that this temporal period coincides with that between censuses). A girl married at a very young age may not have developed biological fertility during this period of time (see Chapter 1); the threat of sterility should not be underestimated given the nature of the censorial oath sworn every five years. Once divorced, it would have been difficult for any husband taking the censorial oath to marry her. The powerlessness of the 'sterile' divorcee is shown graphically in the case of Claudius' daughter Octavia (Suet.*Nero* 35). She married Nero when she was thirteen and was divorced at the age of twenty-two, receiving gifts in the form of estates – later in the same year she was accused of adultery, banished to Pandateria and murdered. Seneca's tragedy, *Octavia,* reveals the anxieties and hopelessness of the spurned young wife with little hope of remarriage and knowledge of her successor, Poppaea. Octavia is an extreme example drawn from the imperial household, but other women defined as sterile and divorced were placed into a similar situation. They were socially dead and had ceased to have a role or purpose within the state, their own family, and importantly in the eyes of their peers. On divorce from their husband they would return to the house of their father or guardian and it was unlikely that they would have been sought out for a second marriage.

However, when we examine the cases in which sterility was cited as a cause, these type of divorces reveal a social practice that preserves the status of the divorced woman. The first and most famous example, Spurius Carvilius' divorce, resulted in the hatred of the people and a general condemnation of his action (Dion.Hal.2.25.6–7; Val.Max.2.1.4). Later examples, such as that of Sulla's third wife, Cloelia (Plu.*Sul.*6.11), were conducted amicably with praise of the woman and gifts. The *Laudatio Turiae* has implicit praise for the husband when he does not divorce his sterile wife even at her instigation (*ILS* 8393). Moreover, divorces for the reason of sterility were also characterised by a rapid marriage on the part of the man to another woman. This allowed for the rumour that the cause of sterility was simply an excuse for the divorce, because the man wished to marry another woman (e.g. Plu.*Sul.*6.11; Dio 59.23.17; Tac.*Ann.*14.60.5). At Rome, where all public actions, particularly those of the elite, were an object of speculation, we can see how the rapid remarriage of a man, after divorcing his wife on the grounds of sterility, would establish the suggestion of an absence of sex within his former marriage and question his ex-wife's fertility (see Laurence 1994 on the mechanics of rumour). Hence, the woman's sterility was placed in doubt and raised the possibility of remarriage and a prevention of the implications of a social death.

By the first century BC it appears that both husband or wife (or their heads of family) could initiate divorce. Divorce, like marriage, appears relatively informal in that all that was required was notification in a letter, or by messenger, from one spouse to the other. There was no state intervention required and no recourse to law unless the return of the dowry was disputed (for a full history of divorce see Treggiari 1991a: 323–64). This informality and the rhetoric of some Roman authors has led to the assumption that divorce was common among the upper classes of Rome in the late Republic and early Principate (cf Bradley 1991: 161; Dixon 1992). It is significant that it is the satirists, in particular, who played on the number of divorces a woman had had as part of their general denigration of women (Mart.*Ep.*6.7; Juv.*Sat.*6.224–30). These sources should not be taken as evidence of a high divorce rate, and, as Treggiari has argued, the rate of divorce may not be as high as previously thought and divorce was not always taken lightly (1991a: 473–82; Appendices 5 and 6; 1991b). Although the young bride might have been able in law to divorce her husband if married without *manus*, to do so she would have required the permission of her father or guardian – the person who had arranged the marriage in the first place. Equally, the language of divorce was engendered to create a language that blamed the wife rather than the husband. Treggiari (1991a: 439) highlights this feature: the husband 'repudiates' or 'dismisses' her, whereas the wife 'goes her separate way' or 'departs'. The language highlights the nature of power within marriage for the young wife. She could be repudiated for the lack of children in the marriage with the blame for their absence placed on her, as opposed to the fertility of the man. She could leave her husband, but the emphasis, even if she was being physically abused, in terms of language highlighted her own female inconsistency rather than a dismissal of the husband.

Divorce had an impact on the life course of a woman even if she had a good chance of contracting a subsequent marriage. The effects of divorce were immediate and disrupting. It could mean leaving the marital home (unless this was part of the dotal arrangement) with little more than personal belongings, and returning to the house of her father or another male relative. It meant the loss of the position of *materfamilias* that had been the foundation of her status as a wife. As the female head of household she absorbed the social persona of her husband, she had authority within the household and influence outside of it via her husband and sons. Women's influence in the public world was, except for a few outstanding exceptions, mediated through their men. On the occasion of divorce all this was potentially lost unless the woman was very wealthy in her own right. If there had been children, a mother also normally lost day-to-day contact with them because, as members of their father's family and not their mother's, they remained in the paternal home, perhaps to be raised by a stepmother. There were of course exceptions to this rule, particularly in the case of small babies, but in general children were raised in their father's house. Children faced a variety of carers throughout their lives and may have lived in several different households with several step parents, but some kept contact with their natural parents (see Chapters 3 and 7). The wife could also have suffered economically. While her dowry should have insured against economic hardship, for a divorced woman it was not quite so straightforward as a simple return of capital. If the fault for the divorce lay with the wife she might forfeit the return of her dowry (*Dig.* 24.3.47). Children from the marriage were partially supported in the ex-husband's house by the retention of a part of the dowry. However, she did not lose property that was hers in her own right. Mothers were expected to leave their property to their children even if they had ceased to live with them and remarried and had additional children (cf *Laudatio Murdiae CIL* VI, 10230). If a woman was to remarry she would need a new dowry, so it appears that financially the wife would be worse off than her ex-husband who might suffer temporary hardship while he returned the dowry (see Dixon 1984a on Cicero and the dowries of Terentia and Tullia).

The status of widows

Marriage could also end prematurely through the untimely death of the husband. A woman's situation as a widow was different from that of the divorcée. Champlin (1991: 120–26) summarises recent discussion on the position of the wife as seen via the testamentary practice of husbands. Seldom did she inherit more than 50 per cent of her husband's estate – in any case, children from the marriage seem to have been preferred by testators over their wives (for further discussion see Chapter 10 below). However, a husband often left his wife the right to use the property in which she had resided until her death or remarriage (Gardner 1986: 163). A husband might also have created an arrangement whereby the widow in effect managed the inheritance of her children and protected their interests. In such a position the inheritance would have come to the children in the form of property or dowry at the time of majority or marriage, a mother acting as *de facto* tutor. Inheritance laws were concerned with protecting the patrimony for the children and only benefited the widow by virtue of the fact that she was considered to have her children's best interests at heart (Dixon 1988: 62–5; Gardner 1986: 150–4; Saller 1991: 41). With this general pattern of inheritance in Roman society, there was a need particularly for young widows to remarry in order to regain their status as a wife and access to a husband's social and economic resources. The Augustan marriage laws also provided an incentive for widows to remarry. It seems that in a large proportion of cases, remarriage was common (for a full treatment of remarriage see Humbert 1972).

Women widowed at a relatively young age faced a series of choices, some more realistic than others. Those without children and still in the power of their father would probably have returned to the natal family home and hope to remarry (cf. Tullia). Those with children might have faced a different series of choices: to remain a widow and raise their husband's children, to remarry – in which case the children might have remained with her and be raised by a stepfather – or be raised by their paternal relations. For very wealthy widows the choice of husband might now have been more of their own making. McGinn cites Tacitus (*Ann.*4.4) wherein Tiberius tells Sejanus that he cannot agree to his offer to marry Livia Julia, and that anyway, having already been widowed, Livilla could make her own decision with the advice of her mother and grandmother (McGinn 1999: 622). Those who were legally independent and wealthy had a wider range of choices available. They could choose, as did Cornelia, mother of the Gracchi, not to remarry. After her husband's death she enjoyed a life that was accorded respect: in her own house, entertaining important visitors, arranging her daughter's marriage and encouraging her sons' political careers. She expected support from her children and family and enjoyed enhanced status as a *univira* (Tac.*Dial.*28; Plu.*T.G.*1.2, *C.G.*19; Val.Max.4.4). Others were not so lucky and remarriage may have proved the sensible option.

However, remarriage need not have been a simple affair. If the widow had children, they had a vested interest in the retention of their inheritance. Her new husband was in many ways viewed as a threat to their financial well-being. Nowhere is this made clearer than in the remarriage of the wealthy widow Aemilia Pudentilla, an example that resulted in Apuleius, her new husband, being taken to court and from this event we have his defence and justification of his actions. He was accused of being a legacy hunter and bewitching Pudentilla into marrying him. Pudentilla had been a widow for at least fourteen years, her husband having died when their sons were aged eight or nine and three or four. Wealthy in her own right, it appears that her deceased husband's family had tried to keep her and her money within the family, her father-in-law betrothing her subsequently to his younger son. Presumably this would also have helped to secure his grandsons' inheritance. Pudentilla did not marry her brother-in-law and on the death of her father-in-law indicated her desire to remarry to her grown-up son, Pontianus (*Apol.*73). The marriage of a wealthy local widow to an outsider became the subject of scandal and legal action. The court case was brought by the father-in-law of Pontianus, who died shortly after his return, and the younger son of Pudentilla, Sicinius Pudens. The ensuing court case highlights the anxiety that surrounded the potential independence of wealthy widows in the Roman mind and the difficulty the Roman male had in finding social space for such women (Fantham 1995). Remarriage of widows might be of benefit to the woman but might present problems in terms of her children's inheritance. We have already seen that step-parents were feared as a potential threat to the inheritance of the children of the first marriage, as with Apuleius above. However the nature of Roman marriage and high mortality rates meant that remarriage and the creation of a series of families was not uncommon. The results of such serial marriages are discussed in Chapter 7 (see also Bradley 1991). They could result in a series of anomalies with stepchildren being older than stepmothers; grandchildren being born close in age to children; and children growing up surrounded by step-siblings (for stepmothers see Watson 1994).

Age and marriage

Marriage changed the identity and status of the participants, most notably in the case of women. The female transition from child to adult was marked by a change in both status and identity. As a child she was the daughter of her father and her identity was dependent on his. A prospective husband would need to approach her father or guardian and negotiate. Once married her identity became associated with that of her husband but also remained strongly associated with her natal family. Her role was in part dependent on her husband's identity and, in particular, age or position in the male life course – a wife with a twenty-five year old husband at the beginning of his political career had a very different life style from one with a husband aged forty, let alone sixty or beyond. This caused a differentiation between wives of the same chronological age but with husbands of different chronological ages (see Chapter 7 for further discussion of age mixing). To give birth created another identity within the marriage – that of mother. A woman's identity was now less dependent on her older husband but was established with reference to her son or daughter. This was proof of her reproductive ability and established her position not simply with reference to her husband, but also his family and her own – she was now not only a wife but also parent to the offspring of two families. To be unable to reproduce and make the transition to this status resulted in divorce and rejection – the consequences of which were low status or social death.

A second marriage was a very different affair. The wife's age and that of her husband would appear to have been closer in these cases. Indeed, as we have shown, there was a greater power for the wife within these marriages that disrupted the ideals of female subordination and *concordia* within the domestic setting. The examples of married women with children, who males identified as deviant or transgressive in their late twenties and thirties, points out their potential power and status. This may have caused many males to prefer to marry a young girl, rather than an older woman who had already had children by another man. Equally, some women of this age group simply preferred to remain as widows or women who had married only once (*univira*).

Their status was reinforced by the death of their husband, and the emergence of their sons into the public realm. Yet, such women could have been attacked for the absence of a husband and though their status may have been high, they were open to attack and ridicule in the male public sphere. The wealthy widow, if she remarried, was deemed to have fallen victim to a legacy hunter or a man intent on cheating her, and her offspring, of her wealth. The anxiety that this stereotype reveals is that of her children, who would have been concerned by a presence of an outsider within their family group. The complexities of family structure produced by remarriage could lead to awkward structures of kinship – maybe as complex as those of the imperial family group created by Augustus. What is clear though is that the variety and meaning of marriage was in part constructed via the ages of the participants – as too old, too young, or simply unsuited. At the same time, their expected behaviour was conditioned by their ages.

7

KINSHIP EXTENSION AND AGE MIXING THROUGH MARRIAGE

In ancient Rome, there was an expectation that its citizens (male and female) would marry and have children throughout their adult lives. It could be described as a duty associated with citizenship, in order that the state maintained a body of citizens that ultimately it could have called upon for its survival. On the other hand, parents and grandparents expected their successors to marry to establish the succession and survival of the family name in the future. More immediately, marriage could be seen as a process by which a family could extend its kin network to include others and to make connections that secured the support of persons beyond their immediate or existing network of relatives (Corbier 1991: 136). In the past the nature of these connections has often been viewed as a determining factor in the politics of the late Republic. However, this is not our concern here; what we wish to show is the potential of marriage as a process of kin extension and that the nature of kin extension varied according to the age of the bride and bridegroom at marriage. Our methodology for approaching this problem is to base our research primarily on the demographic life tables produced by Richard Saller (1994, see Appendix) and to combine these theoretical possibilities with a number of examples drawn from ancient sources. The latter, it has to be stated, are far from representative of all marriages. In particular, Pompey's many marriages reported by Plutarch (*Life of Pompey*) are emblematic *exempla* for a second century AD audience, looking back to the disasters of the first century BC. Other examples that we utilise are necessarily drawn from the letters of Cicero. There is an inevitable reliance on these two sources of information in the discussion of marriage at Rome. This can be seen clearly from Susan Treggiari's index of principal texts cited for her study of *Roman Marriage* (1991a: 547–8). After the legal sources, Cicero is the main author cited and discussed. Other studies of marriage follow this pattern, particularly in the discussion of kin extension – a social phenomenon not covered by Roman law, in that they necessarily rely on certain key examples from the Roman republic based on information from Cicero and Plutarch (e.g. Bradley 1991: 156–76). In short, our knowledge of Roman marriage as a social phenomenon is limited once we step beyond the legal framework. We recognise that our source material influences the way in which we view marriage and this is why we place an emphasis on the need to utilise demographic simulation as a control on these emblemic examples of republican marriage practices.

The starting point for this chapter is a conclusion made by Corbier (1991: 136):

> Matrimonial behaviour was necessarily influenced not by precise political aims but also by prospective inheritance and dowries and by a desire to consolidate or extend kinship and affinity networks.

We take this view and consider it in the context of marriage at different points through the male and female life course. The focus is on how the extension of kin and affinity networks might have varied according to the age of the prospective partners at marriage and remarriage. This approach is combined and underwritten by the work of ancient demographers, which for some time has seen marriage as a determining cultural factor in the overall age patterning of the Roman aristocracy. The discrepancy of female:male marriage ages is said by most writers on the subject to be about fifteen for females and twenty five for males on average. We should point out now that averages always suggest that there are examples below and above the number given. All figures are probable averages: as we all know from our real lives an average summarises a range of numbers on either side of the number listed as simply average and represents a diversity of experience, rather than a numerical exactitude. Saller's useful tables on the average age of living kin provide us with a guide to the kin structures of those getting married (see Appendix). We set out in this chapter a variety of kin structures that depend on the chronological age of the partners at marriage. In doing so, in each case, we discuss examples of marriages within the context of the demographic norms for marriage at those ages across the senatorial order.

The male focus of our sources tends to make all upper class marriages look like alliances between men, with the wife serving merely as a linking mechanism. It is undoubtedly true that prospective son-in-laws did, in effect, choose their father-in-laws and associated networks of kin and *amici* as partners, rather than the bride for herself, (i.e. Agrippa chose Atticus rather than Attica). It is generally accepted that as a male moved up the *cursus honorum* he entered successive brackets of desirability (on *cursus honorum* see Chapter 8), ideally, first as a potential son-in-law, then as a father-in-law. This ideal progression was sometimes subverted by marriage between a man beyond his fiftieth year with a young girl, leaving the individual open to ridicule and with the potential for him to be, ironically, older than his father-in-law. Changes in an individual's political life often brought changes in marital life. However, it is also clear that female fertility and early age of marriage reduced the number of highly desirable partners available. Women, as they progressed through life, were valued first for the connections of their families, particularly their fathers

Plate 7.1 Age distinctiveness in marriage. A funerary relief showing ages of a Republican husband and wife. The husband is represented in this republican relief as a man who has aged, with a lined face and a receding hair line. The wife in contrast is eternally young, maybe a feature that is highlighted by the age of her husband to create an image of a difference in the ages of the couple.

and elder brothers, but also for their potential and then proven fertility. However, it would seem that men regarded young girls or virgin brides as more desirable. The demographics suggest that marrying a daughter off at a relatively young age, certainly before she was twenty, should allow a father to see his grandchildren – so early marriage for daughters was desirable both for political alliances and for certainty of succession. Marriage of a sister was also considered important to the life course of her brothers. There is a common allusion that women had no interest in politics, but as Cooper (1996: 14) has pointed out invisibility in the political realm could have been a source of female power. This observation does not emancipate Roman women *per se*, but it does identify clearly female influence in the political realm via an interest in the success of her father, brothers or husband and his family.

There are some broad parameters that need to be established in the reader's mind prior to our discussion of marriage and kin extension:

- Marriage was not really a matter of choice for men or women in the Roman world. It took different forms but we are concerned here with legal marriage (*conubium*) between members of the upper classes in the last century of the late Republic and early imperial period.
- The purpose of marriage was the procreation of legitimate children, and

the perpetuation of the family in name and the preservation within that family of property, wealth and status.

- Marriage and remarriage was an expected experience for women from the age of fifteen to fifty and for men from twenty-five to sixty.
- Divorce and remarriage usually caused children from the previous marriage to reside in the household of their father.
- There was an ideal of marriage with one partner for life, but at the same time remarriage was strongly encouraged by their kin, society and the state.

First marriage: bride 15 years, bridegroom 25 years

The classic marriage pattern, on which much demographic thinking is based, is that of a man aged twenty-five and a girl aged fifteen. The intentions of such a partnership tend to be elucidated with reference to the example of Cicero. He married Terentia in *c.* 79 BC, at the age of twenty-six or twenty-seven. This was just after he had established himself with his successful defence of Roscius in 80 and in good time for his candidacy for the quaestor-ship in 76 (Shackleton-Bailey 1971: 22–23). This was considered the ideal in the Late Republic but still holds good as a model when the age at first marriage for the male drops to about twenty-two in the Principate. Cicero, as a *novus homo,* needed the networks and the dowry of a well-connected woman and found such a person in Terentia. Ever the traditionalist, Cicero followed the same pattern with his daughter: Tullia married for the first time between 66–63 – her date of birth is unknown but if we assume it was soon after her parent's marriage in 79, this would make her between thirteen and fifteen, at a time in her father's life when he held the magistracies of praetor and consul. Tullia's husband was the nobleman C. Piso Frugi aged about twenty-five (Syme 1986: 276, 330). He had married into the family of a prominent man in political circles (Cicero was praetor in 66 and consul in 63), and no doubt saw this as advantageous for his own nascent political career – he was *mone-talis* in 64 and quaestor in 58 (he died in 57). Cicero had aligned himself with another noble family via the marriage of his daughter at a time when he was at the height of the *cursus honorum* (Treggiari 1991a: 92). Cicero need not be representative of all such marriages, but the detail from his life provides some pointers to the age-related behaviour of a husband and then a father.

To see the role of marriage at these ages in a wider context, we need to investigate the problem with reference to the normative pattern of kin avail-ability on both sides of the partnership. Here, we turn to the simulation model of Richard Saller (see summary Table 7.1 and the Appendix for full details). The bridegroom's family is headed by his father in his fifties, well beyond the age of magistracies but not beyond the age of influence. It should be noted that sixty was seen as an appropriate age to become less concerned with public life at Rome (see Chapter 9). It is notable that both partners'

grandfathers are beyond this point (if alive) and into the time of old age characterised by physical and mental collapse as opposed to that of a *senex* and
wisdom. The bride's family is of greater interest: her father and his siblings
were well within the age range of senior magistracies or had even just held
such a position. Those wishing to make a political alliance via their daughter, at say, the year before the elections for the consulship would have dropped
the marriage age of their daughter to below the fifteen years suggested here.
Such a marriage linked a son at first marriage to a wife with a family whose
political achievement had been made recently or was even being made at the
time. This creates a structural pattern for marriages of this type. It mixes the
ages of the two kinship networks of relatives to establish a greater homo-
geneity amongst the adults.

Table 7.1 Average ages of kin of male aged 25 and female aged 15 at marriage

Kin	Male relatives' age	Female relatives' age
Father	51	47
Mother	47	38
Sibling	25	15
Grandfather	74	66
Grandmother	67	60
Aunt/uncle	49	40
Nephew/niece	4	3

If we turn to another emblematic example of republican marriage, that of
Pompey, we may assert the political implications of marriage. His third
marriage was to Mucia, when he was twenty-six and she was probably
between fourteen and seventeen, as this appears to have been her first
marriage. The couple were together for eighteen years and produced three
children. It also strengthened the link with the Metelli that Pompey had
established with his second marriage to Aemelia, daughter of Metella and
stepdaughter of Sulla. Mucia was well connected to the previous generation,
her father was Q. Metellus Nepos, and to Pompey's contemporaries, she was
half-sister to Q. Metellus Celer and Q. Metellus Nepos (aged twenty-two and
nineteen respectively; see Syme 1986: 245). The connection between them
had mutual benefit: for example the brothers benefited from their sister's
marriage – both were legates of Pompey in the East, Celer in 66, and Nepos
from 67–63. However, this depended on the existence of the marriage, and
the couple's divorce in 60 BC destroyed the cooperation between these two
groups of non-kin.

The examples of Pompey and Cicero are of less importance than the overall
demographic pattern of first marriages. These created connections between
not only the bridegroom and father-in-law, but also between an array of kin
on either side of the marriage. Just as obligations existed between kin, so did

obligations to the in-law's family. The age differences may have structured a system of deference across the marriage. The level of male seniority, if all were living, was: groom's grandfather, bride's grandfather, groom's father, bride's father. The pattern replicates and depends on the age difference between the bride and groom. It points to an asymmetrical pattern that favours the relatives on the groom's side, yet it needs to be noted that the age of the bride's father in his mid-forties is indicative of a person who may have held office recently and/or had an esteemed position within the senate.

Remarriage: bride 15 years, bridegroom 40 years

The pattern of kin extension alters if we change the age of one of the partners. In this case, we have chosen to alter the age of the bridegroom to forty years. This is to highlight how the pattern of kin extension in the second, third or fourth marriage of a man was quite different from that of a first marriage. There are a number of emblematic examples in our source material that point up this possibility. For example, Agrippa married Augustus' daughter, Julia, in 21 BC, at the age of forty-two. This was his third marriage. His first had been to Attica, when he was in his mid-twenties and produced a daughter Vipsania, who was later married to the future emperor Tiberius. This was also Julia's second marriage even though she was only nineteen. Her previous marriage to Marcellus had not produced any children – perhaps due to adolescent sterility on the part of both partners. This time her husband was the same age as her father and they produced five children in eight years. The elder two of these were adopted by their grandfather as his sons – an illustration of the use of a daughter via marriage to create an hereditary line in the absence of a direct lineage via a son (see Corbier 1995).

What we see here is an alliance made by men of a similar age. The bride's father and the bridegroom are of the same generation with siblings of a very similar age. This generation's male parents were for the most part dead and their male children were by no means adults. Marriage, as arranged between a male aged forty and a female aged fifteen, created marriage connections between males of a similar age; without the mixing of ages across three generations as seen in the first example, where we found males aged mid-twenties, in their forties and in their sixties (compare Table 7.1 with 7.2). This created an immediate link within the age group associated with office holding in their late thirties and early forties. Unlike a marriage between a man at twenty-five and a woman at fifteen, this form of marriage does not interlink three generations to create a long and stable marriage alliance across and over those generations.

Table 7.2 Average ages of kin of male aged 40 and female aged 15 at marriage

Kin	Male relatives' age	Female relatives' age
Father	73	47
Mother	65	38
Sibling	40	15
Grandfather	–	66
Grandmother	83	60
Aunt/uncle	64	40
Nephew/niece	11	3
Child	5	–

The age mix here fits a male with an established public career but who lacked heirs. For the bride's family it suited those who required political alliances for the father – who would be coeval with the husband – and the father's brothers. It was likely to be a second or subsequent marriage for the husband. Treggiari argues that middle-aged men who had lost a wife through death or divorce had a preference for a match with a young girl at the beginning of her child-bearing years and the height of her physical beauty (1991a: 401; see also Chapter 6).

The old man and the virgin: bride 15, bridegroom 60

If we increase the age of the male partner in the marriage, we find an even greater variation in the ages of the kin on either side of the marriage. We should also recognise that children who would be in their thirties would exist from previous marriages, and the groom may well have had grandchildren only a little younger than his latest bride. The opportunities for age mixing here are limited. The groom's parents were unlikely to have been alive, and his children were in mid career. The kin mixing is ineffectual and was confused via the existence of children older than the bride. This is pointed up in a number of our sources, and the stupidity of the groom is highlighted to suggest that he was an old man in love – a person to be ridiculed. Cicero and Pompey provide us with examples of this form of ridiculous behaviour. Cicero married his ward, Publilia, after his divorce of Terentia, when he was sixty. Terentia and Cicero had been married for thirty-three years (*Att.*12.11). Terentia accused him of being swept off his feet by Publilia's youth and charm (Plu.*Cic.*41). In contrast, Tiro gave the supposedly more rational and perfectly acceptable explanation – Cicero needed the money to pay his debts and he was already trustee of the girl's fortune (Plut.*Cic.* 41). Whereas Cicero himself explained the match in traditional terms: he needed new alliances within politics (*Fam.*4.13.4; Corbier 1991: 136). The marriage only lasted a very short time – Publilia was divorced the following year, allegedly for being pleased at the death of Tullia, Cicero's daughter (one has a secret sympathy with her). Cicero may have married for money and connections, but he may also have been hoping to have additional children. Tullia was pregnant during the period of the marriage but was already thirty-two years old and on her third marriage and had not yet proven her ability as a mother – she died in childbirth the following year. Marcus, his son, was only nineteen in 46 BC and too young for marriage at this date. This did not prevent the ridicule and incredulity of his friends. In their eyes he was marrying because he was besotted with his young ward.

Table 7.3 Average ages of kin of male aged 60 and female aged 15 at marriage

Kin	Male relatives' age	Female relatives' age
Father	87	47
Mother	78	38
Sibling	58	15
Grandfather	–	66
Grandmother	–	60
Aunt/uncle	74	40
Nephew/niece	32	3
Child	35	–
Grandchild	12	–

Demographically, we see the dramatic differences between the ages of the two families united via marriage. The groom was a little younger than the bride's grandfather and would have had children as old as the bride's mother or father, alongside granddaughters of a very similar age to her and also approaching marriage (see Table 7.3). Such a marriage could create some unlikely age structures within the household and kin group. Pompey's last marriage provides the examples: Cornelia, his new wife, was in fact younger than her stepchildren, and her stepdaughter Pompeia had already presented Pompey with a grandchild (Syme 1986: 255). Cornelia was a step-grandmother before she was ever a mother herself. Age mixing of this extreme was seen as subverting the normal life course. More worrying was the fact that a man could produce a new family and perhaps subvert the inheritance of children by an earlier union. Roman law was full of legal gymnastics designed to prevent just this – particularly in the matter of the mother's dowry and inheritance from the maternal line or *bona maternae* (see Gardner 1986: 97–116 for clear summary of the legal position; also Saller 1994: 204–24; Treggiari 1991a: 365–96). Social criticism of these types of marriages may have been warning enough about the potential rivalries and disputes that such age mixing was associated with. The criticism may also express a general distaste for the subversion of the sociobiological norm that suggested a marriage between a male some ten years older than his wife, rather than forty five years older. Disparity in age of this kind, like disparity in wealth or social status, was seen as a bad marriage (Treggiari 1991a: 97).

Remarriage: widows and divorcées

So far our discussion has looked at examples with a focus on female first marriage with a variation in the age of the male partner. However, it is clear that the Augustan marriage laws intended women to be married through the life course up to the age of fifty – the perceived age past which women did not give birth to children. Hence, those who had been married young and were either later divorced or widowed were expected to remarry. Also, as Bradley (1991: 125–76) demonstrates, in practice marriages among the elite frequently ended in divorce and marriage for life was unusual. In any case, we should view the Augustan marriage laws as a reflection of the ideology or views of a society, rather than as the imposition of a new ideal. Thus, it should follow that these views were present within a section of Roman society during and prior to the civil wars that brought Augustus to power (Gardner 1986: 77–8 has a mercifully brief summary of the law). The view was that they should remarry whilst they were capable of reproduction – even though the individual male on marriage might desire his virgin bride to be married only to him or to be a *univira* (i.e. married only once). Hence, we present here examples of the remarriage of widows or divorcées at the age of thirty and forty.

Table 7.4 Average ages of kin of widows aged 30 and 40

Kin	At thirty: relatives' age	At forty: relatives' age
Father	60	69
Mother	52	61
Sibling	29	39
Grandfather	77	82
Grandmother	71	78
Aunt/uncle	53	61
Nephew/niece	8	14
Child	9	16
Grandchild	–	3

Looking at Saller's simulation, we may examine the case of widows aged thirty and forty respectively (Table 7.4). Their fathers would have been over the age of sixty. For the older widow, their children if female are likely to have been of marriage age, but if male were not yet adults. For the younger widow, her children would have been below the age of ten. Hence, in both cases, the widows' male relatives in the older and younger generation were either pre or post-magisterial office holding age. Their importance may have been found with their brothers. Their ages would have been right within the period of magistracies within the *mos maiorum*. For the Roman republic, Clodia always seems a bit of a distraction from the activities of her brother as tribune in 58 BC. The textual fact that Cicero had made slander about incest in passing and in court points to the closeness of the siblings in public. It is also clear that this group of siblings are a classic example of *consortium* (the pooling of resources by siblings on the death of their father). Bannon demonstrates on the basis of Varro (1997: 49; see *RR*3.16.1–2) that Appius Claudius, the eldest brother and consul in 54, had been appointed guardian over three younger sisters and two younger brothers (Gaius praetor in 56 and Publius tribune in 58). This consortium shared the father's estate equally. Not surprisingly, we also find them acting in each other's interests in public life. This cohesion was brought to bear in their attack on the Cicero brothers led by Clodius with the aid of his elder brother Appius (Bannon 1997: 96–7). The role of their sister in the *consortium* is not obvious but once she was widowed in 59 BC, aged thirty-six, she presumably was no longer tied by considerations of her husband's family and naturally returned to the *consortium* of Claudian siblings. Her life style, as seen through Cicero's *Pro Caelio,* was that of a woman out of control. In terms of kin pressure, she only had her brothers and they were Cicero's enemies. Hence, Clodia, the widow, was an open target for Cicero's invective against her in court. She did not have the protection of marriage against such slander, nor that of her parents' age or influence, and the accusation of incest reflected the closeness of the siblings in private and public life. It is the cultural construction of marriage, in this case its absence, and the accident of Clodia's husband's death that created many of the conditions for the rhetoric utilised by Cicero (see Chapter 6). Cicero was not in conflict with any one of the Claudian siblings but with all of them. The unity of siblings and the reliance on them for the support of middle-aged widows should not be underestimated. This is certainly not unique to the example of Clodia (Hallett 1984: 158) – sisters gained political power at Rome as well as a share of their father's wealth.

The influence of women, such as Clodia, should not be underestimated. A family loyalty that can be identified may have caused the female lineage to pursue the causes of the male line in politics through their partners by marriage or adultery. The collapse of Tullia's third marriage was caused by the affair between her husband, Dolabella, and Clodia's daughter, Metella, in 47 BC – nine years after the trial of Caelius Rufus (Cic.*Att.*11.23). Dolabella, the son-in-law of Cicero, was also supporting the proposed erection of a statue to Publius Clodius – the man who had caused Cicero's exile in 58 BC. It would seem that Dolabella's allegiance in politics had shifted away from Cicero to that of the Claudii, his bitter enemies. To make this shift all the more humiliating and clear to the public, Dolabella had very publicly committed adultery and announced his support for the commemoration of an enemy of Cicero. This raises the whole question of the entanglement of marriage and politics. It would seem that in marriage, men were careful to ensure that their daughters, if possible, married men who were not enemies of their *amici.* Tullia's marriage to Dolabella had been arranged whilst he was away, in 51–50 BC, by Terentia and Tullia herself. Much to his embarrassment, they chose Dolabella who was prosecuting his friend Appius Claudius (Cic.*Fam.*3.12). There had been a lack of choice at the time of the marriage, partly caused by Tullia's age and in part by the impoverishment of many of the suitors (Treggiari 1991a: 128–9). It was her third marriage and to date she had not produced any children, which must have been a further factor in dissuading men from marrying her. In terms of politics, Cicero, although a senior senator, in 50 BC was absent from Rome and had numerous enemies – not an attractive father-in-law, still tainted by his enmity to Clodius, as well as having a very conservative nature. Dolabella married Tullia, but could later signify his distance from his father-in-law via adultery as well as politics. This does not reduce the role of women in marriage to mere pawns to be utilised in the arena of male politics. Metella, as a member of the next generation of the Claudii (the age of her kin follows our first example above), was pursuing the politics of the original *consortium* of siblings by causing the divorce of Tullia, and embarrassment to her father. This identifies the strength of the *consortium* of the Claudii in its opposition to Cicero and the pursuit of its ambitions through its female line. This factor would become more apparent in the imperial household, where the Julio-Claudian dynasty was constructed through marriage and adoption, and organised as a *consortium* on a grand scale. A major factor, in the succession within the imperial household, was the very fact that women survived their husbands (because they were often younger) and promoted their sons' interests (see Corbier 1991, 1995 and Chapter 8 below).

Marriage and the life course

The examination of the examples given above does not recreate the individual's experience of marriage and kin relations, instead they are intended as a guide to the purpose of marriage at certain ages within the hypothesis that marriage extended kin and affinity networks. These were most effective in a typical first marriage of a male in his twenties and a female in her teens and can be seen to have promoted connections across three generations of males, often at the age of magistracy. Marriage by males later in life to a woman at first marriage did not replicate this pattern. Instead, these marriages created linkages within a generation and might be associated with shorter term affinities or were an alternative to the long term partnerships. Cicero, in the 40s BC, married Publilia to extend his social and political connections, shortly before Tullia had married Dolabella as the best out of a series of poor quality suitors. It did not reinforce Cicero's existing affinities, but there was a need for Tullia to be married and to produce children for herself and grandchildren for Cicero. Widows presented an anomaly within Roman society if under fifty years of age. Their fathers or husbands were dead and there was no obvious male kin who would have had authority over them. Hence, between the ages of thirty and fifty, their siblings and in particular brothers were of greater significance. In terms of the life course, this seems a little unexpected since the female siblings would have left home for marriage aged fifteen and socially, if not legally, became part of another household. However, the nature of widowhood and the associated rhetorical slanders of Cicero in the *Pro Caelio* points to a continuing bond between siblings after marriage and certainly into the time of a brother's magistracies and beyond into the next generation. Remarriage, if it occurred, may have reflected the public role of a brother. This suggests that the role of marriage within the female life course would reflect the presence or absence of male relatives. Initially, the father was crucial in the arrangement of marriage of a daughter and we might say that daughters were desirable for men in politics – sons did not mature to marriage until after the major phase of magistracies in a father's life.

The implications of a desire by the Roman elite to extend their kinship networks created a very different family structure from that of western culture today. The temptation to see the Roman familial groupings shaped by death and divorce and reformed by remarriage in the light of a western couple married for life with 1.1 to 1.8 children would be mistaken. Marriage at Rome incorporated the woman into a new kin group whilst continuing to maintain the link to her own family and kin. The power relations of this alliance, maintained through her marriages, were constantly being negotiated and subject to change. The most noticeable change was when she had children and proved her ability to continue the family into the next generation. Now, both her father-in-law and her father had a grandchild. In the absence of other male children, her father could adopt this child as his son (Corbier 1991: 143) and re-form his own family via his female descendants. Repeated remarriage on the part of men created complicated family structures (see Bradley 1991: 126–30), but this does not mean that there was no sentiment within Roman marriage or family. Roman children were born into this changing familial format, and were socialised within its expectations. In a social world in which the death of loved ones was a frequent experience, as was divorce, we should not rule out the possibility of love and affection. However, the bond between siblings, children and their parents was stronger than the tie of marriage. Demographically, the longest lasting relationship in the life course was between siblings, followed by that of child and mother and finally that of child to father. These factors were counteracted in part by social custom and law that made the father's position and will all embracing and, potentially at least, despotic (see Saller 1994: 102–54). Marriage extended familial ties; on divorce or bereavement, remarriage was expected by other blood relatives to ensure that their collective network of affinity and kinship was maintained. Throughout the life course this network was under constant change but that does not preclude bonds of love, affection or sentiment between its members.

8

AGE AND POLITICS

There has been much discussion over the last hundred years or so of the purpose of the legislation at Rome that regulated the order and age in which persons held magistracies – often referred to as the *cursus honorum*. This debate has revolved around the reconstruction of the laws and the implications of these for political life at Rome (see Astin 1958; Badian 1964: 140–56 for summaries of discussion). The principle concern has been that of the period down to Julius Caesar's death in 44 BC, with little connection with the discussion of the *cursus honorum* under the emperors (Birley 1981: 15–35; Syme 1958: appendix 19 for summary of the subject). The discussion of the period of the Roman Republic and that of the Roman Emperors has often been conducted separately with little or no connection between the two historic periods. The emphasis on constitutional niceties has been overemphasised to exclude the social dimension of the *cursus honorum* for individuals within the political elite. We wish in this chapter to relate the changes in the *cursus honorum* from the second century BC through to the first century AD as a way of highlighting its role in the life course, and the alteration of the view of age and stages of life over a period of three hundred years.

The age of politics in the Republic

Marcus Tullius Cicero was proud not only of the fact that as a new man, that is a person whose family had not been amongst the senators before, he had held the consulship, but also that he had been elected to each magistracy on the way up the *cursus honorum* in what he called 'my year' (Cic.*Leg.Agr.*2.3–4, *Off.*2.59, *Brut.*323). What he refers to by this phrase is the first year in which he was permitted to stand. This provides us with an important reference point for understanding the minimum age of political success at Rome. Cicero was elected quaestor at the age of thirty, praetor at the age of thirty-nine and consul at the age of forty-two. Here we see the age of politics as that associated with the thirty- to forty-somethings at Rome, but we need to ask why there was such a structure in place to prevent anyone under the age of thirty from holding office and why there were clear restrictions on the order and age at which offices could be held.

Prior to 180 BC, there seems to have been little by way of restriction on the order in which offices were held. However, in that year, we know that a tribune of the plebs, Lucius Villius, introduced a law to fix the ages at which each magistracy might be sought and held (Liv.40.44.1). No details are given of the nature of the rules and we need to reconstruct these from known cases. These have been dissected by Astin (1958) to demonstrate that, prior to further reform by Sulla in the first century BC, there was generally a fixed order of office holding: quaestor followed by praetor followed by consul. We may set the age of election to the quaestorship with reference to the requirement that political office could only be held if a citizen had undertaken ten years' military service (Polyb.6.19.4). This would have been counted from the age of *tirocinium* or seventeen years of age. Hence a minimum age for the quaestorship can be established at twenty-seven. Astin (1958: 34–6) highlights the ages of office holding of fourteen individuals, whose date of birth we know with precision.

Table 8.1 Known ages of Magistracies prior to Sullan Reforms (for sources see Astin 1958: 34–6)

	Quaestor	Aedile	Praetor	Consul
L. Licinius Crassus				44
Q. Mucius Scaevola				44
M. Antonius	39			43
L. Cornelius Sulla	30		44	49
G. Marius			40	49
M. Aemilius Scaurus				44–45
Scipio Aemilianus		36/7		
Fabius Maximus Aemilianus			35+	39+
C. Laelius			39+	43+
Ser Sulpicius Galba			36–40	43–47
C. Papirius Carbo				40–43
Tiberius Gracchus				40–43
M. Livius Drusus				39–42
Gaius Gracchus				39–42

As can be seen from Table 8.1, the data is partial at best and contains more information on the higher magistracies. However, some general conclusions can be made from these ages of office holding: a man had to have been quaestor before praetor or consul. The ages at which offices were obtained were thirty as a minimum for the quaestorship and the late thirties or early forties as a minimum age for praetor or consul.

The pattern that we have seen in the examples above broadly follows that of Cicero in the first century BC. What is clear from our sources is that during his dictatorship, Sulla reformed the *Lex Annalis* to regulate the order of office holding and the ages at which offices could be held. The major reform was to make the quaestorship open to anyone, regardless of military service, aged thirty (Keaveney 1982: 173–4); that two years needed to elapse between magistracies (for discussion see Badian 1964); and that to hold any magistracy the quaestorship was necessary first. In addition, no individual could hold the same magistracy within a ten year period, and in some way – the sources do not specify how – patricians were advantaged over those from plebian families. The requirements of a minimum age for the quaestorship and a biennium between offices created the series of minimum ages that an individual could hold office: thirty-six for the aedileship, thirty-nine for the praetorship and forty-two for the consulship.

How this worked in practice may be seen from known examples from the last thirty years of the Republic. Our information on office holding is considerably fuller due to the survival of Cicero's discussion of his political allies and enemies, but we are hindered by the fact that the date of a person's birth rarely comes down to us two thousand years after these events. However, in all cases we know that the minimum age of a person was thirty at the elections for the quaestorship. Hence, we may follow the progression of quaestors through the *cursus honorum* (Table 8.2). Cicero held the praetorship at the minimum age that he could nine years after his quaestorship, but should we see this example as unusual? The average gap between the quaestorship and the praetorship down to 49 BC was nine years, with a maximum in some cases of fourteen years. This places all candidates at a similar age or stage within their political careers in the elections.

Another magistracy regarded as essential to the successful election to the praetorship was that of the aedileship, whose responsibilities could include the holding of games. Again, looking at the overall pattern of gaps between the aedileship and praetorship and the subsequent break between praetor and consulship (Table 8.3), we find a pattern that replicates that of Cicero. There is a two year gap between the holding of a magistracy and standing in the next election, which creates a three year gap between magistracies in nearly all cases (confimed by Cic.*Fam.*10.25). Badian (1964: 145) argues that the holding of the position of aedile was in effect a statement of intention to stand for the election to praetor. We might add that the similar pattern between praetor and consul suggests that by standing for aedile, a senator was embarking on a magisterial career, whereas other ex-quaestors may have been satisfied with their position within the senate. Again the effect of the regulations of the *Lex Annalis* is to place all candidates for office at a similar stage with the same breaks between office. This creates a structure to Roman political life in which candidates are of an equal age, if competing in the first possible year, or what Cicero refers to as his year, and equal magisterial experience in all cases. With hindsight, Cicero (*Fam.*10.25, Badian 1964: 145) advised a candidate for the office of aedile that it was easier to be elected in your year, or the first year that you could stand for office.

Table 8.2 The careers of known Quaestors 81–49 BC (data from Broughton 1952)

	Quaestor	Praetor	Consul
P. Cornelius Lentulus	81	75, 73	71
A. Manlius (Torquatus)	81	70	
L. Julius Caesar	77		64
P. Autronius Paetus	75		65 (designate)
M. Tullius Cicero	75	66	63
Cn. Cornelius Lentulus Marcellinus	74	60	56
P. Cornelius Lentulus Spinther	74	60	57
L. Licinius Murena	74	65	62
Ser. Sulpicius Rufus	74	65	51
C. Octavius	73	61	
M. Valerius Messalla Niger	73	64?	61
L. Valerius Flaccus	71	63	
L. Calpurnius Piso Caesoninus	70	61	58
M. Plaetorius Cestianus	70	64	
C. Vergilius Balbus	70	62	
C. Julius Caesar	69	62	59, 48, 46–4
Q. Tullius Cicero	68	62	
M. Aemilius Scaurus	66	56	
L. Caecilius Rufus	66	57	
L. Domitius Ahenobarbus	66	58	54
P. Plautius Hypsaeus	66	55	
Q. Ancharius	65	56	
M. Claudius Marcellus	64	54	51
M. Porcius Cato	64	54	
P. Sestius	63	54 (latest)	
P. Vatinius	63	55	47
M. Iuventius Laterensis	62	51	
M. Nonius Sufenas	62	51	
M. Curtius	61	50?	
P. Servilius Isauricus	60	54	48, 41
C. Trebonius	60	48	45 (suffect)
L. Aemilius Paullus	59	53	50
M. Favonius	59	49	
M. Cornelius Vincianus	56	48?	
L. Minuccius Basilus	55	46	
C. Sallustius Crispus	55	46	
C. Cassius Longinus	54	44	
M. Iunius Brutus	54	44	
M. Antonius	52		44, 34, 31 (designate)
C. Antonius	51	44	
L. Antonius	50		41

Table 8.3 The careers of known Aediles 81–49 BC (data from Broughton 1952)

	Aedile	Praetor	Consul
L. Licinius Lucullus*	79	78	74
Cn. Aufidius	79	77	
Q. Hortensius Hortalus	75	72	69
D. Iunius Silanus	70	67 (latest)	62
P. Sulpicius Galba*	69	66	
M. Caesonius**	69	66	
M. Tullius Cicero**	69	66	63
M. Plaetorius*	67	64?	
Q. Gallius**	67	65	
Q. Voconius Naso**	67	60 (latest)	
Q. Caecilius Metellus**	67	63	60
M. Calpurnius Bibulus*	65	62	59
C. Julius Caesar*	65	62	59
Q. Tullius Cicero**	65	62	
L. Calpurnius Piso Caesoninus*	64		58
C. Octavius**	64	61	
P. Cornelius Lentulus Spinther*	63	60	57
L. Domitius Ahenobarbus*	61	58	54
L. Appuleius Saturninus**	61	58	54
P. Licinius Crassus Dives**	60	57	
M. Aemilius Scaurus*	58	56	
P. Plautius Hypsaeus*	58	55	
Q. Caecilius Metellus*	57	55	52
Q. Fabius Maximus*	57	48	45 (suffect)
C. Cosconius**	57	54	
P. Clodius Pulcher*	56	52 (stands for election)	
L. Aemilius Paullus*	55	53	50
A. Plautius*	54	51	
M. Aemilius Lepidus*	53	49	46, 42
M. Favonius	52	49	
M. Caelius Rufus*	50	48	
C. Vibius Pansa Caetronianus	49	46?	43

Notes

* = certain Curule Aedile

** = certain Plebian Aedile

Elections were contested and there were losers as well as winners (Broughton 1991), but the contest was always between one's chronological peer group. This can be seen as the real purpose of the *Lex Annalis* which was to ensure the fairness of elections and to prevent those who, in the eyes of Republican Romans, were seen to be too young from standing. The latter were defined as those rash youths who were under the age of thirty (Cic.*Phil*.5.47–8, see Chapter 5). However, in spite of the fairness of the law, it would seem that patricians were favoured over plebians. The former were members of *gentes* (families) tracing their ancestry back to the aristocracy of early Rome and can

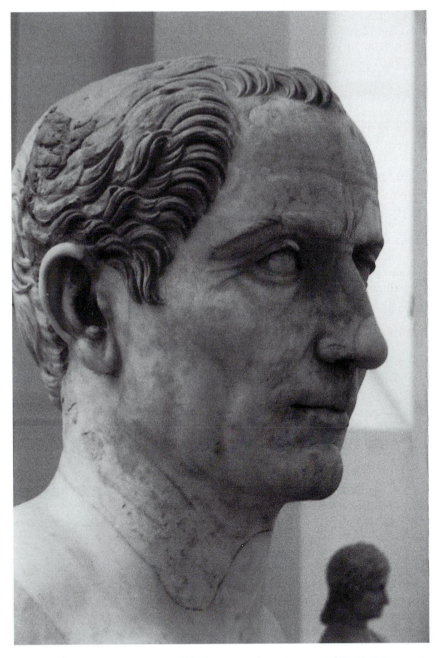

Plate 8.1 Julius Caesar was 56 years old when he was assassinated. This image from the Naples Museum shows him with receding hair, his hair is brushed forward to cover his baldness. The lines around his eyes and the furrow of his brow add to the image of a man who is no longer young (compare Suet.*Jul.*45).

be seen to have been a privileged status group. The distinction between patricians and plebians affected which offices could be held; only a plebian could be a tribune of the plebs or plebian aedile. Conversely, the curule aedileship was only open to patricians. Badian (1964) identifies a privileging of patrician politicans over their plebian counterparts. By analysing the career patterns between quaestor and consul, he found that some members of the senate had an accelerated career over Cicero following the minimum age at which he could hold each magistracy. Cicero has a break of seven years between quaestor and praetor, whereas patricians, including Julius Caesar, were associated with shorter spaces between magistracies (see Table 8.4). Julius Caesar held the quaestorship at the same age as Cicero, but then held the praetorship and consulship two years ahead of the Ciceronian norm; this pattern is found in other cases that can be securely identified as patricians pursuing a magisterial career at the earliest possible age or in their year (Badian 1964: 150). This implies that patricians were privileged – the gap between offices was shorter and they had an accelerated path through the magisterial offices. No doubt this was a measure to maintain the prominence of these ancient *gentes* in a time of considerable social mobility (Burton and Hopkins 1983a).

Table 8.4 Senatorial careers deviating from the Ciceronian norm (for discussion see Badian 1964: 141–4) – dates given in BC

	Quaestor	Aedile	Praetor	Consul
M. Tullius Cicero (norm)	75		66	63
C. Claudius Marcellus	87?		80	
L. Licinius Lucullus	87?	79	78	74
P. Cornelius Lentulus Sura	81		74	71
L. Valerius Triarius	81		78?	
Q. Hortensius Hortalus	80?	75	72	69
Q. Gallius		67	65	
P. Autronius Paetus	75			65
L. Valerius Flaccus	71/70		63	
Q. Tullius Cicero	68?	65	62	
P. Nigidius Figulus		60?	58	
M. Aemilius Scaurus	66?	58	56	
Q. Domitius Ahenobarbus	66	61	58	54
P. Vatinius	63		55	47
Q. Caecilius Metellus Scipio		57	55	52
P. Clodius Pulcher		61	56	52
P. Servilius Isauricus	60		54	48
L. Aemilius Paullus	59?	55?	53	50
Cn Plancius	58	54		
M. Caelius Rufus		50	48	

The redefinition of the age of responsibility

The elaborate controls over when a person held office and the *cursus honorum* as a whole were challenged by events after Julius Caesar's murder. Octavian, at the age of nineteen during the autumn and winter of 44 BC and into the summer of 43 BC, was to place a challenge to the entire age structure of the Republic and, more importantly, challenge the very basis for such age restrictions themselves (famously summarised in *Res Gestae* 1). This series of events is well recorded in the richest period of Cicero's letters and allows us to see not only attitudes towards Caesar's adopted son (Octavian), but also the perception of his actions in the context of his age. It will be argued that the period also sets a pattern of behaviour later emulated by youthful emperors: for example Caligula and Nero in their dealings with older men and, in particular, senators.

In the surviving letters of Cicero we first find mention of Octavian in letters sent to Atticus in November 44 BC (*Att.*16.8, 16.9, 16.11, 16.14, 16.15). Octavian asks for his advice in dealing with Antony. Cicero understands the purpose behind the future emperor's actions as war, and with Octavian as the commander in that war, but Cicero sees at the same time the child, the boy, or at the most a youth. In other words, not really an adult and a person who lacked *gravitas*, in spite of popularity and an ability to be the counter to Antony. These private letters to Atticus are a marked contrast to Cicero's speeches in the senate on 20th December 44 BC (*Phil.*3) and 1st January 43 BC (*Phil.*5.42–8). In these speeches, the orator speaks of the young man as sent by the gods to save them from evil and refers to the young man's or boy's almost divine virtue and intelligence. He also makes the case for a youth to obtain power earlier than the *Leges Annales* permitted. He does this tellingly with a reference to Alexander of Macedon, who he points out was dead before the age at which a Roman was permitted to hold the consulship according to the *Leges Annales*; and that Octavian had already displayed his virtue and should not be prevented from advancement by his age. He also highlights other exceptions to the *Leges Annales* from the Roman past to reinforce his point. The proposal to the senate was to recognise that Octavian should be treated as a pro-praetor with *imperium* to command his army against Antony; he would be a member of the senate and express his opinion with other praetorians; he would be able to seek further office at elections as if he had held the quaestorship in 44 BC (*Phil.*5.46; *Ad M.Brut.*1.15). Effectively, the senate was creating the first constitutional exceptions that took account of a son of a monarch at Rome. These measures ratified by the senate would become a regular feature of the empire, for example the definition of Augustus' powers in 27 BC. More importantly in terms of age, time and again throughout the imperial period, the senate was the body that proposed that the sons of the imperial family were to hold magistracies at an age far younger than they might hold such posts under the traditional *Leges Annales*. One might say that on first January 43 BC, the Roman Revolution was decided in the senate and youth won the day through the proposal and oratory of an old man. Certainly, this was how Brutus was to see it (Cic.*Ad M.Brut.*1.16).

The passing of the decree giving Octavian *imperium* was not the end of the matter. Cicero, in the surviving letters from 43 BC, praises his 'young friend' (*Fam.*11.7) and claims that Octavian had raised his army to defend himself and Cicero's friends in the first place and the *res publica* in the second (*Fam.*12.25). There were doubts in Cicero's mind, because Octavian was so young and could be easily swayed by the advice of others (*Ad M. Brut.*1.10) and in particular the rumour that Cicero had said he should be honoured and then given the push (*Fam.*11.20, 11.21), or the youth might simply not be up to it because he was so young (*Ad M. Brut.*1.10). Others had a similar feeling: Decimus Brutus, the commander of another army in Italy against Antony, was suspicious and exasperated by the actions of one so young. Clearly, Octavian did not follow Decimus' advice in May (*Fam.*11.10) with an implication that this may have been caused by the inherent rashness of a young man. Plancus, the consul elect, saw this as the explanation: his mind had been diverted or he had been badly advised (*Fam.*10.24). These views were confirmed when it was clear that Octavian expected to hold a consulship. Brutus saw this as the means to despotism, and expected, now that he had been raised up so quickly and at such a young age, that Octavian was the ideal candidate to take on that role (Cic.*Ad M. Brut.*1.4a). He asks: 'What do you think will be the mentality of one who thinks himself in a position to covet any office of power with the backing, not of a slaughtered tyrant but the senate itself?'. These views of the age of Octavian played into his hands: he was content to be subordinate to Cicero and to refer to him as 'father' (Cic.*Ad M.Brut.*1.17), but at the same time any action of his contrary to his advice could simply have been put down to his age. Later when the triumvirate became unpopular, Antony took the blame because he was older than Octavian (Plu.*Ant.*21). Strategically, the latter was able to exploit the ideological expectations of senators that a youth would change his mind, might be able to be influenced strongly by one person, was generally rash and would have few qualms in terms of mercy to his enemies (e.g. Suet.*Aug.*13). Indeed, it would seem that during the triumvirate and coincidently whilst he was under the age of thirty, Octavian acted the tyrant (or should we say a Caligula or Nero with power at too young an age); afterwards we see the restrained head of state or *princeps* (Suet.*Aug.*27 sees the distinction).

Age and politics in the Empire

At the end of the civil wars Octavian returned to Rome and in 27 BC, at the age of thirty-four, changed his name to Augustus. In the previous year, he had purged the senate of some 190 undesirables (Dio 52.42), added new *gentes* (families) to the existing patrician families (Syme 1986: 4), and begun work on the tomb for the new dynasty. Throughout his principate, we find him

Plate 8.2 Augustus as priest. His statues remained consistently young-looking throughout his life.

concerned with regulating the lives of Rome's elite: the senators and equites (see especially Talbert 1984: 9–27; Birley 1981 on age and, engagingly, Nicolet 1984 on the political implications of these changes). This was not done instantly but piecemeal according to his thinking from his mid-thirties. There is some variation in his interests and his preoccupations according to his own age. It is worth remembering this and how old or where Augustus

113

was in the life course when considering his actions. We will highlight his age at times, but, for the reader, he was born on 23 September 63 BC and the calculation can be easily made. His age in 27 BC may explain his actions. He dropped the minimum age at which a Roman citizen could hold the quaestorship to their twenty-fifth year as opposed to their thirtieth. There were, as in the Republic, offices of tribune or aedile of the plebs to be held by those from plebian families, and the curule aedileship for those of patrician origins after a two year interval, followed by another two year interval before the praetorship. Hence, a senator in the empire could hold the praetorship at the age of thirty and could follow on to the consulship at thirty-one or two. Compared to the Republican magistrates, their imperial counterparts were some nine to ten years younger. The reasons for this decrease may be sought in the age of Augustus himself in 27 BC – thirty-four. It would have been difficult for him to call himself *princeps* if the annually elected consuls were older than himself. Similarly, his experience of responsibility at a young age may have caused him later in 13 BC to insist that entry in the senate depended upon being one of the annual magistracies know as the *vigintiviri* (Dio 54.26.5), who were attached to the mint, the courts or concerned with the streets or roads of Rome (Birley 1981: 4–8). After holding this office in their late teens, candidates tended to move on to hold the position of military tribune with a legion when nineteen (Birley 1981: 8–12, note 20 on age) – the same age at which Augustus had raised his army against Antony, Brutus and others. The *res publica* was restored with reference to one man's experience of life that was exceptional to all Republican precedents.

Claude Nicolet (1984) has demonstrated that Augustus had three major concerns in the regulations passed that affected the lives of the aristocracy of Rome. He wished in short to ensure or enhance the birth, the merit and the wealth of the members of the senate to create Rome's pre-eminent order as those associated with the senate. In 18 BC, as Curator of Laws and Morals in anticipation of the secular Games in the following year, he raised the property qualification for membership of the senate from 400,000 sesterces to one million sesterces (Dio 54.17.3). The senate was also purged of unworthy members at the same time (Dio 54.13–14). Legislation on the marriage of the members of the senate, their children and grandchildren was enacted (on legislation see Treggiari 1991a: 277–98). This law prevented marriage between these persons and freed slaves or *infames* (actors, gladiators, pimps, prostitutes). The emphasis in the legislation on not only the senator but also their children and grandchildren points to an ideal of an heriditary senate, a fact made apparent by the ability of only the senators and their sons to wear the *latus clavus* (tunic with broad purple band), that anticipated membership of the senate for the sons of senators (Nicolet 1984: 93, citing Dio 59.9.5; Talbert 1984: 216–20 on dress). Another feature of the empire that made the sons of senators prominent was the Troy Games performed by young boys from patrician families, often alongside the children of the imperial family (e.g. Dio 54.26).

These new regulations placed a special emphasis beyond the senators of the moment to their offspring as future senators. In effect, a form of social engineering was now in place to create a set of senatorial families. We may add that the unpopular inheritance tax of AD 6 and 13 did not apply to children or grandchildren of the deceased (Nicolet 1984: 110; Dio 55.25.5, 56.28.6); this may also have been aimed at the prevention of the dispersal of the senatorial property qualification to others outside the agnatic line.

We have already seen how the age of office holding dropped under Augustus in terms of the age at which a person could hold a magistracy. However, Talbert (1984) has defined a three speed senatorial cursus that depended on status. He suggests that there was little competition for the lower magistracies such as the *vigintivirate*, the quaestorship, tribunes and aediles (Dio 54.26); in contrast there was strong competition for the praetorship (Talbert 1984: 19). In response, the number of praetorships increased from ten to sixteen in AD 11 and from fourteen to eighteen in the later part of the first century AD. Equally, the number of consulships increased with the addition of six monthly suffect consulships taken up on 1 July from 5 BC. The number of these posts was greatly increased by Augustus' successors with between six and ten suffect consulships under the Flavians. In effect, the senior magistracies became open to a greater number of people. Also, promotion to a praetorian position could be made at an earlier age via the patronage of the emperor (compare Octavian's advancement in 43 BC by the senate). Competition, in many ways, was curtailed. However, the speed of the interval between a praetorship and a consulship depended on status. Talbert's analysis (1984: 20–21) suggests that patrician senators could expect to be consul by the age of thirty-two to thirty-three, whereas sons of senators from a plebian family would have to undertake more posts away from Rome prior to the consulship at the age of about thirty-eight to forty-two. *Novi homines,* or first generation senators, would have held the consulship at forty-two or forty-four. Hence, the career of a patrician was faster than his plebian counterpart. It comes as no surprise that we find the adlection into the patricians as a feature of the senate under the Flavians (see examples in Jones 1979). Careers could also be accelerated by a year for the birth of each child under the marriage laws. Hence, sons of senators from patrician *gentes* could have been consuls in their late twenties or early thirties in the empire.

The significance of these changes

What these major changes meant for the individual at Rome can only be seen with reference to the few examples for whom we have a near complete record of their careers. The future emperor Vespasian was born in AD 9 (for details of Vespasian's career see Levick 1999) and was always going to be very much a *novus homo*. We may assume that he took up the *toga virilis* in 25/26 at the age of sixteen. After this he served as a military tribune prior to the *vigintivirate* in 31 and, after a break in his public career, he served as quaestor by the age of twenty-five or twenty-six (Levick 1999: 8–9). On his return, there was little time in 36 to canvass amongst the senators for election to the aedileship, which he lost. In the following year, the first year of Caligula's principate, he was duly elected. He was later to be elected to the office of praetor a year after the minimum age allowed and finally he held a suffect consulship in 51 at the age of nearly forty-two (Levick 1999: 19). This career, through the principates of Tiberius, Caligula and Claudius, demonstrates how the new pattern of age and office holding was conducted. Compared to Cicero, the most successful *novus homo* of the Republic, Vespasian held offices earlier below the consulship. The gaps between offices were filled by service in the provinces with the army; whereas for Cicero service in the provinces was seen as an endurance, now it was an expected part of the career of a senator. This can be seen in the career of Agricola (Tacitus' father-in-law). He was born in AD 40 in Gallia Narbonensis. He held the post of military tribune in Britain during the Boudiccan uprising. He was quaestor at the age of twenty-four, tribune of the plebs at twenty-six and stood for the praetorship at twenty-eight (see Chapter 4). It is notable that some of these ages are earlier than the *Leges Annales* would permit, but because he was married and had two children his career was accelerated by two years in line with the Augustan marriage laws. However, again as with the pattern of age and office holding of Vespasian, there was a significant gap between the praetorship and the consulship, not held until his thirty-seventh year after the command of the twentieth legion in Germany and Britain. After the consulship, Agricola was the governor of Britain.

There is a major change from the Republic to Empire in the nature of the age at which an individual gains public responsibility. Whereas Cicero in his mid-twenties gained a reputation via the public trial of Verres, the ex-governor of Sicily, Vespasian and Agricola had held public responsibility in the *vigintivirate* and were on the point of holding the quaestorship, an office for which Cicero was not eligible prior to the age of thirty. In their late twenties, senators in the empire were already on an upward spiral to the praetorship. In contrast, in the Republic, this was an office held some ten years later shortly before the consulship. Where we see similarity is in the age of holding the consulship in our examples. The accelerated career structure in the empire only applied to this office if the candidate was a patrician. This group had also been privileged under the Republic, but only by a few years (as we saw at the beginning of this chapter). In the empire, their status was reinforced and we can suggest that the patrician sons of senators had a different experience of the life course to those of the plebian senators and the *novi homines* entering the senate for the first time.

9

GETTING OLD

In Western societies of the late twentieth century, the transition into the 'third age' has been marked most usually by retirement from work and living on a pension from the age of sixty or sixty-five. The major feature that has defined this stage of life has been the absence of work and the presence of earnings derived from physical or mental labour (see Hockey and James 1993). The Roman world did not define old age in the same way or mark it with a transition at a set age. These factors cause old age to appear different and present us with a challenge to understand this stage of life within its context, rather than with reference to modern conceptions of pensions and retirement in the West. The latter, that have defined our understanding of the old, may well disappear within the lifespan of the present generation in work – already the twenty-first century has opened with a discussion of the merits of removing the statutory retirement age in Britain. It will be interesting to see if there will be a redefinition of the characteristics of old age, as the over sixty-fives are drawn back into work. Equally, the ageism experienced in the workplace today may change in its form in the future too. Our understanding of the Roman concept of old age, unlike much of the life course, is informed by the personal voices of the elderly. This is in part caused by a fundamental feature of old age at Rome: it was a period of time in which a person had greater *otium* (leisure), but needed to utilise that leisure to enhance or preserve their mental faculties. This led some of the elderly to write philosophical treaties and, not surprisingly, the focus of many of these was their experience of old age. Indeed, it could be stated that the ancient experience of old age, in many ways, informed the notions of endurance that developed stoic philosophy adopted by both young and elderly.

At Rome, old age did not entirely depend on a simple measurement of chronological age of the individual, but also took account of a person's physical and mental health. There was no retirement age as such, or system of pensions. The majority of the population presumably did not have the luxury to do anything other than to work until they dropped. The position the individual held in later life was dependent on the status, wealth and character that they held in earlier life. Only in the mythical golden age of the past were the elderly respected for their years (*contra.* Dupont 1992: 232). There was, however, for those who could afford it, a very strong concept of a retreat from public life, and an idea that with increasing years another stage of the life course was reached. This featured, if not a total withdrawal from public life, at least an absence of office holding – a feature of the central phases of adult-hood.

In ancient texts, the chronological age at which old age began varies. The categorisation of *seniores* or *senex* starts anywhere between forty-six and sixty (for sources see Suder 1978). There seems to be a general consensus that at some time between these ages, and certainly after the age of sixty, the individual entered a new stage of the life course and was defined by themselves or by others as simply old. There was no obvious rite of passage that marked this transition, rather social expectations changed. Their role and obligations as citizens reverted to those of a child. Once they reached the age of sixty they were not eligible for military service – a characteristic feature of adult life in Republican Rome. As they were no longer participants in the army, they ceased to be able to vote in the *comitia centuriata* (the assembly of the centuries). The Roman saying 'sixty year olds over the bridge' ('*sexagenarios de ponte*': Varro in Nonius 523.21; Macrobius *Sat* 1.5.10) referred to the fact that men over sixty were no longer allowed to vote – the *pontes* being the narrow gangways into the voting enclosures. In the Empire men over sixty were also excused attendance at the Senate; judges and local *decuriones* could retire but could retain their title (Sen.*Brev.Vit.*20.4). Equally, in the Augustan marriage laws, a man was not expected to be married or to produce further children for the state. In short, a man over the age of sixty was freed from public duties (Varro in Nonius 523.24) but at the same time deprived of many of the essential signifiers of citizenship – useful to the state and valued by his fellow citizens. Interestingly, from the second century AD, the age at which a man was excused from the public duties of providing *munera* (for example games) was raised to the age of seventy (*Dig.*50.4). This marks a change to extend obligations to those who were both of high status and older.

We have often made the point in this book that the Roman conception of age and ageing, as written, embodied the point of view of the adult male citizen. In progressing through life a Roman male passed from a period where he lacked power to one in which he gained authority, status and the right to legitimate action within the public and private sphere. In his youth and early adulthood he was deemed to be at the height of his physical and sexual power; in middle age he reached the heights of political authority. Old age represented a loss of all these forms of empowerment, it was characterised by the decline of physical and mental faculties and a loss of authority in the public arena accompanied by an increasing dependence on others and general sense of vulnerability. While the potential for social marginalisation was great, the Roman institution of *patria potestas* protected old men from the demands of unscrupulous sons (Saller 1994: 102–32). Old men retained legal control over their *familia* unless they could be declared incapable in law; and however physically decrepit a parent became, they maintained some control over the younger generation by the threat of disinheritance (on wills, see Chapter 10). Individuals in old age were also at pains to resist the stereotypical images of this stage of life – in a mode of discourse familiar to many members of the third age or their younger sons and daughters today. If the potential for marginalisation for men was great, it was even more so for elderly Roman women – they all but disappear from the story except as stereotyped evil witches, grasping widows and stepmothers, or lustful hags. In contrast to the surviving evidence for men, we simply do not have access to the ways in which women resisted these stereotypes drawn up by younger male poets and satirists. However, the ultimate means of resistance for many widows may have been their will and the potential to disinherit their sons and daughters.

Old age had never brought guaranteed respect or right to position, but the Roman virtue of *pietas* enshrined the idea of respect for one's parents and an obligation to look after them in their old age in return for the care they had shown already. At the same time that Octavian/Augustus placed an emphasis on his youth, there was a promotion of the ideal of *pietas*. This can be clearly demonstrated with reference to the description or image of Aeneas carrying his aged father, Anchises, out of the burning city of Troy (note his wife is left behind in contrast). The emperor Antoninus Pius allegedly earned his epithet because he gave his arm to his father-in-law, weakened by age (SHA *Hadrian* 24). An elderly person might have expected their children or heirs to have been the first call for support in their declining years, children, however, might have had other ideas. In the second century AD, a series of legal rulings were passed on the question of parent-child obligations and on when a son was obliged to support his aged father: was he under a natural obligation even if emancipated? Was a grandson constrained by a similar obligation? (*Dig.*25.3.5; Parkin 1997: 133). If you lacked children you might have a spouse on whom to depend, but in the final resort an individual was left to their own resources. Those resources may have included the legal obligation of freed slaves to support their former masters, if they were in a position to do so (*Dig.*25.15.3).

A philosophy of old age

The image of the ideal Republican is that of the well known veristic statue of the patrician carrying two portrait heads – the features that signify his status are his bald head, furrowed brow, and the deeply etched lines of his face. Thought to be based on death masks, the common image of Republican man is of the older individual (Plate 9.1; see examples in Kleiner 1992; Ramage and Ramage 1995). These images evoke the individual's gravitas (serious-ness), the fact that he has devoted his time to the state and his family's well-being. The ageing process was clearly shown on his face and these signs

Plate 9.1 Republican holding two portrait busts of ancestors. Although not the original heads, the intention of the veristic tradition is clear. Here are middle-aged men who have served the state in war and politics and have their civic virtue etched in the lines on their faces.

reflected his civic standing. The ideal of the Roman Republic was one that accorded increased status the older a man became, as illustrated by the *Lex Annalis*, which set a minimum age limit for all the major magistracies (for discussion see Chapter 8). As a man grew older so did the number of honours and positions he had held and could have aspired to. Alongside this accumulation of public honour, the institution of paternal power meant that control and authority were always vested in the older generation, which was reinforced through an ideology of *pietas* towards parents (Saller 1994: 130–32). As age increased, if things followed the expected course or according to a man's or family's aspirations, he could expect to rise up the career ladder, to increase his wealth and to widen his social and economic networks through the marriages of his children. Through his adult life, these would increase to an extent where the direct control of all these connections would become looser, since some would depend on connections via his grandchildren, but ideally his control over such connections should have continued until his death. There are clear indications here, although in some ways marginalised, that the old retained the reins of power and we might expect that old age was a time to be cherished and an opportunity to bask in the glory of a lifetime fulfilled. However, there are indications to the contrary: Valerius Maximus reports that respect for old age was an 'ancient custom' of a past golden age. The days when young men accompanied their fathers to the Senate, waited at the door to escort them home, waited on older guests before seating themselves at dinner and rarely spoke at meals were clearly over (2.1.9). One of the phenomena of the late Republic was that young men no longer 'waited their turn' in line with traditional practices (*mos maiorum*) or as decreed by the *Lex Annalis*. As we saw in Chapter 8, there was a general distrust of the young – epitomised by Cicero's relationship to Octavian in 43 BC. The triumph of Octavian at Actium was also associated with the abandonment of the traditional veristic portraiture of the Republic in favour of the image of eternal youth found in the statuary and on the coinage of Augustus, but the ideals of the Republic were to be returned to under the Flavians less than a century later.

This background of change places into context one of the most significant texts on the role of old age. In 44 BC, in his early sixties, Cicero wrote a defence of old age, *Cato Maior de Senectute,* and dedicated it to his friend Atticus who was sixty-five. The text is set out as a dialogue between Scipio Aemelianus and Cato the Elder, with the occasional aside from Gaius Laelius, and placed in the past, at approximately 150 BC when Cato was eighty-three years old (Powell 1988; Parkin 1998: 25). It is an extended philosophical tract that does not detail the actual lived experience of old age but rather attempts to negotiate space for older members of society who have much to offer in terms of experience to those younger than themselves. The dialogue opens with Scipio's surprise that old age is not a burden to Cato though it weighs down other men (2.4). Cato's response denies that old age is the root of the problem, but instead suggests that those who lack the character to live a virtuous and happy life are going to find any age burdensome (2.4 and cf. 18.62–66). In repost, Laelius points out that Cato has the advantages of resources, wealth and social position (3.8) and this viewpoint is conceded by Cato, who admits that his view is that of a comfortable member of the upper class with good health. The dialogue than passes on to discuss Roman heroes or *exempla* from the past who have done great deeds despite encroaching age and to list and refute a number of common complaints about getting old. Cato recognises that old age will prevent men from doing great physical feats but this does not stop them being mentally active. He sees the wisdom and experience of the elderly as useful to the state and suggests keeping the memory active by exercising it (6–8). There is also a pertinent comment, given the political situation at the time of writing, about states in past history being overthrown by the young but sustained and restored by the old (6.20).

The physical weakness of old age is inevitable but there are still activities that he can do – he could still potentially make public speeches but was now in a better position to instruct Scipio and Laelius on the art of rhetoric (9.28). Cato also partly attributes the loss of physical strength to the dissipation of youth (10.30). This physical weakening is why the old are exempt from holding offices in which such vigour is needed, but this does not mean that old men cannot perform certain duties (11.34). It is the duty of every man to resist old age, to adopt a good regimen of health, practise moderate exercise and eat frugally (11.36 and cf. Spurinna below) in order to have the energy for intellectual exercise and the study of philosophy. Here, we see old age treated in the manner of a disease, which needs to be endured but can be overcome by the virtuous man by following a regimen. Another common complaint, the decline in sexual prowess and pleasure, is welcomed by Cato as a positive of old age as it only detracted from higher pursuits (12.41ff). Likewise the desire to over-indulge in food and drink also passes and allows Cato to enjoy his moderate diet and delight more in conversation (14.46). One activity that has grown in pleasure as Cato grew older is farming and agriculture – these are deemed suitable activities for an ageing man, although one does not imagine that Cato is actually out harvesting, digging irrigation ditches and pruning the vines himself: his is clearly an executive role (15.51–4). Cato's final reason why old age is to be feared is that it means death is not far away (19.66). His reaction to this is typically Stoic: 'After death the sensation is either pleasant or there is none at all' (20.74). The study of philosophy prepares the individual for the inevitability of death and Cato looks forward to his time in the afterlife, where he will meet his father again (23.84–85).

This treatise reflects some of the realities and anxieties of Cicero at the age of sixty-two. Philosophy had become his consolation and refuge in the 40s BC while he was still coming to terms with the death of Tullia (see Chapter 10)

122

and the changed political situation (see Chapter 8). Perhaps it was also an articulation of an anxiety about his own future and that of his fellow senators in the political upheaval of the period when young men were taking over. The dialogue is set in the mythical past, like the *exempla* of Valerius Maximus, at a time when the elderly still held influence and authority (cf. Parkin 1998: 25). Cicero might praise the idea of a withdrawal from the public world but he was writing within a tradition that held the idea of *otium*, leisure for intellectual pursuits, as a reward for labouring in the political and civic arena, and as a necessity to maintain the mental faculties. Conversely there is also an apparent anxiety about being sidelined when one still has much to offer in terms of the experience and wisdom of years. A similar anxiety was expressed by Plutarch, writing one hundred and fifty years later, in *'On whether an old man should engage in public affairs'* (*Moralia* 783b – 797f). He regarded withdrawal from public life as shameful and contemptuous. The virtues of old age, of wisdom, experience and good judgement are precisely those that best qualify a man for public service. He thought it was not suitable for men to retire to domesticity, a situation more suited to women. Clearly, as old age approached, men were concerned about their role in life. It was apparently no easier in the Roman period to let the younger generation – men in their forties – take over, than it is for some today. These treatises represent an attempt to rationalise philosophical ideals and the potential realities of growing old. They are pragmatic in the recognition of the advantages and disadvantages of old age and are an attempt to negotiate some social and political space for the elderly, but still do not really tell us of the lived experience of old age for most Romans.

A life less different?

The complexity of the individual experience of becoming old is revealed by two descriptions of the personal experiences of old age. These texts need not represent the entire range of experience of the phenomenon, but they provide revealing details of the complexity and anxieties associated with ageing. In a letter to Calvisius Rufus, Pliny sets out the ideal old age for the upper class Roman male; the description of Spurinna's life in retirement illustrates the type of activities that were thought to be suitable and life enhancing once one had withdrawn from public life.

> Every morning he stays in bed for an hour after dawn, then calls for his shoes and takes a three-mile walk to exercise his mind and body. If he has friends with him he carries on a serious conversation, if he is alone a book is read aloud... then he sits down, the book is continued, or preferably the conversation; after which he goes out in his carriage accompanied by his wife (a model of her sex) or one of his friends, a pleasure recently mine... After a drive of seven miles he will walk another mile, then sit again or

retire to his room and his writing, for he composes lyric verses in both Greek and Latin with considerable success; ...when summoned for his bath (in mid-afternoon in winter and an hour earlier in summer) he first removes his clothes and takes a walk in the sunshine if there is no wind, and then throws a ball briskly for some time, this being another form of exercise whereby he keeps old age at bay. After his bath he lies down for a short rest before dinner, and listens while something light and soothing is read aloud...Dinner is brought in on dishes of antique solid silver, a simple meal but well served...Between courses there is often a performance of comedy, so that the pleasures of the table have a seasoning of letters, and the meal is prolonged into the night, even in summer, without anyone finding it too long amid such pleasant company.

The result is that Spurinna has passed his seventy-seventh year, but his sight and hearing are unimpaired, and he is physically agile and energetic; old age has brought him nothing but wisdom. This is the sort of life I hope and pray will be mine, and I shall eagerly enter on it as soon as the thought of my years permits me to sound a retreat. Meanwhile innumerable tasks fill my time, though here again Spurinna sets me a reassuring example, for he also accepted public offices, held magistracies and governed provinces as long as it was his duty, and thus his present retirement was earned by hard work.

(Plin.*Ep*.3.1)

Other commentators (Parkin 1998; Minois 1989) have noted that while Pliny might aspire to the ordered life, healthy exercise, simple diet and intellectual pursuits that filled Spurinna's well earned retirement he also recognised that there was another side to old age – that of the decrepitude of Domitius Tullus. Domitius Tullus's wealth had not helped him to a happy old age, instead he was so 'crippled and deformed in every limb' that he even had to have his teeth brushed by his slaves and was looked after by a devoted wife (*Ep*.8.18). The Romans admired those who lived to a good old age and treated both their bodies and mind with respect. Spurinna gained Pliny's admiration because of his regimen. His carefully ordered physical regime implied his high moral qualities. While poor Pliny did not live to achieve either version of retirement – he died while governing Bithynia in *c*. AD 112 – most Romans, male and female, must have viewed the onset of old age with some trepidation and the realistic thought that either fate could be theirs.

A letter by the stoic Seneca (*Ep*.12; cf Parkin 1998: 27) shows recognition of personal experience: Seneca visits an estate of his to discover that the building is falling apart through old age and makes the comparison through metaphor and simile to that of his body in old age.

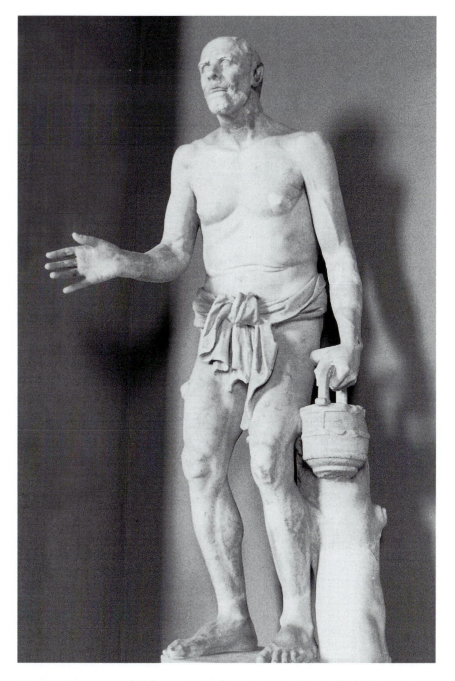

Plate 9.2 Roman copy of Hellenistic original depicting an old man. The body is no longer erect, the veins are clearly shown and the flesh has lost the tight muscularity of the adult body.

Wherever I turn, I see evidence of my increasing senility. I was visiting an estate of mine outside Rome and complaining of the expense of repairing the dilapidated building. My manager assured me that it was not the result of neglect on his part: he was doing all he could, but the fact was that the building was old. Actually, the house was built under my own supervision – what is to happen to me, if stones of the same age as myself are in such a crumbling state? I was upset at what he had said, and took advantage to show my temper. 'These plane-trees are obviously not being looked after' I said; 'There are no leaves on them, the branches are knotted and parched, and the bark is flaking off these squalid trunks. That would not happen if someone was digging around them and watering them properly.' He swore by my own *genius* (spirit) that he was doing all he could, that there was no respect in which he was falling short – the fact was that the trees were old. Between ourselves, I planted them myself, I saw them put out their first growth of leaves. I walked up to the entrance. 'Who,' I said, 'is that decrepit fellow? How appropriate that he should be posted by the door – he's about to take leave of us. Where on earth did you get hold of him? What possessed you to steal a corpse from someone else?' But the chap said to me, 'Don't you recognise me? I'm Felicio – you used to give me puppets at the Saturnalia. I'm the son of Philostius. I was your playmate when we were little children.' 'The man's completely mad,' I said, 'Now he's turned into a little boy and playmate of mine. Could be true though – he's as toothless as a child.'

(Translation from Wiedemann and Gardner 1991: 95–6).

The comments illustrate the potential vulnerability of the aged; they become like children, physically weak and dependent on others. They also highlight the different rate of ageing between the master and the slave. The living conditions of each had a dramatic effect on their physical well being. Following these comments Seneca moved swiftly into philosophical debate – or denial we might say – on the pleasures of old age. This letter is one of a collection addressed to Lucilius written in the last two years of Seneca's life. While these letters are arguably part philosophical essays in disguise, based on the letters of Epicurus, and Lucilius most likely completely fictional (Griffin 1992: 416–8) they were composed while Seneca was in his late sixties and living in retirement away from the court. Several of them cover various themes of old age: the fear of death (4, 24, 26, 30, 61, 63); retirement (4, 19, 24); reverting to childish behaviour (4); physical disintegration of the body and the treatment of its various ailments (26, 30, 54, 55, 65). Such thoughts obviously preoccupied Seneca in his later life. While he rationalised away the fear of death through philosophy and looked to the positive aspects of being retired, Seneca was suffering from continued ill-health, particularly asthma or a shortness of breath which he referred to as 'practising how to die' (*meditationem mortis; Ep.*54.2). He recognised that old age affected the body more than the mind. The irony of old age was that the body declined just at the point in life when peace of mind (*tranquilitas*) and modesty were achieved as a result of the wisdom gained from the experiences of a long life (26.2–3; *cf.* 30). Stoicism is clearly expressed in his attitude toward the negative aspects of old age and approaching death, a personal view that was taken over into the retelling of his suicide by Tacitus. Seneca's death, ordered by Nero, was long and drawn out because his austere regimen had caused his body to become so emaciated that cutting his wrists could not result in death. The strength of his body, despite his willingness to face death, implied his high moral standing (*Ann.*15.63). Seneca's discussion of old age is underpinned by Stoicism, maybe not surprisingly since philosophy was the mental panacea for the old. The personal voice or experience is understood via the mental exercise of philosophy.

The old woman: a continuing cause for male concern

Elderly women disappear from the sources even more insidiously than elderly men, no personal treatises written by women in old age survive to counter the views of younger male authors and, in particular, the poets and satirists. It is a common misconception that widows are old women in ancient literature. We have shown in previous chapters that widows could have been at a very young age when they lost their husband. It is unclear whether women, if they survived the dangerous years of childhood and childbearing, would have had longer life expectancies than men (for discussion see Parkin 1992: 92–106). What the sources do reveal is a concern for the behaviour of women once they have passed the age of fertility. It is these women who feature extensively in satirical literature. The male Roman world had to deal with a reality that presented a number of legally independent but economically dependent elder women. That is, women who stood outside the social roles of wife and mother but might lack the means to support themselves. It also had to deal with those who were legally and financially independent, that is, had the means and the social status to act for themselves. As with other stages in the female life course there is a biological marker that can signify the passing into a new period of life. Where the age of menarche marks the transition from virgin to wife and mother, so the menopause can be used as a biological marker for transmission into a fourth stage in the female life course. Once a woman was beyond child bearing her status underwent a change. It was understood that reproductive life would cease at some point. Authorities disagreed about just when this was; Pliny the Elder, following Aristotle, thought that most women reached menopause somewhere between forty and fifty (*NH*7.14.61; *HA*585b3–5) and Soranus endorsed this, but added that some women might not reach menopause until sixty (*Gyn.*1.4.20; Amundsen and Diers 1970). Augustus' marriage laws accepted this age range in that they insisted on remarriage for widows under fifty; only once past this age was a woman

Plate 9.3 Roman copy of Hellenistic original depicting an old person. Here the flesh sags, especially the breasts, and the bones show beneath the skin. Physical weakness and vulnerability are clearly expressed. The gender of this image is still under debate by art historians.

exempt from penalties. Given the stress of the laws on reproduction it seems likely to conclude that the lawmakers thought a women under fifty should have been expected to reproduce. We have no idea how women dealt with the menopause or whether they even had a name for it, but we can assume they recognised that they were no longer fertile.

One elderly lady who lived an enjoyable old age and managed to raise her grandson to a standard of personal austerity admired by Pliny was Ummidia Quadratilla (*Ep.*7.24). Ummidia died at the age of seventy-nine in good health and unimpaired intellect. She had occupied her leisure time in playing draughts and being entertained by her personal troupe of mime actors. She never allowed her grandson to witness these performances and thus did not let the inappropriate side of her life corrupt him. She also left a will that Pliny approved of. Unmoved by those who paid fawning attention to her, she bequeathed two-thirds of her property to her grandson and a third to her granddaughter, and very little to her freedmen actors. She thus earned Pliny's admiration on two counts (three, if you count consulting him on the grandson's education): leaving her property within the family and raising a good citizen. She is also attested as a patroness of her local town of Casinum (*CIL*X.5183). Ummidia was undoubtedly a wealthy woman who could afford her own pleasures and her own care in her old age. We have to assume that one of the reasons that elderly women all but disappear from the sources is partly that they disappear from life – without resources or children to care for you once the infirmities of age arrived you probably did not survive for long.

Old women, however, were stock characters of comedy and satire. The sexually voracious old hag had a pedigree that reached back to Aristophanes (cf *Ecclesiasuzae* 1065ff – three old women fighting over a young man who lusts after a girl. New laws passed by the women of Athens compelled him to have sex with one of them first). The character of the wealthy wife (*uxor dotata*) who could make excessive demands, sexual and otherwise, on her husband was common in the comedies of Plautus (e.g. *Aulularia* 534–5; *Mostellaria* 690–97 cited in Walcot 1991: 19–20; Rosivach 1994: 110). In the satires of Horace, Martial (cf. 3.93; 10.90) and Juvenal (*Sat.*6) old women are described in terms of gross physical decrepitude and inappropriate sexual desire. Horace's *Epodes* 8 and 12 are particularly vindictive attacks on old women and their sexual appetites. The depiction of hanging breasts, flabby stomach, black teeth, and wrinkled body in *Epode* 8 is particularly vivid. In *Epode* 12 a man of indeterminate years is repulsed by the sexual attentions of on old woman (for full discussion see Richlin 1983: 109–16). The humour is created not just by the grotesque imagery but by the inappropriate behaviour of women beyond the age of childbearing. The sexual appetites of both men and women were considered to be part of an earlier stage of life, but here the women are doubly inappropriate as the instigators of such attention even if prostitutes (compare *Odes* 1.25, 3.15 and 4.13; Esler 1989). To seek out the sexual attentions of an elderly woman as the young Otho did was clear evidence of an underhand agenda (Suet. *Otho* 2). Sexual vigour was considered suitable to a young man but even his ardour was assumed to cool as he grew older; sexual attractiveness was suitable for a woman as a young wife and mother, not for an elderly woman.

The end of life

It is clear that vulnerability, both physical and mental, was considered characteristic of old age. These physical and mental inabilities were recognised by Roman writers and commentators of all kinds and played for laughs. Rosivach's study (1994) on the negative stereotypes of old women lists witches, drunks, superstition and garrulousness among other characterisations, but it is as well to remember that such negative stereotyping was not confined to women. Juvenal's *Satire* 10 does for old men what Horace does for old women. He lists physical deformities from the bald head, running nose, quivering limbs and voice, loss of taste and loss of sexual ability. He then passes on to the indignities of having to be shouted at, having to take food from another's fingers, and finally the loss of memory – an image so ghastly that the individual was the shame of his family and not even approached by legacy hunters (lines 190–240).

As potential victims of legacy hunters, the vulnerability, both mental and physical, of the elderly was manifest (a viewpoint confirmed in the satirical role reversal in Lucian *Dial.mort.* 5–9). Legacy hunting particularly offended the Roman sense of *pietas* and family duty because it would send money and property outside the bloodline. As we have already seen (Chapter 6), Apuleius was accused of such motivation when he married the widow Pudentilla, the prosecution upping her age to sixty to make their point. As marriage was considered a union for the production of children and carrying on the family, and sexual activity suitable only to the fertile time of a woman's life, it was thought that the only reason for a widow to remarry past this point in her life, especially if her children were already adult, was because someone was after her money. Ummidia Quadratilla had not given in to those who paid court to her, as we have seen. Pliny reports with disapproval on M. Aquilius Regulus, who played both sides of the legacy game. He acquired a legacy from the dying widow of his enemy Piso by fooling her into thinking he could predict her recovery; he encouraged doctors to improve the health of Velleius Blaesus until he had changed his will, then berated the doctors for keeping Blaesus alive; while witnessing the signing of Aurelia's will forced her to write a codicil giving him the fine clothes she was wearing for the occasion (*Ep.* 2.20). To Pliny's satisfaction Regulus was unsuccessful on the latter two counts, Blaesus left him nothing and Aurelia outlived him. Regulus had emancipated his own son so that the boy could inherit from his mother (while still under *potestas* the boy could not inherit). Regulus then indulged his son, Pliny's implication being in the hope of inheriting from him. Unfortunately the boy did predecease his father, leaving Regulus prey to legacy hunters himself (*Ep.*4.2).

It was not unknown for the elderly to express tiredness with life (*taedium vitae*) as age took its toll, ill health became unbearable, or outside influences made life untenable. Refusing food (*inedia*) was considered an honourable and even heroic method of taking your own life (Van Hooff 1990). Atticus did so at age seventy-eight with severe intestinal illness (Nepos *Atticus* 21–22), as did Pliny's 'guardian and mentor', Corellius Rufus, who tired of fighting the excruciating pain in his feet, having tried to control it by a strict regimen. In the end he refused all food and died (*Ep.*1.12). It is all very well for the aristocracy to exit from life with dignity and out of choice. The less fortunate may come to the fate of the old man in one of the poems of the *Greek Anthology* (cited in Van Hooff 1990: 35):

> Worn by age and poverty, no one stretching out his hand to relieve my misery, on my tottering legs I went slowly to my grave, scarce able to reach the end of my wretched life. In my case the law of death was reversed, for I did not die first to be buried, but I died after my funeral.
>
> (*Anth.Pal.*7. 336)

Clearly as we reach old age and begin to notice its effects the mind begins to focus on the subject of approaching death. It is a universal of human nature to be anxious about how we will cope with the practicalities of life as we grow more debilitated, at whatever age this happens. However we do not wish to give the impression that all ancient sources viewed old age as a time of misery and doom. Growing older was inevitable but it could have its pleasures, and not just the philosophical activities that the aristocratic minds of Cicero and Seneca project. If given a choice no doubt the upper class Roman would prefer to imagine that she or he would age gracefully and enjoy a comfortable life like those of Ummidia or Spurinna.

10

DEATH AND MEMORY

Death, as we have seen in Chapter 1, could occur at any point during the Roman life span with a concentration of deaths in childhood, early adulthood, in childbirth, and later, after about fifty years of age. This pattern and its associated greater frequency of death than that experienced in the West today would suggest that during the Roman life course an individual witnessed the loss of relatives at every stage. Famously, the grandsons of Augustus, Gaius and Lucius, died in early adulthood. Events Augustus recalled in the *Res Gestae* (14) on his death, recounting in the same passage the honours they had held and their achievements even though still young:

> My sons, Gaius and Lucius, of whom Fortuna bereaved me in their youth, were for my honour designated consuls by the Senate and People of Rome when they were fourteen, with the provision that they should enter on that magistracy after the lapse of five years [i.e. at the age of nineteen]. Further, the senate decreed that from that day when they were led to the forum they should take part in the public councils. Furthermore each of them was presented with silver shields and spears by the whole body of the Roman *equites* and hailed *princeps iuventutis* (emperor of youths).

The emphasis, in this public text, was on the honours decreed to these two young men and the recognition of their value in life by the public bodies: the Senate and People of Rome and the *equites*. It is this which is highlighted here as a memorial to their brief lives. The role of the goddess Fortuna (Luck) illustrates a resignation to the deaths of the young, who had such great potential in their later lives in the eyes of their parents (compare Suet.*Aug.*65). Little appears here of the private grief Augustus experienced, instead we have a statement about the status of his adopted sons in the eyes of other Romans. This illustrates a facet of Roman commemoration – a life is seen from the point of view of the community or its public manifestation. In funerary inscriptions, the offices held by a man are recalled and his public prominence measured; or in the case of women their role as wives or mothers. This form of representation displayed the public values of Roman society, but need not reveal the private emotions associated with the act of commemoration itself. Often, we find that the funeral and construction of a tomb make statements about the public view of the dead – maybe to increase the social value of the living through association with a memory of the deceased. Hence the commemoration of the dead and their memory through story telling or history added value to the status of the surviving relatives. This will be the focus of our opening discussion.

Death, within the family, was a common experience (see Chapter 1) at all stages of the life course. It caused families and their relations to reconfigure their forms of property holding, and could result in a change in the relative statuses of these kin to one another. A powerful vehicle for guiding these changes was the will of the deceased that ensured for the transfer of property and thus equally status to relatives after death. The will as a feature of Roman society will be examined, with a view to understanding the thoughts or the ideological preconceptions behind the process of the resocialisation of family members of different ages on the death of a *paterfamilias*. This process of death and resocialisation would have been experienced frequently by the period of adulthood. The loss of siblings during childhood would have been a common experience. For parents, the loss of at least one of their children would have been expected. However, this does not imply that they were immune to that loss. The statements in inscriptions from Rome that refer to an age of death are most common for those who were under the age of twenty-five and were made by their parents. The statement of age, in these cases, represents a summation of the tragedy of death. Their son or daughter had not lived to fulfil their potential; there was little to say in commemorating them apart from their age or their youth (Chapter 5). The number expressed the emotion of loss and was quite different from the enumeration of offices, statements of marriage etcetera found in inscriptions associated with male and female adults.

The dead did not simply occupy the minds of the living at the time of their departure. Festivals of the deceased and celebrations at the family tomb caused them to have a presence within the lives of the living members of a family. These rituals, that took place within the context of the tomb and its associated inscriptions, provided a context for the continuing survival of a bond between the living and the dead. For those growing up in Rome, they were not just born into a family and household (see Chapter 2), they were also born into a structure of ancestry associated with the burial places of these persons. These latter and their associated rituals provide us with an indication of a system of family memory and ideology that provided *exempla* which the next generation might live by. The deceased, in effect, continued to live after death via the memory of others, alongside their predecessors and ancestors. A complicated panoply of memory aids can be seen to have existed that were most prominent in the funeral, the epitaph, the will and festivals that commemorated the deceased, as well as an ancestral mask in the *atrium* of the home (see Flower 1996). These actions reveal the interplay of individuals at different stages in the life course and the interaction of generations that form the larger structure: the Roman life cycle. Through death, the individual and the events of their life course passed into memory and history.

The funeral

Funerals would have varied greatly according to the age and status of the deceased. Our information on the Roman funeral tends to refer to the death of those who had lived well into adult life and had fulfilled their social obligations as citizens. Polybius (6.53–54) provides a description of the process of a funeral of a leading man at Rome. The body was brought to the forum in procession with many of the deceased's relatives wearing the death masks of their famous ancestors and dressed according to the ancestor's highest public office: if a praetor or consul a purple bordered toga, if a censor a purple toga, if a person who had triumphed a gold embroidered toga (see Flower 1996: 91–127 for full discussion). In the forum, these relatives sat on curule chairs and the body of the deceased was displayed in an upright position. A grown up son, if one existed, gave a eulogy on the deceased's life. The choice of a male heir here was significant; it emphasised the continuity into the future of the deceased father. It also highlighted to all the inherited role of the son, after the death of his father – he was going to replace him in society. The speaker would have recalled the achievements and accomplishments of the ancestors of the man who had died addressing each of their death masks beginning with the most ancient. Hence the life of the deceased was recalled first and then placed alongside the lives of that person's ancestors. In effect this integrated the life of the deceased into an ancestral series of lives, whilst those watching the speaker thought of the future survival of that ancestry in the son's family or future family. The eulogy at a person's funeral was the first time an account was made of that person's life, in the future at another funeral a similar account would have been given after all the other ancestors' lives had been recalled. After the body had been taken from the forum, a mask of the deceased was made and kept in the house of his next of kin to be worn at funerals in the future.

Polybius viewed these events as a way in which the grief and loss of an individual family became a public concern for all citizens present in the forum. Moreover, the images of ancestors and recall of the deceased's life created an image or series of aspirations for the young to live by and indicated the notion of enduring hardships for the common good of Rome. However, there is another way of seeing the funeral and its imagery. The deceased was undergoing a transition from the world of the living into that of the dead. His position was liminal, neither within the community of the living nor that of the dead. By recalling his life and then the lives of other family members, a series of lives or a history of the family was recounted.

This history was chronological, beginning with the earliest and ending with the penultimate death. The fact that the deceased's life was recalled first could be seen as a means of integrating the recent past into this historical sequence of lives that formed the life course of the family name and the collective memory of the family. In seeing the funeral as a public event and the concern of all citizens rather than just a private family affair, Polybius highlighted how the naming of individuals, and in particular those who were consuls, created a sense of history and historical time. After all, annalistic history was based upon the naming of the consuls each year as a means to place events into a chronological sequence. Hence, we can see the funeral as a family or public history into which the deceased was being placed (compare Flower 1996: 126–7).

The funeral oration was not exclusive to men. Women who lived into old age were often given a public funeral (Plu.*Caes.*5). At the funeral of Julius Caesar's aunt, who had been married to Gaius Marius, the speech, as recalled by Suetonius, is suggestive of the nature of the content of these eulogies to women:

> The family of my aunt Julia is descended by her mother from the kings and on her father's side is akin to the mortal gods; for the Marcii Reges go back to Ancus Marcius and the Julii, the family of which ours is a branch, to Venus. Our stock therefore has the sanctity of kings, whose power is supreme over mortal men, and the claim to reverence which attaches to gods, who hold sway over kings themselves.
>
> (*Jul.*6)

Here, emphasis is placed on the ancestry of women as an integral element of the family itself. It is significant that on the death of his wife, in the same year, Julius Caesar made a public speech, contrary to custom, for the young woman – seen later by Plutarch as a popular measure (Plu.*Caes.*5). Also, the funerals provided an opportunity for Caesar to display the death masks of Marius and his family (Flower 1996: 124). This would have linked him to his ancestors from the past and provided a reminder to the viewer of the ancestry of the speaker as well as the deceased (Plu.*Caes.*5). In effect, the recall of Marius on these occasions re-established a controversial phase of Roman history and to a certain extent, through the audacity and daring of the speaker, reinvented the person of Marius as a potent symbol for the present. In no way should we see the funeral oration as simply a matter that concerned the deceased; it recalled, re-established and reinvented the memory of individuals from Rome's past. The speech, like all forms of rhetoric, could have manipulated or created ancestral memory of the past according to the needs in the present of the speaker. Those may have been simple – the acceptance of a son as a worthy successor – or, in the case of Caesar, the creation of a new context for political thought and ideology.

Plate 10.1 Minucia Suavis, died age 14 years (Rome). The inscription reads: To the shades, Minucia Suavis wife of Publius Sextilus Campanus. She lived 14 years, 8 months and 23 days. Tiberius Claudius Suavis, a most pious father, made this.

Grief and commemoration

The need to commemorate female relatives did not solely apply to those with ancestry stretching back into time. Cicero, a *novus homo* (new man), felt a need to establish a shrine for his daughter Tullia. She died after giving birth to a son in January 45 BC (Rawson 1975: 222–28). Her father was transfixed by grief causing him to avoid both public appearances in the forum at Rome or at his houses where Tullia had lived part of her life. He in fact became rather reclusive in a new house at Astura (*Fam.4.6*). Servius Sulpicius Rufus in a letter of consolation to Cicero (*Fam.4.5*) summarises Tullia's life:

> She saw you her father, a praetor, then a consul, and an augur; she was married to men from noble families; she enjoyed almost all of life's blessings. And she departed from life when the Republic died. How, then, can you or she complain about fate on this account?

No stigma was attached to the fact Tullia had been divorced twice before her death in her early thirties. What was emphasised instead was that she was married to members of Rome's nobility, whilst she saw her father's success in public life. The two seem inseparable and the passage characterises the way in which Roman men related the female life course to their own public actions. The affection between father and daughter was described in the letter as inherent in both his and her status: affection is enhanced by status and status enhanced affection. Other more typical examples of affective ties are clear in other letters (*Att.2.8* on willingness to attend games that Tullia wishes to see, 4.1 on loyally welcoming her father's return from exile at Brundisium; the bond of affection between Tullia and Atticus' wife, Pilia, *Att.4.4a, 4.16*).

Cicero wished to build a shrine to his daughter so that she would not be forgotten. An almost daily correspondence with Atticus took place during March and May 45 BC to buy a property for this purpose (see *Att.12*). Arpinum, his home town, was rejected, because few would travel that way and see the shrine (*Att.12.12*). Tusculum, where she had died, was also rejected for the same reason (*Att.12.37*). Astura was seen as unsatisfactory (*Att.12.19*). What he wanted was a property on the far bank of the Tiber, which was in the public eye (*Att.12.19*). These suburban properties did not come cheap, a thousand *iugera* (620 acres) property had recently been sold for 11,500,000 *sestertii* (*Att.13.31*), and Cicero began to call in debts, and to sell silver plate and other luxury items (*Att.12.23, 12.25*). The other problem was simply to find a suitable property for the project that was actually for sale. Given these difficulties, he considered buying on the coast near Ostia (*Att.12.30*). Demands of the site seem to have been paramount over size or scale of existing buildings, presumably to create the necessary topographical prominence of the shrine to his daughter (*Att.12.27, 12.34*). It is difficult to establish the nature of the shrine from the letters. Cicero was adamant that it should not be a tomb, because the monument was to commemorate his daughter's apotheosis (*Att*.12.36). His greatest worry was whether such a monument would survive in the future with changes in ownership of land (*Att*.12.19, 12.36). The desire for a shrine clearly was seen as a little odd by Atticus and other friends of Cicero. However in the context of modern work on the need for continuing bonds between the living and the dead, it makes rather more sense. Also, if we remember that Cicero as a *novus homo* was not associated with major monuments at Rome, we can then see that the prominent shrine to his daughter would create a greater presence in the city. We might even say to commemorate a daughter in this way, in the context of Cicero's feelings about the loss of freedom in the 40s BC, would have also been a statement about the nature of politics.

Remembering the child

There was a major difference between the funerals of adults and children. In contrast to the elaborate rituals, processions and panegyrics given in front of citizens during the day, children were cremated at night and interred into the tomb by daybreak (Serv.*Aen*.1.727, 6.224, *Dan*.11.143; Sen.*Brev.Vit*.20.5; Tac.*Ann*.13.17; Rose 1923; Flower 1996: 95–6). The category of child was defined for males as those who wore the *toga praetexta* and would have included most males under the age of sixteen (Tac.*Ann*.13.17; Liv.45.40–41). Few examples survive that refer to female funerals, however it is clear that virgins were treated differently in death. For example, the process of execution could not be applied to a female virgin (Dio 58.11). This indicates that there was a different treatment of the female body in death generally, the nature of which remains less than clear from our extant source material. It has been argued that funerals of children occurred at night to prevent attention being drawn to a family's loss (Flower 1996: 96–7). This view seems to be proven by the literary references to funerals themselves. However, the commemoration of children in cemeteries is strongly attested, even though most demographers would regard infants as under-represented generally (Parkin 1992: 6). For example the inscriptions that attest age of death using the *vixit* (s/he lived) formula from Rome demonstrate that children were commemorated (see Table 10.1 below). The evidence displays a classic pattern of age rounding with a particular stress on age ten, twenty and twenty-five (Duncan-Jones 1990). This causes the ages represented to be inaccurate, but there are other features of the numerical distribution of ages represented that display other social and cultural biases. These reveal features of mortuary practice. Not surprisingly, there is a significant bias in the data towards the under seven year olds – probably a reflection of a greater number of deaths within these early years of the lifespan at Rome. There is a quite significant drop in the number of individuals represented after the age of ten

Plate 10.2 The Isola Sacra Cemetery (Ostia and Portus). Note the appearance of different styles of commemoration.

with a significant concentration on the representation of eighteen year olds – outnumbering all age rounded figures (five, ten, fifteen, twenty, twenty-five). This points to the importance of this age within the life cycle. At eighteen, the male was no longer wearing a *toga praetexta* and would have traditionally completed his year of military training. In other words, he would have become a citizen in every sense – civil and military. It would not be true to say that all those represented in the inscriptions here had done so, however it points to a tradition that eighteen marked a transitional point as much as twenty-five, the youngest age of office holding, also did. These two ages are also highlighted as transitional points in the public life of the elite at Rome. Cassius Dio (52.20), in a speech accredited to Maecenas in 29 BC, states that at eighteen a male could be put onto the list of knights, because it was possible to discern his physical and mental abilities at this age; but nobody should join the senate until the age of twenty-five. Thus, eighteen can be seen to have been a transitional point in the life course.

Table 10.1 Epigraphic evidence for age in *vixit* formula under the age of 26 (Rome)

Age	Number
0–1	67
1–2	51
2–3	84
3–4	74
4–5	85
5–6	70
6–7	63
7–8	57
8–9	55
9–10	56
10–11	71
11–12	32
12–13	42
13–14	35
14–15	38
15–16	32
16–17	35
17–18	40
18–19	82
19–20	55
20–21	65
21–22	28
22–23	52
23–24	39
24–25	30
25–26	76

Therefore, although children were not commemorated by the elaborate funerals so prominent in our literary sources, they appear in the tombs of the deceased or in the large *columbaria* of the major families in the cemeteries outside the city of Rome. This would suggest that children were not publicly mourned but were a loss for the family in terms of the continuation of its name, sacred rites, and household or *domus* (Liv.45.40–41).

The living and the dead

The commemoration of the dead did not end with the funeral and the place-ment of the ashes or body within the tomb. Mourning, both private and public, occurred after the funeral. The period of mourning was limited legally: for women a whole year, whereas for men a few days (Dio 56.34–42; 58.2). Hence, for Cicero to grieve for his daughter and to attempt to build a shrine to her may have been seen as unusual if not immoral. For most people, the family tomb or simple marking of the grave with an amphora (see Plate 10.2) was the place at which the dead were commemorated. A series of annual festivals each February reminded the living of the role of their predecessors and ancestors. The festival known as the Parentalia saw the members of most families leave the city and go to the cemetery and the place that was associated with their ancestors (on the festival see Scullard 1981: 74–6; Toynbee 1971: 63–4). This activity took place at some point between the 13 and 21 of February. On leaving the city, the family would have seen the offerings in the road and in the streets of the cemeteries to the parents of the family. These offerings were basic and set up on a broken piece of pottery: an offering of corn, a tile wreathed in a garland, a few grains of salt, bread soaked in wine or simply some flowers (Ovid *Fasti* 2.537–555). The festival, although a private affair that focused attention on the family's forebears, was said to have been introduced by Aeneas who on his arrival in Italy had a need to commemorate his dead father. In other words, the ancestors of the family were integrated with a historical perspective of the founding mythology of the city itself.

During the period of the Parentalia, temples were closed and weddings forbidden (Ovid *Fasti* 2.557–70), which we may see symbolically as halting the life course of individuals and the city until the *manes* or ghosts of those from the past had been honoured. The Parentalia was followed on the twenty-second of February by the Caristia, which involved the kin relatives of a family meeting to offer incense and food to the Lares (household gods). The emphasis of the festival as portrayed by Ovid (*Fasti* 2.617–38) was on the concord and agreement of the family. Unkind or disrespectful thoughts and actions were to be kept away from the meeting. Ovid lists these as the mother who was harsh to her offspring, the son yearning for the death of his father or mother, the mother-in-law maltreating her daughter-in-law. The reality of family conflict was overlaid by an ideology of harmony and respect for the deceased.

The sequence of festivals is interesting. The procedure of honouring the dead at the tomb and then a meeting of the family to quell quarrels in front of the Lares mirrors the sequence at a person's death – burial in the tomb and then the resocialisation of the family after the funeral itself. The emphasis placed on concord was also present after the funeral. The need for so doing arose from the will and transmission of the deceased's property.

Wills were seen as very truthful statements of the deceased's wishes, in contrast to their public life that had involved rhetoric and speech making. There was also immense public interest in the content of other people's wills (see Champlin 1991 for a thorough treatment of Roman testamentary practice). Our modern literature on wills has generally placed a strong emphasis on the inheritance pattern from men to women or from men to their children, as opposed to the testamentary practices of both men and women. We need to be aware that in a subject extensively dominated by legal sources, there is a possibility of gender being confused and masked by the use of legal terminology. Here, the legal definition of *paterfamilias* as property owner of either male or female gender is of particular significance (*Dig.*50.16; Saller 1999: 185). This compounds the general problem in our legal sources of gender stereotyping that expects or attributes property to men. If we look at the surviving wills, we find that where the gender of the testator is known, most are by men with a significant proportion written by women (85% and 15% respectively, Champlin 1991: 46). In the overall pattern of testation, children were preferred over all others (Champlin 1991: 119–120). This included the marriage partner of the deceased, whether in their first, second, third or fourth marriage, but care was taken to ensure that the marriage partner's life did not suffer through this pattern of inheritance. For example, a wife would have been given an allowance to continue living the style of life she had been used to, in her place of residence, until her death (Champlin 1991: 120–1). Hence, children from earlier relationships tended to be preferred over all others in general. The preference for children over wives displays an anxiety about the possibility that the wife would remarry after the death of a husband and that the property would have passed to others outside the deceased's family. Equally, we might say that the continuity of the familial line was the fundamental concern to the deceased, rather than distrust of marriage partners and fear of future marriages. Not surprisingly, male children were given preference over female children. The reason given for this by Roman lawyers was that they would have needed more to live off, if they were to pursue a public career. Again, another reason may simply be that daughters once married would not have perpetuated the name of the deceased. It needs to be stressed that the female line was not unimportant, although it may not be frequently visible within our source material. Women were also leaving wills which likewise privileged their children over all others (Dixon 1988: 47–9). Where examples do appear, we find a significance and a memory of the maternal line to exist (e.g. Polybius, 31.26–9, on the female lineage of Scipio Aemilianus). Certainly, the transfer of property down the generations was expected from mother to child (Cic.*Caec.*12). More significant, perhaps, was the fact that lineage within the imperial family could be traced via mothers as well as fathers. For example, Caligula was said to trace his ancestry as much through his mother Agrippina, and his grandmother Julia, the daughter of Augustus, as via his father Germanicus – the son of Augustus' sister (Suet.*Cal.*7, 23; see Corbier 1995 for further examples). Memory of kin from the past was not limited to men only.

The place of the dead in the life course

Although the remains of the dead were buried or placed in tombs outside the city itself, their presence was felt within the lives of the city's inhabitants. Rome, and its associated buildings and monuments, was an arena for the recall of the past. Death masks were kept in the *atrium* of the home. The statues of the famous men (or Rome's ancestors) were the focus of didactic examples for the young to recall and emulate. This included individuals from beyond a person's ancestors, a *novus homo* (new man, e.g. Cicero) could appropriate another man's ancestors as the rhetorical occasion demanded, but for most the emphasis was placed firmly on the need to present or reinvent the past actions of prominent individuals within the present. The writer of a will at Rome had the opportunity to influence how their memory might survive with the division of property alongside this as an important adjunct. Equally, the building of one's own tomb as a preparation for the moment of death was not uncommon. These two factors point to a concern with the recall of a life after death by adult males. Children in contrast were commemorated simply by their parents and presented as a loss for the world as well as the parents, because in adulthood they would have capitalised on the indications of a life to come. Women were recalled for their lives married to famous men and became a vehicle for reference to key male ancestors and their children. Their name and memory was incorporated into a male systematised method of retelling the past.

11

AGE AND AGEING IN THE ROMAN EMPIRE AND BEYOND

In this final chapter, we wish to draw out a number of general points raised through the book. It is not intended as a summary of the key characteristics of the Roman life course, which have been discussed in the individual chapters already. Instead we raise issues not only for the study of the life course, but also for the more general historical approach to the reading of texts and writing of ancient history and archaeology, as well as some implications of our work for the modern study of gerontology. We wish to stress that the life course was not simply a series of stages that can be studied in isolation from each other; for instance, it is impossible to study Roman childhood without reference to the stages of life from which it is viewed. There is an importance in understanding each stage, or mode of transition between stages, in relationship to the whole life course of a society. For us, the life course should be viewed as an informal social institution that provided a structure to Roman society. The interaction between age cohorts that can only take place via the demographic simulation produced by Richard Saller (1994) aids our understanding of texts or inscriptions that provide information at the specific level of individual action.

Issues for ancient history and archaeology

The emphasis placed on the study of age and the life course in this book has raised a number of general issues for the study of ancient history and archaeology. We have set out to demonstrate that age, as well as gender and status, accounted for the actions of individuals we find referred to in the texts we read to construct or reconfigure the lives and actions of people in the Roman past. Age was something that was experienced and, at the same time, created an expectation of certain forms of behaviour. The young and the old were marginalised in this world of ages, in preference to men in middle age. However, in our texts, some men were forever represented and seen from a perspective of their old age. This is particularly apparent in the writing of Roman emperors. Tiberius never seems to have had a youthful stage in Suetonius' *Life* – he takes on the character of his age and personality once emperor. Equally, the young did not have the possibility of wisdom but in many cases resorted to the typical behaviour that characterised youthful excesses – they could achieve success only with help from their older advisors or the senate. The exception, of course, was Octavian; but this only marked him out as divine and somehow different from all the others – thus reinforcing the stereotypes of age related behaviour amongst others in society.

We see the interplay of ages within society as a factor in the transmission of a stable social system that might incorporate new ideas, architectural forms, dress, food, forms of production etcetera, yet was inherently conservative in outlook. Marriage did not simply involve an asymmetry between partners, but also mixed the ages of the husband's and wife's families. The sons and sons-in-law would appear to have looked to their elders for advice and we might say that marriage was a form of patronage, in which the son-in-law was in an unequal relationship with his more senior father-in-law. He was also expected to respect his own father. The position of first marriage in the male life course was situated within the ancient discourse of human development to coincide with the period at which a male was perceived to have ceased to have been impulsive and to have calmed his more irrational desires. It was a time in which he could have been trusted to enter into decisions in a considered manner. His wife, often much younger, was seen or idealised as subordinate. In reality, this subordination may have been short lived and we can identify wives who did not conform to the male idealisation of the virgin bride. Certainly, in second or third marriages, we can find examples of wives dealing with the dynamics of their lives and capable of asserting their viewpoint. The power of women, particularly in their late twenties or thirties, is displayed in the male representation of such women in rhetoric and historical writing as deviant or transgressive. They were, as far as our male writers were concerned, taking on a male role; and thus competing both socially, economically and, through their male relatives, politically. However, we do not find these traits associated with younger women, who had not given birth to heirs. Age and motherhood gave different meanings and access to social institutions.

Often in the ancient texts we only see a representation of the outward or public expression of social institutions. This is particularly true of marriage and the family, where information leads us to the legal or societal norms, which are expressed in discussion of the institution. The private face of these structures is often expressed in very personal terms, from a very limited number of sources. This inevitably causes certain examples of particular individuals and their families to take on a greater meaning in the discussion undertaken – some we have named and discussed, others we have not included in that discussion. It is impossible to include every text and every variation on the theme of the marriage and the family. However, what we have shown is the variety of forms according to age. There are other examples that could be included, but these would confirm the general pattern of variation according to the age of the participants. However, we are aware that it is often difficult, if not impossible, to situate these social experiences within a framework of chronological age of the participants. When we do have such information, the sample size is reduced further. However small our data set, it remains an invaluable insight into the private realm of the participants that can be elucidated through demographic simulation.

Our representation in this book of the meaning of age and the life course has of necessity depended on ancient texts, which were produced by a male elite. This could be seen as a deficiency of the book. We do not cover the life course of others within the Roman social system. What were the features of the life course of a slave? In many ways, this question, like others, cannot be answered. Our sources romanticise their relationship to their slaves – a trait of stoicism or of the pragmatism of Cato. We may imagine or empathise a life course of birth, capture, transport, sales and freedom or old age in slavery or birth, rearing, sale, resale etcetera. However, the slave even when freed was subject to the ideology of the life course of the freeborn citizen. They were freed at a certain age, but their life history would have continued to have been dominated by an early life within slavery or an absence of freedom. The efforts of Petronius' Trimalchio to gain acceptance, even with the ironic display of his life history (*Sat.*29) demonstrate the life course of the freeborn as a mode of expression, aspiration and ideology. Equally, we may question whether the ordinary citizens experienced the life course in a similar manner with the same stages, but, with our current information, we would be unable to give an answer based on ancient evidence. Instead, we may suggest that age as an explanatory system, found within accounts of the actions of historical *exempla*, or heroes of the Roman past, might suggest that there was a common under-standing of actions or explanations of behaviour according to the age of the participants. Moreover, the rhetoric of the *cursus honorum* was something that citizens understood and were invited to participate in by voting in the assem-blies and at elections. More importantly, maybe, the experience of military service in the Republic was organised with a set of age criteria in mind. An experience of a system based on a series of stages of life drawn up by the elite does not mean that the lives of ordinary citizens conformed to the experiences we find in the writings of Cicero or Seneca. However, it does indicate a universal acceptance of these age related concepts and an ideology of age that descends from the elite down to other sectors at Rome.

The study of age related concepts in our literary sources raises the question of how age was represented through visual imagery and material culture. The images arranged throughout the text offer a view of the representation of persons from the past at different ages. The intersection of these forms with stories of the young, mature and aged from mythology and history is appar-ent. In many cases, their meaning is dependent on a generic and widespread knowledge of myth and history with memory aids in the form of inscriptions. Statuary and sculptural friezes may be the most apparent forms of material culture through which age was expressed. However, the usage of objects to define a person as young or old was also at play in the Roman empire. We have highlighted the usage of objects in childhood, rites of passage, and in burials in the text. These demonstrate a mode of expression of continuity, and change of personal identity through the life course that parallels the discussion and action associated with these objects and more perishable items, such as textiles. There is much more that could be done, particularly in the field of burials, where biological age may be cross-referenced to the usage of burial goods (Gowling 2001). Maybe more importantly, it is in burial that we may begin to understand the spread of what we have defined as the life course at Rome across the empire.

The life course approach adopted in this book offers a framework for the study of temporal experience in the Roman world. Time, as measured in BC and AD today, gives meaning and order to a series of events from the past. In the writing of political history, chronological explanation has been at the forefront of the current historical narratives with reference across to the political structures of the assembly and the senate (e.g. Lintott 1994). Recent efforts to include a role for the populace in political history (Millar 1998) have been welcomed. We would argue that there is also a role for an understanding of the structure of politics from the point of view of the life course as well. The experiences of sections of the population at different ages provided an overall structure to political thinking at Rome. There is a deeper temporal structure that ancient historians only occasionally contemplate – how many people at Rome had lived through the agrarian laws of the Gracchi, who later would have viewed the politics of events leading up to the social war? How would information about these interrelated events in our historical narratives today have been explained or remembered across the generations at Rome? This takes the temporal arrangement of politics away from the dominant texts, with their emphasis on the role of the individual leading statesman, and considers ways in which these histories may have been considered within the context of family time. The non-hereditary nature of the Roman aristocracy is well known (Hopkins 1983), but how did the authority of a family member who had held the consulship influence the ideas and actions of younger relatives who did not achieve such heights of power? There is also the difficult question of how we should view the life course at Rome within the context of the migration in Italy during the first millennium BC? When did the structure of the Roman life course come into being? This question cannot be answered, since the ancient view was that it had been invented by Romulus in a mythical past.

As a conception of time, the life course of a society provides us with a different way to understand specific actions. It neither conforms to the historical demands of the *longue durée* associated with much archaeological thought (see papers in Gilchrist 2000), nor the chronological specificity of known dates associated with many historical narratives (Pilcher 1995: 20–21). It presents us with a human conception of time as a lived experience, in which there was an expected future for all individuals (however improbable) of living into old age. At the same time, the interplay of ages within the social world of the household and kinship networks structured the nature of memory and social interaction or expectation. How different the Roman life course was from other systems in other contemporary states seems at present unclear. The archaeological study of age related funerary practices is still in its infancy, and we may begin to understand the variation between Roman burial practices according to age and other societies from beyond the Roman sphere in the future (see Gowling 2001). The affect on the structure of the life course of societal changes in late antiquity and early medieval Europe is a counterpoint to the study of difference across and beyond the Roman empire. The recovery of difference in the life course is possible across space and time, but at present the data may not be available in a form for undertaking such a study.

Issues for gerontology

Rome was a classic pre-industrial, yet urbanised, society. The forms of its social institutions have been studied from a variety of perspectives. There are now key works on marriage, the family and demography, that have informed the work presented in this book. Rome is not simply an example to display the workings of a life course approach; it is also important for the study of gerontology. The social institutions and legal frameworks of Rome have an importance for our understanding of later forms of the life course. This is not to say that Rome is the origin of later conceptions of the life course with a linear development over time. Instead, we would point to the role of Rome as a key inspiration for the invention of tradition and the creation of new social institutions and legal frameworks (see papers in Wyke and Biddiss 1999). At the same time, we would wish to highlight the concepts of age and many of the characteristics of the modern western life course that existed at Rome.

Our study of the Roman life course has highlighted a number of factors that may inform the current development of the study of the life course and gerontology (for summary of theories of the life course see Pilcher 1995; Quadagno 1999: 21–42). We would strongly argue against a theory that placed a stress on the role of modernisation in the creation of the current age structures and, in particular, the marginalisation of the elderly or the creation of the stages of life – specifically childhood. Certainly, at Rome, the elderly were expected to disengage with public life and certain commitments as citizens – although, as such, there was no retirement age. Childhood, as has been recognised by others, was a specified period of the life course at Rome. The Roman concept of the life course was not tightly bound to the measurement of chronological age in its later stages. Attempts were made, however, to link the recognised stages of life to a chronology of ageing. Indeed, chronological age would appear to have been measured inaccurately once a person reached adulthood or citizenship. This would imply that parental measurement of children's age was not only accurate but also charted the stages of development in childhood. It is unfortunate that our sources do not treat these developments discursively to reveal their meaning. Instead, we find adults romanticising games and other childhood activities.

It has become clear from our examination or charting of the Roman conception of age and ageing that there was not a standard experience of the life course, although we have also found that there was an expectation or explanation of another person's behaviour according to their age or stage of life. This is where we have found a role for the social construction of age and ageing, which reveals that there was never a natural procedure through life or biological norm of age. This highlights how age was not simply a phenomenon rooted in nature, but was a human societal creation that referred often to the natural world – for example the visible life course of plants or animals. Roman understanding of the life course viewed disengagement by an individual from the main events of public life as inevitable, but, at the same time, stressed a continuity between all earlier periods of the life course from youth onwards and as a precondition for an enjoyable old age. There was no age of retirement, but there was an expectation of withdrawal from politics and warfare after the age of sixty.

Throughout this book, we have emphasised the differences in the experience and the social construction of the life course according to gender. This has highlighted some anomalies. It would appear that women on marriage, via age differentiation, were expected to be subordinate to their husbands. However, throughout their married lives, they owned property and in later life might have outlived their husbands. These two factors caused disquiet amongst males, since the transmission of property could be disrupted by the actions of the survivor of the marriage. Roman law endeavoured to prevent such occurrences happening. However, it is clear, in later life elite women could have had control of considerable amounts of property and influence. We would not say, though, that this was a general pattern; while the practice of testators was to leave their wives and daughters well off, most of their wealth was left to their male heirs – on the grounds that public duty caused them to have a greater need for money and property.

It would be incorrect to say that Rome was a gerontocracy. The old engaged in philosophy as a leisure pursuit and wrote discourses or defences of the condition of old age. It is certain that the experience or endurance of old age and its associated illness were an inspiration for stoic philosophies. However, a greater dominance was given to an Aristotelian ideal that both the young and the old were equally lacking in judgement: it was the adult males who in mid-life blended the positive qualities of the young and the old and were the ideal people to lead or command. The old themselves advocated a role in which the old advised and guided the young – hence ironing out the extremes to create artificially the qualities naturally associated with a middle aged man. We also see at Rome a number of competing elaborations of the basic Aristotelian differences. This was done with reference to astrological signs and chronological measurement, which produced a more scientific (in the ancient sense) reading of the life course. In practice, qualities of the young or the old might have been emphasised for the benefit of the participants.

Finally, the ancient characterisation of the life course has influenced the thinking of modern sociologists is uncertain. Much thinking from classical antiquity was assimilated or reinvented within modernity and modernisation. The coincidence of many roles of the citizen disappearing at sixty or just after, the time of retirement for many in western societies, might imply some form of reception or reference, conscious or subconscious, to the reading of classical texts in the late nineteenth and early twentieth centuries (see Wyke and Biddiss 1999). Indeed, the reception of texts from antiquity, whether in Aristotle, Cicero or Seneca, may have shaped not only modern thought, but that of other historical epochs (see Shahar 1998 for the middle ages). It may be that the seventeenth century Calvinist conception of the stages of life culminating in old age was a product of the reinterpretation of texts from a classical past. Today, it is easy to see the influence of ancient thought in many modern institutions – but less easy to prove how people from the past, who read Latin for pleasure in their leisure time, were influenced by its concepts and thinking. The Roman life course appears very modern, but beyond this modernity lies an alien reality.

APPENDIX

The following tables are taken from Richard Saller's book *Patriarchy, Property and Death in the Roman Family;* a full explanation as to how the tables were constructed is given in that book (1994: 9–70). For our purposes, these life tables provide a guide to the nature of the kinship universe across the life cycle at Rome. The figures to one or two decimal points suggest to the demographically unitiated a high level of accuracy, but it needs to be remembered that the figures are an average figure of all variations across society. Hence, where a reader may think of an example from the ancient world quite different to the average given, there will be another example at the opposite extreme of that experience that would cause the figure given as the average to represent those extremes.

Two tables are given as 'level 3' and 'level 6' for the senatorial elite, as discussed in the book. The reason two different sets of data are presented is that our estimates of the average life expectancy at birth vary from twenty-five years to thirty-three years. Again we stress here, in response to a general misunderstanding by classicists of average life expectancy, that these averages include those who did not survive the first years of life and those who lived into their eighties and beyond. These figures do not mean that everyone was dead by twenty-five or thirty-three! The tables represent the demographic possibility of a sustainable population into which are placed the paramaeters of the age of marriage, the frequency of remarriage, our understanding of Roman fertility patterns etc. It is a procedure utilised by historical demographers for other periodisations and has been seen as a means to estimate or model: the nature and number of living kin at a specified age; the proportion of people at a specific age who would have at least one kin relative in each category; and finally the average age of those living kin. In effect, these three tables give us a view into the changing familial structures of the life course.

We stress again, as our final thought on these tables, that the figures are not intended to replicate exactly the Roman life course or all cases; they cannot because there was no single or unified lived experience of birth, marriage, parenting and death. Instead, the model produces a set of probabilities and simplifies the complexities of societal choice to produce a generalised view of kinship universes at different ages. It is the variation of the figures according to age that can inform us or make us aware of the changing kinship patterns according to age.

Table A: Saller Table 3.2.a: Female 'senatorial', Level 3 West: mean number of living kin

Kin	EXACT AGE OF EGO (YEARS)														
	0	5	10	15	20	25	30	35	40	45	50	55	60	65	70
Husband	·	·	·	0.6	1.0	1.0	1.0	1.0	1.0	0.9	0.9	0.9	0.7	0.5	0.3
Parent	2.0	1.8	1.6	1.4	1.2	1.0	0.8	0.6	0.4	0.3	0.2	0.1	0.0	0.0	0.0
Father	1.0	0.9	0.8	0.7	0.5	0.4	0.3	0.2	0.1	0.1	0.1	0.0	0.0	·	0.0
Mother	1.0	0.9	0.8	0.8	0.7	0.6	0.5	0.4	0.3	0.2	0.1	0.1	0.0	0.0	0.0
Sibling	1.2	1.9	2.0	1.9	1.8	1.7	1.5	1.4	1.3	1.1	0.9	0.8	0.6	0.4	0.3
Brother	0.6	0.9	1.0	1.0	0.9	0.8	0.8	0.7	0.6	0.5	0.5	0.4	0.3	0.2	0.1
Sister	0.6	1.0	1.0	1.0	0.9	0.8	0.8	0.7	0.6	0.6	0.5	0.4	0.3	0.2	0.2
Child	·	·	·	·	1.2	1.8	2.0	2.1	2.1	2.1	1.9	1.8	1.6	1.4	1.2
Son	·	·	·	·	0.6	0.9	1.0	1.1	1.1	1.0	1.0	0.9	0.8	0.7	0.6
Daughter	·	·	·	·	0.6	0.9	1.0	1.1	1.1	1.0	1.0	0.9	0.8	0.7	0.6
Grandparent	1.8	1.5	1.1	0.8	0.6	0.4	0.2	0.1	0.0	0.0	0.0	·	·	·	·
Grandfather	0.8	0.6	0.4	0.2	0.1	0.1	0.0	0.0	0.0	0.0	0.0	·	·	·	·
Grandmother	1.1	0.9	0.7	0.6	0.4	0.3	0.2	0.1	0.0	0.0	0.0	·	·	·	·
Maternal grandfather	0.5	0.4	0.3	0.2	0.1	0.1	0.0	0.0	0.0	0.0	0.0	·	·	·	·
Paternal grandfather	0.3	0.2	0.1	0.1	0.0	0.0	0.0	0.0	0.0	·	0.0	·	·	·	·
Maternal grandmother	0.6	0.5	0.5	0.4	0.3	0.2	0.1	·	·	·	0.0	·	·	·	·
Paternal grandmother	0.5	0.4	0.3	0.2	0.1	0.1	0.0	0.0	0.0	0.0	0.0	·	·	·	·
Grandchild	·	·	·	·	·	·	·	0.2	0.8	1.6	2.5	3.1	3.5	3.6	3.5
Grandson	·	·	·	·	·	·	·	0.1	0.4	0.8	1.2	1.5	1.7	1.8	1.7
Granddaughter	·	·	·	·	·	·	·	0.1	0.4	0.8	1.3	1.6	1.8	1.8	1.8
Aunt/uncle	3.2	2.9	2.6	2.3	2.0	1.7	1.4	1.1	0.8	0.5	0.3	0.2	0.1	0.0	0.0
Aunt	1.6	1.4	1.3	1.2	1.0	0.9	0.7	0.6	0.4	0.3	0.2	0.1	0.1	0.0	0.0
Uncle	1.6	1.5	1.3	1.1	1.0	0.8	0.7	0.5	0.4	0.2	0.1	0.1	0.0	0.0	0.0
Maternal aunt	0.9	0.8	0.7	0.7	0.6	0.5	0.4	0.4	0.3	0.2	0.1	0.1	0.0	0.0	0.0
Paternal aunt	0.7	0.7	0.6	0.5	0.4	0.4	0.3	0.2	0.1	0.1	0.0	0.0	0.0	0.0	0.0
Maternal uncle	0.9	0.8	0.7	0.7	0.6	0.5	0.4	0.3	0.2	0.2	0.1	0.1	0.0	0.0	0.0
Paternal uncle	0.7	0.7	0.6	0.5	0.4	0.3	0.2	0.2	0.1	0.1	0.0	0.0	0.0	0.0	0.0
Nephew/niece	0.0	0.0	0.1	0.5	1.1	1.9	2.6	3.1	3.2	3.2	3.0	2.8	2.5	2.3	2.0
Nephew	0.0	0.0	0.1	0.2	0.5	1.0	1.3	1.5	1.6	1.6	1.5	1.4	1.3	1.1	1.0
Niece	0.0	0.0	0.1	0.3	0.6	0.9	1.3	1.5	1.6	1.6	1.5	1.4	1.3	1.1	1.0

Note: · indicates no occurrences in simulation; 0.0 indicates less than 0.1
Demographic analysis of 'senatorial', Level 3 West population: Gross Reproduction Rate: 2.29; Net Reproduction Rate: 1.00; Mean Age at Maternity: 22.45

Table B; Saller Table 3.2.b: Female 'senatorial', Level 3 West: proportion having living kin

Kin	EXACT AGE OF EGO (YEARS)														
	0	5	10	15	20	25	30	35	40	45	50	55	60	65	70
Husband	.	.	.	0.60	0.97	0.97	0.96	0.96	0.95	0.95	0.94	0.92	0.70	0.51	0.35
Parent	1.00	0.99	0.96	0.92	0.84	0.75	0.65	0.52	0.40	0.27	0.16	0.09	0.04	0.01	0.00
Father	1.00	0.89	0.78	0.67	0.54	0.41	0.31	0.21	0.12	0.07	0.03	0.01	0.00	.	.
Mother	1.00	0.93	0.85	0.75	0.67	0.58	0.50	0.41	0.32	0.23	0.14	0.08	0.03	0.01	0.00
Sibling	0.60	0.82	0.80	0.79	0.77	0.75	0.73	0.70	0.66	0.62	0.56	0.51	0.42	0.34	0.24
Brother	0.41	0.59	0.60	0.58	0.56	0.54	0.51	0.48	0.45	0.41	0.35	0.30	0.23	0.18	0.12
Sister	0.41	0.60	0.60	0.58	0.56	0.53	0.50	0.47	0.44	0.40	0.36	0.32	0.27	0.21	0.14
Child	.	.	.	.	0.73	0.81	0.82	0.82	0.81	0.81	0.79	0.76	0.73	0.70	0.66
Son	.	.	.	.	0.47	0.58	0.61	0.62	0.62	0.61	0.58	0.54	0.51	0.47	0.42
Daughter	.	.	.	.	0.46	0.58	0.61	0.62	0.62	0.61	0.59	0.55	0.52	0.48	0.45
Grandparent	0.89	0.82	0.71	0.58	0.45	0.32	0.18	0.09	0.04	0.01	0.00	.	.	.	.
Grandfather	0.62	0.48	0.33	0.22	0.14	0.07	0.03	0.01	0.00	0.00	0.00	.	.	.	.
Grandmother	0.78	0.70	0.60	0.48	0.38	0.27	0.16	0.08	0.03	0.01	0.00	.	.	.	.
Maternal grandfather	0.48	0.37	0.26	0.17	0.11	0.06	0.03	0.01	0.00	0.00	0.00	.	.	.	.
Paternal grandfather	0.28	0.18	0.11	0.07	0.03	0.01	0.00	.	.	.	.	.	.	.	.
Maternal grandmother	0.61	0.53	0.45	0.36	0.29	0.21	0.13	0.07	0.03	0.01	.	.	.	.	.
Paternal grandmother	0.45	0.38	0.29	0.20	0.14	0.08	0.04	0.01	0.00	0.00	0.00	.	.	.	.
Grandchild	.	.	.	.	.	.	.	0.16	0.38	0.56	0.66	0.71	0.72	0.73	0.73
Grandson	.	.	.	.	.	.	.	0.09	0.25	0.41	0.53	0.59	0.62	0.62	0.62
Granddaughter	.	.	.	.	.	.	.	0.09	0.28	0.43	0.54	0.61	0.62	0.63	0.63
Aunt/uncle	0.93	0.91	0.89	0.86	0.82	0.77	0.70	0.61	0.51	0.38	0.26	0.16	0.08	0.03	0.01
Aunt	0.76	0.74	0.70	0.67	0.62	0.56	0.50	0.42	0.33	0.24	0.16	0.10	0.05	0.02	0.01
Uncle	0.77	0.74	0.70	0.65	0.60	0.54	0.45	0.37	0.29	0.20	0.13	0.07	0.03	0.01	0.00
Maternal aunt	0.55	0.52	0.49	0.46	0.42	0.38	0.34	0.28	0.23	0.18	0.13	0.08	0.04	0.02	0.01
Paternal aunt	0.49	0.46	0.42	0.38	0.34	0.30	0.24	0.19	0.13	0.08	0.04	0.02	0.01	0.00	0.00
Maternal uncle	0.55	0.52	0.49	0.46	0.42	0.37	0.31	0.26	0.20	0.15	0.10	0.06	0.02	0.01	0.00
Paternal uncle	0.50	0.46	0.42	0.36	0.31	0.27	0.20	0.15	0.11	0.07	0.04	0.02	0.00	0.00	0.00
Nephew/niece	0.00	0.01	0.06	0.23	0.41	0.57	0.65	0.69	0.69	0.68	0.68	0.67	0.65	0.63	0.61
Nephew	0.00	0.01	0.04	0.15	0.30	0.45	0.54	0.58	0.60	0.59	0.57	0.56	0.54	0.51	0.48
Niece	0.00	0.01	0.04	0.16	0.30	0.44	0.53	0.58	0.59	0.58	0.57	0.55	0.53	0.50	0.47

Note: . indicates no occurrences in simulation; 0.00 indicates less than 0.01

Table C; Saller Table 3.2.c: Female 'senatorial', Level 3 West: mean age of living kin

EXACT AGE OF EGO (YEARS)

Kin	0	5	10	15	20	25	30	35	40	45	50	55	60	65	70
Husband	.	.	.	27.0	31.2	35.5	39.0	42.5	45.4	47.6	49.2	50.1	53.3	55.9	57.8
Parent	27.8	32.5	37.2	41.9	46.5	50.8	55.1	59.1	63.2	67.3	71.1	75.1	79.2	82.9	87.5
Father	32.6	37.3	42.0	46.7	51.3	55.7	60.2	64.6	68.9	73.4	77.7	81.7	87.5	.	.
Mother	23.0	27.9	32.8	37.7	42.6	47.3	51.9	56.3	61.0	65.6	69.9	74.5	78.8	82.9	87.5
Sibling	4.2	6.1	10.1	14.8	19.7	24.6	29.5	34.4	39.3	44.1	49.1	53.8	58.4	63.0	67.1
Brother	4.2	6.1	10.0	14.8	19.6	24.5	29.3	34.3	39.2	43.9	48.8	53.6	58.3	62.8	67.0
Sister	4.2	6.1	10.1	14.8	19.7	24.7	29.6	34.6	39.5	44.3	49.3	54.0	58.6	63.1	67.3
Child	.	.	.	.	2.0	5.0	8.6	12.3	16.3	20.5	25.2	30.1	34.9	39.7	44.5
Son	.	.	.	.	2.0	5.0	8.6	12.4	16.3	20.6	25.4	30.2	35.0	39.7	44.5
Daughter	.	.	.	.	2.0	5.0	8.5	12.2	16.2	20.4	25.0	29.9	34.8	39.6	44.4
Grandparent	50.6	54.6	58.2	61.8	65.3	68.6	71.8	75.0	78.5	81.3	87.7	.	.	.	.
Grandfather	54.9	58.9	62.6	66.1	69.8	73.5	76.9	79.5	82.5	86.3	89.0	.	.	.	.
Grandmother	47.5	51.9	55.9	59.9	63.8	67.4	70.9	74.5	78.0	80.8	87.0	.	.	.	.
Maternal grandfather	52.1	56.4	60.4	64.2	68.2	72.4	76.1	79.5	82.5	86.3	89.0	.	.	.	.
Paternal grandfather	59.8	63.9	67.7	71.3	75.6	79.0	82.7	.	.	.	.	.	.	.	.
Maternal grandmother	43.9	48.5	52.9	57.3	61.5	65.6	69.4	73.5	77.4	80.6	87.0	.	.	.	.
Paternal grandmother	52.3	56.8	60.7	64.6	68.9	72.5	76.3	80.2	84.6	86.8	87.0	.	.	.	.
Grandchild	.	.	.	.	.	.	.	1.1	2.8	4.6	6.5	9.1	12.1	15.7	19.6
Grandson	.	.	.	.	.	.	.	1.1	2.8	4.5	6.4	9.0	12.0	15.7	19.6
Granddaughter	.	.	.	.	.	.	.	1.1	2.8	4.7	6.6	9.2	12.2	15.7	19.6
Aunt/uncle	25.8	30.5	35.2	39.9	44.5	48.9	53.1	57.3	61.1	64.8	68.2	71.6	74.0	76.7	80.7
Aunt	26.0	30.7	35.4	40.2	44.9	49.4	53.5	57.6	61.3	65.0	68.3	71.5	74.1	77.0	82.1
Uncle	25.7	30.3	34.9	39.5	44.1	48.5	52.6	56.9	60.8	64.7	68.1	71.7	73.8	76.2	76.5
Maternal aunt	21.9	26.7	31.5	36.4	41.2	45.8	50.4	54.8	58.9	63.0	66.8	70.3	73.2	76.2	81.9
Paternal aunt	30.8	35.6	40.3	45.2	49.7	54.1	58.3	62.2	66.0	69.7	72.9	76.0	79.1	81.5	83.0
Maternal uncle	21.5	26.2	30.9	35.7	40.6	45.2	49.7	54.2	58.5	62.7	66.6	70.8	73.7	76.1	75.7
Paternal uncle	30.6	35.4	40.1	44.7	49.2	53.5	57.4	61.9	65.8	69.4	72.0	75.1	73.9	77.2	83.9
Nephew/niece	2.2	2.1	2.5	2.8	4.2	5.7	8.0	10.7	14.1	18.1	22.6	27.2	32.0	36.7	41.4
Nephew	4.8	1.9	2.4	2.9	4.1	5.6	7.9	10.7	14.2	18.2	22.7	27.3	32.0	36.7	41.4
Niece	1.4	2.3	2.6	2.8	4.2	5.9	8.0	10.7	14.1	18.0	22.5	27.1	31.9	36.7	41.3

Note: . indicates no occurrences in simulation; 0.0 indicates less than 0.1

Table D; Saller Table 3.2.d: Male 'senatorial', Level 3 West: mean number of living kin

Kin	EXACT AGE OF EGO (YEARS)														
	0	5	10	15	20	25	30	35	40	45	50	55	60	65	70
Wife	·	·	·	·	·	0.6	0.9	1.0	1.0	1.0	1.0	1.0	0.9	0.7	0.6
Parent	2.0	1.8	1.6	1.4	1.2	1.0	0.8	0.6	0.4	0.3	0.2	0.1	0.0	0.0	0.0
Father	1.0	0.9	0.8	0.7	0.5	0.4	0.3	0.2	0.1	0.1	0.0	0.0	0.0	0.0	·
Mother	1.0	0.9	0.8	0.8	0.7	0.6	0.5	0.4	0.3	0.2	0.1	0.1	0.0	0.0	0.0
Sibling	1.2	1.9	2.0	1.9	1.8	1.6	1.5	1.3	1.2	1.0	0.9	0.7	0.6	0.4	0.3
Brother	0.6	0.9	1.0	0.9	0.9	0.8	0.8	0.7	0.6	0.5	0.4	0.4	0.3	0.2	0.1
Sister	0.6	1.0	1.0	0.9	0.9	0.8	0.7	0.7	0.6	0.5	0.4	0.4	0.3	0.2	0.2
Child	·	·	·	·	·	0.3	1.2	1.7	1.9	1.9	1.8	1.7	1.5	1.4	1.2
Son	·	·	·	·	·	0.2	0.6	0.9	0.9	0.9	0.9	0.8	0.8	0.7	0.6
Daughter	·	·	·	·	·	0.1	0.6	0.9	1.0	0.9	0.9	0.8	0.8	0.7	0.6
Grandparent	1.8	1.4	1.1	0.8	0.5	0.3	0.2	0.1	0.0	0.0	0.0	·	·	·	·
Grandfather	0.7	0.5	0.4	0.2	0.1	0.1	0.0	0.0	0.0	0.0	·	·	·	·	·
Grandmother	1.0	0.9	0.7	0.5	0.4	0.2	0.1	0.1	0.0	0.0	0.0	·	·	·	·
Maternal grandfather	0.5	0.3	0.2	0.2	0.1	0.1	0.0	0.0	0.0	0.0	0.0	·	·	·	·
Paternal grandfather	0.3	0.2	0.1	0.1	0.0	0.0	0.0	0.0	·	·	·	·	·	·	·
Maternal grandmother	0.6	0.5	0.4	0.3	0.2	0.2	0.1	0.1	0.0	0.0	0.0	·	·	·	·
Paternal grandmother	0.4	0.4	0.3	0.2	0.1	0.1	0.0	0.0	0.0	0.0	·	·	·	·	·
Grandchild	·	·	·	·	·	·	·	·	0.0	0.3	1.0	1.8	2.5	2.9	3.1
Grandson	·	·	·	·	·	·	·	·	0.0	0.2	0.5	0.9	1.2	1.4	1.5
Granddaughter	·	·	·	·	·	·	·	·	0.0	0.2	0.5	0.9	1.2	1.5	1.6
Aunt/uncle	3.1	2.8	2.5	2.2	1.9	1.6	1.3	1.0	0.7	0.5	0.3	0.2	0.1	0.0	0.0
Aunt	1.5	1.4	1.3	1.1	1.0	0.8	0.7	0.6	0.4	0.3	0.2	0.1	0.0	0.0	0.0
Uncle	1.6	1.4	1.2	1.1	0.9	0.8	0.6	0.5	0.3	0.2	0.1	0.1	0.0	0.0	0.0
Maternal aunt	0.8	0.8	0.7	0.6	0.6	0.5	0.4	0.3	0.3	0.2	0.1	0.1	0.0	0.0	0.0
Paternal aunt	0.7	0.6	0.6	0.5	0.4	0.3	0.3	0.2	0.1	0.1	0.0	0.0	0.0	0.0	·
Maternal uncle	0.8	0.8	0.7	0.6	0.5	0.5	0.4	0.3	0.2	0.2	0.1	0.1	0.0	0.0	·
Paternal uncle	0.7	0.6	0.6	0.5	0.4	0.3	0.2	0.2	0.1	0.1	0.0	0.0	0.0	0.0	0.0
Nephew/niece	0.0	0.0	0.1	0.5	1.1	1.9	2.6	3.0	3.1	3.1	2.9	2.7	2.5	2.2	1.9
Nephew	0.0	0.0	0.1	0.3	0.6	0.9	1.3	1.5	1.6	1.5	1.5	1.4	1.2	1.1	1.0
Niece	0.0	0.0	0.1	0.3	0.6	1.0	1.3	1.5	1.6	1.5	1.5	1.3	1.2	1.1	1.0

Note: · indicates no occurrences in simulation; 0.0 indicates less than 0.1

Table E; Saller Table 3.2.e: Male 'senatorial', Level 3 West: proportion having living kin

Kin	EXACT AGE OF EGO (YEARS)														
	0	5	10	15	20	25	30	35	40	45	50	55	60	65	70
Wife	.	.	.	.	.	0.59	0.93	0.97	0.97	0.97	0.97	0.96	0.85	0.72	0.58
Parent	1.00	0.99	0.96	0.91	0.85	0.76	0.65	0.53	0.40	0.27	0.17	0.09	0.04	0.01	0.00
Father	1.00	0.90	0.78	0.66	0.54	0.43	0.32	0.22	0.13	0.07	0.03	0.01	0.00	.	.
Mother	1.00	0.91	0.83	0.75	0.66	0.58	0.49	0.41	0.31	0.22	0.15	0.08	0.04	0.01	0.00
Sibling	0.60	0.83	0.81	0.80	0.78	0.76	0.73	0.69	0.66	0.61	0.56	0.49	0.42	0.34	0.23
Brother	0.40	0.59	0.60	0.59	0.57	0.54	0.51	0.48	0.44	0.40	0.35	0.30	0.24	0.18	0.11
Sister	0.41	0.60	0.60	0.58	0.56	0.53	0.50	0.46	0.43	0.39	0.35	0.30	0.25	0.20	0.14
Child	.	.	.	.	.	0.26	0.69	0.77	0.78	0.78	0.76	0.73	0.71	0.68	0.65
Son	.	.	.	.	.	0.14	0.44	0.56	0.58	0.58	0.56	0.53	0.50	0.47	0.43
Daughter	.	.	.	.	.	0.14	0.46	0.56	0.58	0.58	0.56	0.53	0.51	0.48	0.45
Grandparent	0.89	0.81	0.70	0.55	0.41	0.27	0.15	0.08	0.03	0.01	0.00				
Grandfather	0.60	0.47	0.33	0.22	0.13	0.07	0.02	0.01	0.00	0.00	.				
Grandmother	0.76	0.68	0.58	0.45	0.34	0.23	0.13	0.07	0.03	0.01	0.00				
Maternal grandfather	0.46	0.35	0.25	0.17	0.10	0.05	0.02	0.01	0.00	0.00					
Paternal grandfather	0.27	0.19	0.11	0.06	0.03	0.01	0.00	0.00							
Maternal grandmother	0.59	0.51	0.42	0.33	0.25	0.18	0.11	0.06	0.03	0.01	0.00				
Paternal grandmother	0.43	0.35	0.28	0.20	0.12	0.07	0.03	0.01	0.00	0.00					
Grandchild								.	0.02	0.20	0.41	0.58	0.65	0.68	0.67
Grandson								.	0.01	0.12	0.30	0.45	0.53	0.57	0.58
Granddaughter								.	0.01	0.13	0.30	0.45	0.53	0.57	0.59
Aunt/uncle	0.93	0.91	0.88	0.84	0.80	0.75	0.68	0.59	0.48	0.36	0.24	0.13	0.07	0.03	0.01
Aunt	0.75	0.72	0.68	0.64	0.59	0.54	0.47	0.40	0.32	0.23	0.15	0.09	0.05	0.02	0.01
Uncle	0.77	0.73	0.68	0.64	0.59	0.52	0.44	0.35	0.27	0.19	0.12	0.06	0.03	0.01	0.00
Maternal aunt	0.53	0.51	0.48	0.44	0.41	0.37	0.33	0.28	0.23	0.17	0.12	0.07	0.04	0.02	0.01
Paternal aunt	0.48	0.44	0.40	0.37	0.32	0.28	0.22	0.17	0.12	0.08	0.04	0.02	0.01	0.00	
Maternal uncle	0.54	0.51	0.48	0.44	0.40	0.35	0.30	0.24	0.19	0.14	0.09	0.05	0.02	0.01	0.00
Paternal uncle	0.50	0.46	0.41	0.37	0.32	0.27	0.21	0.15	0.10	0.06	0.03	0.02	0.00	0.00	0.00
Nephew/niece	0.01	0.02	0.07	0.24	0.43	0.58	0.67	0.70	0.71	0.70	0.70	0.69	0.68	0.66	0.63
Nephew	0.00	0.01	0.05	0.16	0.31	0.45	0.54	0.59	0.60	0.59	0.58	0.57	0.54	0.52	0.48
Niece	0.00	0.01	0.05	0.16	0.31	0.46	0.55	0.60	0.61	0.60	0.58	0.57	0.55	0.52	0.49

Note: . indicates no occurrences in simulation; 0.00 indicates less than 0.01

Table F: Saller Table 3.2.f: Male 'senatorial', Level 3 West: mean age of living kin

Kin	\multicolumn{15}{c}{EXACT AGE OF EGO (YEARS)}
	0	5	10	15	20	25	30	35	40	45	50	55	60	65	70
Wife	.	.	.	.	.	17.8	21.3	25.6	30.0	34.1	38.2	41.7	46.3	50.5	54.4
Parent	28.0	32.8	37.5	42.1	46.7	51.1	55.3	59.5	63.6	67.5	71.1	75.0	78.5	82.2	87.3
Father	32.7	37.5	42.3	46.9	51.4	56.0	60.5	64.8	69.5	73.7	77.6	82.4	88.2	.	.
Mother	23.2	28.1	33.1	37.9	42.8	47.5	51.9	56.6	61.2	65.7	69.8	74.1	78.3	82.2	87.3
Sibling	4.3	6.3	10.2	14.9	19.8	24.7	29.6	34.5	39.3	44.2	49.0	53.6	58.2	62.7	67.0
Brother	4.3	6.2	10.1	14.8	19.6	24.6	29.4	34.4	39.2	44.0	48.8	53.5	58.1	62.6	66.9
Sister	4.4	6.3	10.4	15.0	19.9	24.8	29.7	34.6	39.4	44.4	49.2	53.7	58.3	62.8	67.1
Child	.	.	.	.	.	0.9	2.8	5.7	9.4	13.9	18.7	23.7	28.6	33.5	38.4
Son	.	.	.	.	.	0.9	2.8	5.6	9.4	13.8	18.6	23.6	28.4	33.3	38.3
Daughter	.	.	.	.	.	0.9	2.8	5.7	9.5	13.9	18.8	23.8	28.7	33.7	38.5
Grandparent	50.8	54.7	58.4	62.1	65.5	68.8	72.1	75.4	79.2	83.4	87.3	.	.	.	.
Grandfather	55.0	59.0	62.7	66.6	70.1	73.7	77.0	80.5	84.2	90.0	.	.	.	.	.
Grandmother	47.7	52.0	56.3	60.1	63.9	67.5	71.2	74.8	78.9	83.2	87.3	.	.	.	.
Maternal grandfather	52.2	56.4	60.5	64.6	68.8	72.5	76.1	79.6	84.2	90.0	.	.	.	.	.
Paternal grandfather	59.8	63.7	67.6	71.7	74.6	78.7	82.3	87.1	.	.	.	.	.	.	.
Maternal grandmother	44.4	48.8	53.3	57.3	61.6	65.6	69.7	73.7	78.3	83.0	87.3	.	.	.	.
Paternal grandmother	52.3	56.6	60.7	64.8	68.7	72.6	77.0	80.6	84.6	87.7	.	.	.	.	.
Grandchild	.	.	.	.	.	.	.	.	0.5	1.7	3.3	5.0	7.3	10.2	13.6
Grandson	.	.	.	.	.	.	.	.	0.5	1.7	3.3	5.0	7.2	10.2	13.6
Granddaughter	.	.	.	.	.	.	.	.	0.4	1.7	3.3	5.1	7.3	10.2	13.6
Aunt/uncle	26.1	30.9	35.5	40.2	44.8	49.2	53.4	57.5	61.2	64.7	68.3	71.4	74.4	77.7	81.4
Aunt	26.1	30.9	35.7	40.4	45.0	49.5	53.7	57.7	61.4	65.0	68.5	71.5	74.9	78.2	82.5
Uncle	26.2	30.8	35.4	39.9	44.6	48.9	53.0	57.2	60.9	64.3	68.0	71.2	73.6	77.0	79.8
Maternal aunt	22.0	26.9	31.8	36.6	41.4	45.8	50.4	54.7	58.9	62.7	66.6	70.3	74.2	77.9	82.5
Paternal aunt	30.8	35.7	40.5	45.2	49.8	54.5	58.9	62.9	66.7	70.5	74.4	77.7	80.0	83.1	.
Maternal uncle	22.2	26.9	31.6	36.4	41.1	45.6	50.0	54.5	58.5	62.4	66.5	69.9	72.8	76.1	79.7
Paternal uncle	30.8	35.4	40.1	44.6	49.1	53.5	57.6	61.7	65.7	68.9	72.5	75.5	79.6	84.4	80.7
Nephew/niece	1.7	2.6	2.8	3.2	4.5	6.1	8.2	10.9	14.4	18.5	23.0	27.7	32.5	37.3	41.9
Nephew	1.8	2.7	2.9	3.3	4.6	6.2	8.3	11.0	14.5	18.6	23.1	27.8	32.6	37.3	41.8
Niece	1.5	2.6	2.7	3.2	4.4	6.0	8.1	10.8	14.4	18.3	22.8	27.6	32.3	37.2	42.0

Note: . indicates no occurrences in simulation; 0.0 indicates less than 0.1

Table G; Saller Table 3.3.a: Female 'senatorial', Level 6 West: mean number of living kin

Kin	EXACT AGE OF EGO (YEARS)														
	0	5	10	15	20	25	30	35	40	45	50	55	60	65	70
Husband				0.6	1.0	1.0	1.0	1.0	1.0	1.0	1.0	0.9	0.7	0.6	0.4
Parent	2.0	1.8	1.7	1.5	1.4	1.2	1.0	0.8	0.6	0.4	0.3	0.2	0.1	0.0	0.0
Father	1.0	0.9	0.8	0.7	0.6	0.5	0.4	0.3	0.2	0.1	0.1	0.0	0.0	0.0	0.0
Mother	1.0	0.9	0.9	0.8	0.7	0.7	0.6	0.5	0.4	0.3	0.2	0.1	0.1	0.0	0.0
Sibling	1.1	1.8	1.9	1.9	1.8	1.7	1.6	1.5	1.3	1.2	1.1	0.9	0.8	0.6	0.4
Brother	0.5	0.9	0.9	0.9	0.9	0.8	0.8	0.7	0.7	0.6	0.5	0.5	0.4	0.3	0.2
Sister	0.5	0.9	0.9	0.9	0.9	0.8	0.8	0.7	0.7	0.6	0.5	0.5	0.4	0.3	0.2
Child					1.3	1.9	2.0	2.1	2.1	2.1	1.9	1.8	1.7	1.5	1.3
Son					0.7	0.9	1.0	1.0	1.0	1.0	1.0	0.9	0.8	0.7	0.6
Daughter					0.7	0.9	1.0	1.0	1.0	1.0	1.0	0.9	0.8	0.8	0.7
Grandparent	2.2	1.9	1.5	1.1	0.8	0.6	0.3	0.2	0.1	0.0	0.0	0.0	0.0		
Grandfather	1.0	0.8	0.6	0.4	0.3	0.1	0.1	0.0	0.0	0.0	0.0				
Grandmother	1.2	1.1	0.9	0.7	0.6	0.4	0.3	0.2	0.1	0.0	0.0	0.0	0.0		
Maternal grandfather	0.6	0.5	0.4	0.3	0.2	0.1	0.1	0.0	0.0	0.0	0.0				
Paternal grandfather	0.4	0.3	0.2	0.1	0.1	0.0	0.0	0.0	0.0						
Maternal grandmother	0.7	0.6	0.6	0.5	0.4	0.3	0.2	0.1	0.1	0.0	0.0	0.0	0.0		
Paternal grandmother	0.5	0.5	0.4	0.3	0.2	0.1	0.1	0.0	0.0						
Grandchild								0.3	1.1	1.9	2.7	3.3	3.6	3.6	3.6
Grandson								0.1	0.5	1.0	1.4	1.6	1.8	1.8	1.8
Granddaughter								0.1	0.5	1.0	1.4	1.7	1.8	1.8	1.8
Aunt/uncle	3.3	3.0	2.8	2.6	2.3	2.0	1.7	1.4	1.1	0.8	0.5	0.3	0.2	0.1	0.0
Aunt	1.6	1.5	1.4	1.3	1.1	1.0	0.9	0.7	0.6	0.4	0.3	0.2	0.1	0.0	0.0
Uncle	1.7	1.5	1.4	1.3	1.1	1.0	0.8	0.7	0.5	0.4	0.2	0.1	0.1	0.0	0.0
Maternal aunt	0.9	0.8	0.8	0.7	0.6	0.6	0.5	0.4	0.4	0.3	0.2	0.1	0.1	0.0	0.0
Paternal aunt	0.8	0.7	0.6	0.6	0.5	0.4	0.4	0.3	0.2	0.1	0.1	0.0	0.0	0.0	0.0
Maternal uncle	0.9	0.8	0.8	0.7	0.7	0.6	0.5	0.4	0.3	0.3	0.2	0.1	0.1	0.0	0.0
Paternal uncle	0.8	0.7	0.6	0.6	0.5	0.4	0.3	0.2	0.2	0.1	0.1	0.0	0.0	0.0	0.0
Nephew/niece	0.0	0.0	0.1	0.4	1.1	1.9	2.6	3.0	3.2	3.1	3.0	2.8	2.6	2.4	2.1
Nephew	0.0	0.0	0.0	0.2	0.5	0.9	1.2	1.5	1.6	1.5	1.5	1.4	1.3	1.2	1.0
Niece	0.0	0.0	0.0	0.2	0.6	1.0	1.3	1.5	1.6	1.6	1.5	1.4	1.3	1.2	1.1

Note: . indicates no occurrences in simulation; 0.0 indicates less than 0.1

Demographic analysis of 'senatorial'; Level 6 West population; Gross Reproduction Rate: 1.84; Net Reproduction Rate: 1.01; Mean Age at Maternity: 21.78

Table H: Saller Table 3.3.b: Female 'senatorial', Level 3 West: proportion having living kin

| | EXACT AGE OF EGO (YEARS) | | | | | | | | | | | | | | |
Kin	0	5	10	15	20	25	30	35	40	45	50	55	60	65	70
Husband	.	.	.	0.62	0.97	0.98	0.97	0.97	0.96	0.95	0.95	0.95	0.75	0.55	0.38
Parent	1.00	0.99	0.97	0.94	0.89	0.82	0.74	0.65	0.53	0.40	0.27	0.15	0.07	0.03	0.01
Father	1.00	0.91	0.82	0.72	0.62	0.51	0.41	0.30	0.20	0.12	0.06	0.03	0.01	0.00	0.00
Mother	1.00	0.94	0.87	0.80	0.73	0.66	0.59	0.51	0.42	0.32	0.22	0.13	0.06	0.03	0.01
Sibling	0.59	0.82	0.81	0.80	0.79	0.77	0.75	0.72	0.70	0.66	0.62	0.57	0.51	0.42	0.32
Brother	0.38	0.59	0.59	0.58	0.56	0.54	0.53	0.50	0.47	0.43	0.39	0.34	0.29	0.23	0.16
Sister	0.39	0.58	0.58	0.56	0.55	0.53	0.51	0.49	0.47	0.44	0.40	0.36	0.32	0.26	0.20
Child	.	.	.	.	0.78	0.83	0.83	0.84	0.84	0.83	0.82	0.80	0.77	0.74	0.70
Son	.	.	.	.	0.50	0.60	0.62	0.62	0.63	0.61	0.59	0.56	0.53	0.50	0.45
Daughter	.	.	.	.	0.50	0.61	0.62	0.62	0.62	0.61	0.59	0.57	0.54	0.51	0.47
Grandparent	0.96	0.91	0.83	0.73	0.60	0.45	0.29	0.17	0.08	0.04	0.01	0.00	0.00	.	.
Grandfather	0.74	0.63	0.49	0.36	0.24	0.14	0.06	0.03	0.01	0.00	0.00	.	.	.	.
Grandmother	0.86	0.80	0.72	0.61	0.50	0.38	0.26	0.15	0.08	0.03	0.01	0.00	0.00	.	.
Maternal grandfather	0.59	0.48	0.38	0.28	0.19	0.12	0.06	0.02	0.01	0.00	0.00	.	.	.	.
Paternal grandfather	0.38	0.28	0.19	0.11	0.06	0.03	0.01	0.00	0.00	.	.	.	.	.	.
Maternal grandmother	0.70	0.63	0.55	0.47	0.39	0.29	0.21	0.13	0.07	0.03	0.01	0.00	0.00	.	.
Paternal grandmother	0.54	0.46	0.36	0.27	0.20	0.13	0.06	0.03	0.01	0.00	0.00	.	.	.	.
Grandchild	.	.	.	.	.	.	.	0.21	0.47	0.63	0.71	0.75	0.76	0.76	0.76
Grandson	.	.	.	.	.	.	.	0.12	0.33	0.50	0.59	0.64	0.66	0.66	0.65
Granddaughter	.	.	.	.	.	.	.	0.12	0.34	0.49	0.59	0.64	0.66	0.66	0.66
Aunt/uncle	0.95	0.93	0.92	0.90	0.87	0.83	0.78	0.71	0.61	0.50	0.37	0.24	0.14	0.06	0.03
Aunt	0.78	0.75	0.72	0.70	0.66	0.62	0.57	0.50	0.42	0.33	0.23	0.15	0.09	0.04	0.02
Uncle	0.79	0.76	0.73	0.70	0.65	0.60	0.53	0.45	0.37	0.28	0.20	0.12	0.06	0.03	0.01
Maternal aunt	0.56	0.54	0.51	0.48	0.45	0.42	0.39	0.34	0.30	0.24	0.18	0.12	0.07	0.04	0.02
Paternal aunt	0.51	0.48	0.45	0.42	0.38	0.34	0.29	0.23	0.18	0.12	0.07	0.03	0.02	0.01	0.00
Maternal uncle	0.57	0.55	0.52	0.49	0.46	0.42	0.37	0.32	0.27	0.21	0.15	0.10	0.05	0.02	0.00
Paternal uncle	0.51	0.48	0.44	0.40	0.35	0.31	0.26	0.20	0.14	0.09	0.05	0.03	0.01	0.00	0.00
Nephew/niece	0.00	0.01	0.05	0.22	0.43	0.58	0.67	0.71	0.71	0.71	0.70	0.69	0.68	0.67	0.65
Nephew	0.00	0.00	0.03	0.14	0.30	0.44	0.54	0.58	0.59	0.59	0.58	0.57	0.55	0.52	0.49
Niece	0.00	0.01	0.04	0.15	0.32	0.46	0.56	0.60	0.60	0.60	0.59	0.58	0.56	0.54	0.52

Note: . indicates no occurrences in simulation; 0.00 indicates less than 0.01

Table 1: Saller Table 3.3.c: Female 'senatorial', Level 6 West: mean age of living kin

Kin	EXACT AGE OF EGO (YEARS)														
	0	5	10	15	20	25	30	35	40	45	50	55	60	65	70
Husband	·	·	·	27.3	31.6	35.8	39.8	43.4	46.7	49.1	50.7	52.0	55.6	58.4	60.5
Parent	27.1	31.8	36.6	41.2	45.8	50.2	54.6	59.0	63.0	67.2	71.3	75.3	78.8	83.1	88.3
Father	32.1	36.9	41.6	46.2	50.8	55.3	59.9	64.5	68.8	73.1	77.7	82.3	84.7	88.9	93.9
Mother	22.0	27.0	31.9	36.8	41.6	46.4	51.0	55.7	60.3	64.9	69.6	73.9	78.2	83.0	88.0
Sibling	3.9	5.9	10.1	14.7	19.5	24.4	29.3	34.3	39.2	44.1	48.9	53.8	58.5	63.1	67.4
Brother	3.8	5.8	10.1	14.7	19.5	24.3	29.2	34.1	39.0	43.9	48.6	53.5	58.3	62.9	67.3
Sister	3.9	5.9	10.1	14.8	19.6	24.5	29.4	34.4	39.4	44.4	49.2	54.1	58.7	63.3	67.5
Child	·	·	·	·	2.2	5.5	9.4	13.6	17.7	21.9	26.6	31.5	36.4	41.2	46.1
Son	·	·	·	·	2.2	5.5	9.5	13.6	17.7	21.9	26.6	31.6	36.4	41.3	46.0
Daughter	·	·	·	·	2.1	5.4	9.4	13.5	17.6	21.8	26.6	31.5	36.3	41.2	46.1
Grandparent	50.2	54.3	58.1	61.8	65.3	68.9	71.9	75.4	78.7	82.4	87.1	88.8	94.6	·	·
Grandfather	54.6	58.7	62.7	66.5	70.0	73.6	76.9	80.5	85.6	89.0	91.4	·	·	·	·
Grandmother	46.8	51.1	55.3	59.3	63.3	67.2	70.7	74.6	78.0	81.8	87.0	88.8	94.6	·	·
Maternal grandfather	51.4	55.7	59.8	64.1	68.2	72.3	76.1	80.0	85.1	89.0	91.4	·	·	·	·
Paternal grandfather	59.8	64.1	68.2	72.2	75.9	79.6	83.0	87.2	91.7	·	·	·	·	·	·
Maternal grandmother	42.9	47.4	52.0	56.3	60.6	64.8	68.9	73.1	77.1	81.3	86.4	88.8	94.6	·	·
Paternal grandmother	51.9	56.3	60.4	64.5	68.8	72.9	76.8	80.7	85.2	88.3	94.1	·	·	·	·
Grandchild	·	·	·	·	·	·	·	1.2	3.1	5.0	7.4	10.3	13.7	17.5	21.5
Grandson	·	·	·	·	·	·	·	1.2	3.1	5.1	7.4	10.3	13.7	17.4	21.5
Granddaughter	·	·	·	·	·	·	·	1.2	3.1	5.0	7.4	10.2	13.7	17.5	21.5
Aunt/uncle	25.8	30.6	35.3	40.0	44.6	49.2	53.6	57.7	61.7	65.6	69.2	72.5	76.0	79.0	80.9
Aunt	25.9	30.7	35.5	40.3	44.9	49.5	53.8	58.0	62.1	65.8	69.3	72.7	76.2	79.0	80.4
Uncle	25.8	30.5	35.1	39.8	44.4	48.9	53.3	57.5	61.3	65.2	69.0	72.3	75.7	78.8	82.0
Maternal aunt	21.3	26.2	31.0	35.9	40.8	45.5	50.3	54.9	59.3	63.4	67.3	71.4	75.0	78.5	80.2
Paternal aunt	31.1	36.0	40.8	45.6	49.9	54.5	58.8	62.9	67.2	71.1	75.0	78.0	82.2	82.9	84.1
Maternal uncle	21.4	26.2	31.0	35.8	40.5	45.2	49.8	54.3	58.6	63.0	67.2	70.9	74.6	78.6	81.6
Paternal uncle	30.9	35.7	40.3	45.1	49.7	54.3	58.7	62.9	66.9	70.7	74.6	77.5	81.9	81.1	85.1
Nephew/niece	3.2	3.0	3.0	2.9	4.2	5.9	8.2	11.0	14.7	18.9	23.5	28.3	33.1	37.9	42.6
Nephew	4.0	4.3	3.0	2.9	4.1	5.9	8.1	10.9	14.6	18.7	23.3	28.0	32.8	37.6	42.2
Niece	2.2	2.2	3.0	2.9	4.2	6.0	8.2	11.2	14.9	19.2	23.8	28.6	33.4	38.3	43.1

Note: . indicates no occurrences in simulation; 0.0 indicates less than 0.1

Table J; Saller Table 3.3.d: Male 'senatorial', Level 6 West: mean number of living kin

Kin	EXACT AGE OF EGO (YEARS)														
	0	5	10	15	20	25	30	35	40	45	50	55	60	65	70
Wife	·	·	·	·	0.0	0.6	0.9	1.0	1.0	1.0	1.0	1.0	0.9	0.8	0.6
Parent	2.0	1.8	1.7	1.5	1.4	1.2	1.0	0.8	0.6	0.4	0.3	0.1	0.1	0.0	0.0
Father	1.0	0.9	0.8	0.7	0.6	0.5	0.4	0.3	0.2	0.1	0.1	0.0	0.0	0.0	0.0
Mother	1.0	0.9	0.9	0.8	0.7	0.7	0.6	0.5	0.4	0.3	0.2	0.1	0.1	0.0	·
Sibling	1.1	1.8	1.9	1.8	1.8	1.7	1.6	1.5	1.3	1.2	1.1	0.9	0.8	0.6	0.4
Brother	0.5	0.9	0.9	0.9	0.9	0.8	0.8	0.7	0.7	0.6	0.5	0.4	0.4	0.3	0.2
Sister	0.6	0.9	0.9	0.9	0.9	0.8	0.8	0.7	0.7	0.6	0.6	0.5	0.4	0.3	0.2
Child	·	·	·	·	·	0.3	1.3	1.8	1.9	1.9	1.8	1.7	1.6	1.4	1.3
Son	·	·	·	·	·	0.2	0.7	0.9	0.9	0.9	0.9	0.8	0.8	0.7	0.7
Daughter	·	·	·	·	·	0.2	0.7	0.9	0.9	0.9	0.9	0.8	0.8	0.7	0.7
Grandparent	2.2	1.8	1.5	1.1	0.8	0.5	0.3	0.2	0.1	0.0	0.0	0.0	·	·	·
Grandfather	0.9	0.7	0.5	0.4	0.2	0.1	0.1	0.0	0.0	0.0	0.0	·	·	·	·
Grandmother	1.2	1.1	0.9	0.7	0.6	0.4	0.3	0.2	0.1	0.0	0.0	0.0	·	·	·
Maternal grandfather	0.6	0.5	0.4	0.3	0.2	0.1	0.1	0.0	0.0	0.0	0.0	·	·	·	·
Paternal grandfather	0.4	0.3	0.2	0.1	0.1	0.0	0.0	0.0	0.0	0.0	0.0	·	·	·	·
Maternal grandmother	0.7	0.6	0.5	0.5	0.4	0.3	0.2	0.1	0.1	0.0	0.0	0.0	·	·	·
Paternal grandmother	0.5	0.5	0.4	0.3	0.2	0.1	0.1	0.0	0.0	0.0	0.0	0.0	·	·	·
Grandchild	·	·	·	·	·	·	·	·	0.0	0.4	1.1	1.9	2.6	3.0	3.2
Grandson	·	·	·	·	·	·	·	·	0.0	0.2	0.6	1.0	1.3	1.6	1.6
Granddaughter	·	·	·	·	·	·	·	·	0.0	0.2	0.6	1.0	1.3	1.5	1.6
Aunt/uncle	3.3	3.1	2.8	2.6	2.3	2.0	1.7	1.4	1.1	0.8	0.5	0.3	0.2	0.1	0.0
Aunt	1.6	1.5	1.4	1.3	1.2	1.1	0.9	0.7	0.6	0.4	0.3	0.2	0.1	0.0	0.0
Uncle	1.6	1.5	1.4	1.3	1.1	1.0	0.8	0.6	0.5	0.3	0.2	0.1	0.1	0.0	0.0
Maternal aunt	0.9	0.8	0.8	0.7	0.7	0.6	0.5	0.5	0.4	0.3	0.2	0.1	0.1	0.0	0.0
Paternal aunt	0.8	0.7	0.7	0.6	0.5	0.5	0.4	0.3	0.2	0.1	0.1	0.0	0.0	0.0	0.0
Maternal uncle	0.9	0.8	0.8	0.7	0.6	0.6	0.5	0.4	0.3	0.2	0.2	0.1	0.1	0.0	0.0
Paternal uncle	0.8	0.7	0.6	0.6	0.5	0.4	0.3	0.2	0.2	0.1	0.1	0.0	0.0	0.0	0.0
Nephew/niece	0.0	0.0	0.1	0.5	1.1	1.9	2.6	3.0	3.1	3.1	3.0	2.8	2.6	2.3	2.1
Nephew	0.0	0.0	0.1	0.2	0.6	1.0	1.3	1.5	1.6	1.6	1.5	1.4	1.3	1.2	1.0
Niece	0.0	0.0	0.1	0.2	0.6	1.0	1.3	1.5	1.6	1.5	1.5	1.4	1.3	1.2	1.1

Note: · indicates no occurrences in simulation; 0.0 indicates less than 0.1

Table K: Saller Table 3.3.e: Male 'senatorial', Level 6 West: proportion having living kin

Kin	\multicolumn{15}{c}{EXACT AGE OF EGO (YEARS)}														
	0	5	10	15	20	25	30	35	40	45	50	55	60	65	70
Wife					0.00	0.59	0.94	0.98	0.98	0.97	0.98	0.97	0.87	0.76	0.64
Parent	1.00	0.99	0.97	0.94	0.90	0.83	0.75	0.65	0.52	0.39	0.25	0.14	0.07	0.03	0.01
Father	1.00	0.90	0.82	0.72	0.62	0.51	0.40	0.30	0.20	0.11	0.05	0.02	0.01	0.00	.
Mother	1.00	0.94	0.88	0.81	0.74	0.67	0.59	0.51	0.41	0.31	0.21	0.13	0.06	0.02	0.01
Sibling	0.57	0.83	0.81	0.80	0.78	0.77	0.75	0.72	0.69	0.65	0.62	0.56	0.50	0.42	0.32
Brother	0.38	0.59	0.59	0.58	0.56	0.54	0.52	0.49	0.46	0.43	0.39	0.34	0.29	0.23	0.16
Sister	0.38	0.59	0.58	0.57	0.56	0.54	0.51	0.49	0.46	0.43	0.41	0.36	0.32	0.26	0.20
Child						0.27	0.73	0.81	0.81	0.80	0.79	0.77	0.75	0.72	0.69
Son						0.15	0.49	0.58	0.59	0.58	0.57	0.55	0.52	0.50	0.47
Daughter						0.15	0.48	0.57	0.58	0.58	0.56	0.53	0.51	0.49	0.46
Grandparent	0.95	0.90	0.82	0.72	0.58	0.44	0.29	0.17	0.08	0.03	0.01	0.00	.	.	.
Grandfather	0.72	0.60	0.47	0.34	0.21	0.13	0.06	0.02	0.01	0.00	0.00		.	.	.
Grandmother	0.85	0.79	0.71	0.60	0.49	0.37	0.25	0.15	0.07	0.03	0.01	0.00	.	.	.
Maternal grandfather	0.57	0.47	0.36	0.26	0.17	0.10	0.05	0.02	0.01						
Paternal grandfather	0.35	0.26	0.18	0.10	0.05	0.03	0.01	0.00							
Maternal grandmother	0.70	0.62	0.54	0.45	0.37	0.28	0.20	0.12	0.06	0.03	0.01	0.00			
Paternal grandmother	0.54	0.46	0.37	0.28	0.20	0.12	0.06	0.03	0.01	0.00	0.00	.			
Grandchild							.	.	0.02	0.26	0.47	0.62	0.69	0.72	0.72
Grandson							.	.	0.01	0.16	0.33	0.48	0.56	0.60	0.60
Granddaughter							.	.	0.01	0.17	0.34	0.49	0.57	0.61	0.61
Aunt/uncle	0.94	0.93	0.92	0.89	0.86	0.82	0.77	0.70	0.61	0.50	0.37	0.24	0.14	0.06	0.02
Aunt	0.78	0.76	0.74	0.70	0.67	0.62	0.57	0.50	0.43	0.34	0.24	0.16	0.09	0.04	0.01
Uncle	0.77	0.75	0.72	0.69	0.64	0.59	0.53	0.44	0.35	0.27	0.19	0.11	0.06	0.03	0.01
Maternal aunt	0.55	0.53	0.51	0.49	0.46	0.43	0.39	0.35	0.30	0.24	0.18	0.12	0.07	0.03	0.01
Paternal aunt	0.51	0.49	0.46	0.42	0.39	0.35	0.29	0.24	0.18	0.12	0.08	0.04	0.01	0.01	0.00
Maternal uncle	0.56	0.53	0.51	0.48	0.45	0.41	0.37	0.31	0.25	0.19	0.14	0.09	0.05	0.02	0.01
Paternal uncle	0.51	0.48	0.44	0.41	0.36	0.32	0.26	0.20	0.14	0.09	0.05	0.03	0.01	0.00	0.00
Nephew/niece	0.00	0.01	0.05	0.22	0.43	0.59	0.68	0.71	0.71	0.71	0.70	0.69	0.68	0.67	0.65
Nephew	0.00	0.01	0.03	0.15	0.31	0.46	0.56	0.60	0.60	0.59	0.58	0.57	0.55	0.53	0.51
Niece	0.00	0.01	0.03	0.15	0.32	0.46	0.56	0.59	0.60	0.60	0.59	0.57	0.56	0.54	0.52

Note: . indicates no occurrences in simulation; 0.00 indicates less than 0.01

Table L; Saller Table 3.3.f: Male 'senatorial', Level 6 West: mean age of living kin

Kin	EXACT AGE OF EGO (YEARS)														
	0	5	10	15	20	25	30	35	40	45	50	55	60	65	70
Wife	.	.	.	.	19.8	17.9	21.5	25.9	30.5	34.7	38.6	42.4	47.0	51.5	55.8
Parent	27.2	32.0	36.7	41.4	45.9	50.5	54.8	59.2	63.4	67.3	71.2	75.3	79.5	83.8	87.5
Father	32.2	37.0	41.7	46.3	51.0	55.6	60.1	64.5	68.9	73.4	77.6	81.9	86.1	92.1	.
Mother	22.2	27.1	32.0	37.0	41.7	46.6	51.3	56.1	60.7	65.2	69.7	74.2	78.8	83.3	87.5
Sibling	4.0	6.0	10.2	14.9	19.8	24.7	29.7	34.6	39.6	44.5	49.4	54.2	58.8	63.5	67.9
Brother	3.9	5.9	10.1	14.8	19.7	24.6	29.6	34.5	39.5	44.4	49.3	54.0	58.7	63.4	67.8
Sister	4.0	6.1	10.3	15.0	19.9	24.8	29.8	34.7	39.7	44.6	49.5	54.3	58.9	63.7	68.0
Child	.	.	.	.	.	1.0	3.0	6.2	10.3	14.9	19.8	24.7	29.7	34.6	39.5
Son	.	.	.	.	.	1.0	3.1	6.2	10.3	14.9	19.8	24.7	29.7	34.6	39.5
Daughter	.	.	.	.	.	1.0	3.0	6.2	10.3	14.9	19.7	24.7	29.7	34.6	39.5
Grandparent	50.2	54.3	58.2	61.8	65.2	68.8	71.9	75.1	78.5	81.6	86.4	90.5	.	.	.
Grandfather	54.7	58.8	62.7	66.3	69.9	73.7	77.2	80.6	84.5	87.8	93.7	.	.	.	.
Grandmother	46.9	51.3	55.5	59.5	63.4	67.3	70.6	74.3	78.1	81.5	86.1	90.5	.	.	.
Maternal grandfather	51.5	56.0	60.0	64.1	68.3	72.4	76.4	80.2	84.5	87.8	93.7	.	.	.	.
Paternal grandfather	59.8	63.9	68.0	71.8	75.5	79.3	83.2	89.4	.	.	.	.	.	.	.
Maternal grandmother	43.1	47.7	52.1	56.4	60.7	65.1	68.9	72.9	77.0	81.0	85.8	90.5	.	.	.
Paternal grandmother	51.9	56.2	60.3	64.5	68.5	72.4	76.3	80.1	85.0	88.2	93.5	.	.	.	.
Grandchild									0.7	1.9	3.7	5.6	8.1	11.1	14.9
Grandson									0.7	1.9	3.7	5.6	8.0	11.1	14.8
Granddaughter									0.7	1.9	3.7	5.7	8.2	11.2	14.9
Aunt/uncle	25.9	30.6	35.3	40.1	44.6	49.1	53.5	57.7	61.7	65.5	69.1	72.6	76.0	79.2	80.7
Aunt	25.7	30.5	35.3	40.0	44.7	49.2	53.7	57.9	61.9	65.7	69.3	72.9	76.4	79.6	81.5
Uncle	26.0	30.7	35.4	40.1	44.6	49.0	53.3	57.4	61.4	65.1	68.7	72.1	75.5	78.6	79.6
Maternal aunt	21.3	26.1	31.0	35.8	40.7	45.5	50.2	54.8	59.2	63.3	67.4	71.5	75.6	78.5	81.3
Paternal aunt	30.7	35.5	40.3	45.1	49.6	54.2	58.6	62.9	66.8	70.9	74.4	78.3	81.6	86.5	84.7
Maternal uncle	21.6	26.3	31.1	35.8	40.6	45.1	49.8	54.3	58.6	62.7	66.8	70.8	74.4	77.9	79.5
Paternal uncle	30.9	35.7	40.4	45.2	49.7	54.2	58.4	62.6	66.5	70.4	73.7	77.1	80.9	84.0	80.8
Nephew/niece	4.8	3.4	3.3	3.0	4.3	6.1	8.4	11.3	15.1	19.4	24.0	28.7	33.6	38.4	43.1
Nephew	6.7	3.4	2.8	2.8	4.2	6.0	8.4	11.3	15.0	19.3	23.8	28.6	33.4	38.2	42.9
Niece	4.3	3.4	3.7	3.2	4.3	6.2	8.5	11.4	15.2	19.5	24.1	28.9	33.8	38.6	43.3

Note: . indicates no occurrences in simulation; 0.0 indicates less than 0.1

BIBLIOGRAPHY

Amundsen, D.W. and Diers, C.J. (1970) The age of menopause in Classical Greece and Rome', *Human Biology* 42: 79–86.

Aries, P. (1962) *Centuries of Childhood*, Cape: London.

Arieti, J.A. (1997) 'Rape and Livy's view of Roman history', in S. Deacy and K.F. Pierce (eds) *Rape in Antiquity*, London: Duckworth, 209–29.

Astin, A.E. (1958) *The Lex Annalis before Sulla*, Brussels: Collection Latomus 32.

Atkinson, D. (1914) 'A hoard of Samian ware from Pompeii', *Journal of Roman Studies* 4: 27–64.

Badian, E. (1964) *Studies in Greek and Roman History*, Oxford: Blackwells.

Bannon, C.J. (1997) *The Brothers of Romulus: Fraternal Pietas in Roman Law, Literature and Society*, Princeton: Princeton University Press.

Barton, T. (1994) *Power and Knowledge: Astrology, Physiognomics and Medicine under the Roman Empire*, Ann Arbor: University of Michigan Press.

Beard, M. (1980) 'The sexual status of the Vestal Virgins', *Journal of Roman Studies* 70: 12–27.

—— (1995) 'Re-reading (Vestal) virginity', in R. Hawley and B. Levick (eds) *Women in Antiquity: New Assessments*, London: Routledge, 166–77.

—— (1999) 'Erotics of rape: Livy, Ovid and the Sabine women', in P. Setälä and L. Savunen (eds) *Female Networks and the Public Sphere in Roman Society (Acta Instituti Romani Finlandiae 22)* 1–10.

Beard, M., North, J. and Price, S. (1998) *Religions of Rome volume 1*, Cambridge: CUP.

Belmont, N. (1973) *Levana* ou comment, élever' les enfants', *Annales Economies, Sociétés, Civilisations* 29: 77–89.

Bennett, J.W. (1967) *Hutterian Brethren. The Agricultural Economy and Social Organisation of a Communal People*, San Francisco: Stanford University Press.

Berry, J. (1997) 'Household artefacts: towards a re-interpretation of Roman domestic space', in R. Laurence and A. Wallace-Hadrill (eds) *Domestic Space in the Roman World: Pompeii and Beyond*, Journal of Roman Archaeology, Supplementary series 22: 183–95.

Birley, A.R. (1981) *The Fasti of Roman Britain*, Oxford: Clarendon.

Bonner, J.T. (1993 *Life Cycles. Reflections of an Evolutionary Biologist*, Princeton: Princeton University Press.

Boswell, J. (1988) *The Kindness of Strangers: the Abandonment of Children in Western Europe from Late Antiquity to the Renaissance*, Harmondsworth: Penguin.

Bradley, K. (1986) 'Wet-nursing at Rome: a study of social relations', in B. Rawson (ed.) *The Family in Ancient Rome*, London: Croom Helm, 201–29.

—— (1991) *Discovering the Roman Family*, Oxford: Oxford University Press.

Broughton, T.R.S. (1952) *The Magistrates of the Roman Republic*, New York: American Philological Association.

—— (1991) *Candidates Defeated in Roman Elections*, Philadelphia: American Philosophical Society.

Brown, R. (1995) 'Livy's Sabine women and the ideal of *Concordia*', *Transactions of the American Philological Association* 125: 291–319.

Burton, A. (1989) 'Looking forward from Ariès? Pictorial and material evidence for the history of childhood and family life', *Continuity and Change* 4: 203–29.

Burton, G. and Hopkins, K. (1983) 'Political succession in the late Roman Republic', in K. Hopkins *Death and Renewal*: Cambridge: Cambridge University Press, 31–119.

Carcopino, J. (1956) *Daily Life in Ancient Rome*, Harmondsworth: Pelican.

Carp, T. (1980) '*Puer senex* in Roman and Medieval thought', *Latomus* 39: 736–9.

Champlin, E. (1991) *Final Judgements: Duty and Emotion in Roman Wills 200 B.C. – A.D.250*, Berkeley: University of California Press.

Chandler, A.R. (1948) 'Aristotle on mental aging', *Journal of Gerontology* 3: 220–4.

Clay, J.S. (1989) 'The old man in the garden: Georgic 4.116–148', in Falkner, T.M. and de Luce, J. (eds) *Old Age in Greek and Latin Literature*, New York: State University of New York Press, 183–95.

Cohen, D. and Saller, R. (1994) 'Foucault on sexuality in Greco-Roman antiquity', in J. Goldstein (ed.) *Foucault and the Writing of History*, Oxford: Blackwell, 35–59.

Cooper, K. (1992) Insinuations of womanly influence: an aspect of the Christianisation of the Roman aristocracy', *Journal of Roman Studies* 82: 150–64.

—— (1996) *The Virgin and the Bride: Idealised Womanhood in Late Antiquity*, Cambridge MA, Harvard University Press.

Corbier, M. (1991) 'Constructing kinship in Rome: marriage, divorce, filiation and adoption', in D.I. Kertzer and R. Saller (eds) *The Family in Italy from Antiquity to the Present*, Newhaven: Yale University Press, 127–44.

—— (1995) 'Male power and legitimacy through women: the Domus Augusta under the Julio-Claudians', in R. Hawley and B. Levick (eds) *Women in Antiquity: New Assessments*, London: Routledge, 178–93.

Cunningham, H. (1995) *Children and Childhood in Western Society Since 1500*, London: Longmans.

Currie, S. (1996). 'The empire of adults: the representation of children on Trajan's Arch at Beneventum', in J. Elsner (ed.) *Art and Text in Roman Culture*, Cambridge: Cambridge University Press, 153–81.

Delia, D. (1991) 'Fulvia reconsidered', in S. Pomeroy (ed.) *Women's History and Ancient History*, University of North Carolina Press: Chapel Hill and London 173–96.

De Luce, J. (1989) 'Ovid as an idiographic study of creativity and old age', in T.M. Falkner and J. de Luce, (eds) *Old Age in Greek and Latin Literature*, New York: State University of New York Press, 195–216.

DeMause, L. (ed.) (1974) *The History of Childhood*, New York.

Dickmann, J-A. (1997) 'The peristyle and the transformation of domestic space in Hellenistic Pompeii', in R. Laurence and A. Wallace-Hadrill (eds) *Domestic Space in the Roman World: Pompeii and Beyond*, Journal of Roman Archaeology, Supplementary Series 22: 121–36.

Dixon, S. (1983) 'A family business: women's role in patronage and politics at Rome 80–44 BC', *Classica et Medievalia* 34: 91–112.

—— (1984a) 'Family finances: Terentia and Tullia', *Antichthon* 18: 78–101.

—— (1984b) '*Infirmitas sexus*: womanly weakness in Roman Law', *Tijdschrift voor Rechtsgeschiedenis* 52: 343–71.

—— (1985) 'The marriage alliance in the Roman elite', *Journal of Family History* 10: 353–78.

—— (1988) *The Roman Mother*, London: Croom Helm.

—— (1991) 'The sentimental ideal of the Roman family', in B. Rawson (ed.) *Marriage, Divorce and Children in Ancient Rome*, Oxford: Clarendon Press, 99–113.

—— (1992) *The Roman Family*, Baltimore: Johns Hopkins University Press.

Duncan-Jones, R.P. (1977) 'Age-rounding, illiteracy and social differentiation in the Roman Empire', *Chiron* 7: 333–53.

—— (1990) *Structure and Scale in the Roman Economy*, Cambridge: Cambridge University Press.

Dupont, F. (1992) *Daily Life in Ancient Rome*, Oxford: Blackwells.

Edwards, C. (1993). *The Politics of Immorality in Ancient Rome*, Cambridge: Cambridge University Press.

Engels, D. (1980) 'The problem of female infanticide in the Graeco-Roman world', *Classical Philology*, 75: 112–20.

Esler, C.C. (1989) 'Horace's old girls: evolution of a topos', in T.M Falkner and J. de Luce (eds) *Old Age in Greek and Latin Literature*, New York: State University of New York Press, 172–82.

Eveleth, P.B. (1979) 'Population differences in growth: environmental and genetic factors', in F. Falker and J. Tanner (eds) *Human Growth: Neurobiology and Nutrition volume 3*, New York: Plenum, 373–94.

Eyben, E. (1972) 'Antiquity's view of puberty', *Latomus* 31: 677–97.

—— (1993) *Restless Youth in Ancient Rome*, London: Routledge.

Falkner, T.M. and de Luce, J. (eds) (1989) *Old Age in Greek and Latin Literature*, New York: State University of New York Press.

Fantham, E. (1995) '*Aemelia Pudentilla*: or the wealthy widow's choice', in R. Hawley and B. Levick (eds) *Women in Antiquity: New Assessments*, London: Routledge, 220–32.

Finley, M.I. (1989) 'The elderly in Classical Antiquity' in T.M. Falkner and J. de Luce (eds) *Old Age in Greek and Latin Literature*, New York: State University of New York Press, 1–20.

Fischler, S. (1994) 'Social stereotypes and historical analysis: the case of imperial women at Rome', in L. Archer, S. Fischler and M. Wyke (eds) *Women in Ancient Societies: An Illusion in the Night*, Basingstoke: MacMillan, 115–33.

(forthcoming) From *puella* to *matrona*'.

Flower, H.I. (1996) *Ancestor Masks and Aristocratic Power in Roman Culture*, Oxford: Clarendon Press.

Foss, P.W. (1997) 'Watchful *lares* Roman household organisation and the rituals of cooking and eating', in R. Laurence and A. Wallace-Hadrill (eds) *Domestic Space in the Roman World: Pompeii and Beyond, Journal of Roman Archaeology*, Supplementary Series 22.

Foucault, M. (1986) *The Care of the Self: The History of Sexuality, volume 3* trans. R. Hurley, Random House: New York.

Fraschetti, A. (1997) 'Roman youth', in G. Levi and J-C. Schmitt, (eds) *History of Young People in the West. Vol. 1: Ancient and Medieval Rights of Passage*, Cambridge, MA: Belknap Press.

Frier, B. (1994) 'Natural fertility and family limitation in Roman marriage', *Classical Philology* 89: 318–33.

Frisch, R.E. (1978) 'Population, food intake and fertility', *Science* 199: 22–30.

—— and McArthur, J.W. (1974) 'Menstrual cycles: fatness as a determinant of minimum weight for height necessary for their maintenance and onset', *Science* 185: 949–51.

Funaioli, H. (1907) *Grammaticae Romanae Fragmenta*, Lipsla: Teubner.

Galton, F. *et al.* (1883) 'The final report of the Anthropometric Committee', *Report to the 53rd Meeting of the British Association for the Advancement of Science*, London: John Murray.

Gardner, J. (1986) *Women in Roman Law and Society*, Routledge: London.

Gardner, J.F. and Wiedemann, T. (1991) *The Roman Household: A Sourcebook*, London: Routledge.

Garland, R. (1990) *The Greek Way of Life from Conception to Old Age*, Duckworth: London.

Garnsey, P. (1991) 'Child rearing in ancient Italy', in D.I. Kertzer and R.P. Saller (eds) *The Family in Italy from Antiquity to the Present*, New Haven, Yale University Press: 48–65

Garnsey, P. (1999) *Food and Society in Classical Antiquity*, Cambridge: Cambridge University Press.

George, M. (1997) '*Servus* and *domus*: the slave in the Roman house', in R. Laurence and A. Wallace-Hadrill (eds) *Domestic Space in the Roman World: Pompeii and Beyond, Journal of Roman Archaeology* Supplementary Series 22: 15–24.

Giddens, A. (1984) *The Constitution of Society: Outline of the Theory of Structuration*, Cambridge: Polity.

Gilchrist, R. (2000) *Human Lifecycles (World Archaeology* 31.3), London: Routledge.

Gleason, M. (1990) 'The semiotics of gender', in D.M. Haltin, J.J. Winkler and F.I. Zeitlein (eds) *Before Sexuality*, Princeton, NJ: Princeton University Press, 389–415.

Gleason, M. (1995) *Making Men. Sophists and Self-Presentation in Ancient Rome*. Princeton, NJ: Princeton University Press.

Goldsworthy, A.K. (1996) *The Roman Army at War 100BC - AD200*, Oxford: Clarendon.

Gowland, R. (2001) 'Playing dead: implications of mortuary evidence for the social construction of childhood in Roman Britain' in G. Davies, A. Gardner and K. Lockyer (eds) *TRAC2000. Proceedings of the tenth annual Theoretical Roman Archaeology Conference*, Oxford, Oxbow, pp. 152–68.

Gratwick, A.S. (1984), 'Free or not so free? wives and daughters in the Roman Republic', in E. Craik (ed.) *Marriage and Property*, Aberdeen: Aberdeen University Press.

Griffin, M. (1984) *Nero: The End of a Dynasty*, London: Batsford.

—— (1992). *Seneca. A Philosopher in Politics*, Oxford: Clarendon.

Haley, S.P. (1985) 'Five wives of Pompey the Great', *Greece and Rome* 32: 49–59.

Hallett, J. (1984) *Fathers and Daughters in Elite Roman Society*, Princeton, NJ: Princeton University Press.

Hallett, J. and Skinner, M. (1997) *Roman Sexualities*, Princeton, NJ: Princeton University Press.

Harris, W.V. (1982) 'The theoretical possibility of extensive infanticide in the Graeco-Roman world, *Classical Quarterly* 32: 114–6.

—— (1994) 'Child exposure in the Roman empire', *Journal of Roman Studies* 84: 1–22.

Hemelrijk, E.A. (1999) *Matrona Docta, Educated Women in the Roman Elite from Cornelia to Julia Domna*, London: Routledge.

Herbert-Brown, G. (1994) *Ovid and the Fasti: An Historical Study*, Oxford: Clarendon.

Hockey, J. and James, A. (1993) *Growing Up and Growing Old. Ageing and Dependency in the Life Course*, London: Sage.

Hopkins, K. (1965) 'The age of Roman girls at marriage', *Population Studies* 20: 309–27.

—— (1966) 'On the probable age structure of the Roman population', *Population Studies* 20: 245–64.

—— (1983) *Death and Renewal*, Cambridge: Cambridge University Press.

168

—— (1991) 'From violence to blessing: symbols and rituals in ancient Rome', in A. Molho, K. Raaflaub and J. Emlen (eds) *City States in Classical Antiquity and Medieval Italy*, Ann Arbor, MI: University of Michigan Press, 479–98.

Hostetler, J.A. (1974) *Hutterite Society*, Baltimore: Johns Hopkins University Press.

Howell, N. (1979) *The Demography of the Dobe !Kung*, New York: Academic Press.

Huffman, S.L. (1978) 'Postpartum amenorrhea: how is it affected by maternal nutritional status?', *Science* 200: 1155–57.

Humbert, M. (1972) *Le Remariage à Rome*, Milan: Guiffre.

Huskinson, J. (1996) *Roman Children's Sarcophagi: Their Decoration and its Social Significance*, Oxford: Oxford University Press.

—— (1997) 'Iconography: another perspective', in B. Rawson and P. Weaver (eds) *The Roman Family in Italy: Status, Sentiment, Space*, Clarendon: Oxford, 233–38.

Janssen, R.M. (1996) 'Soft toys from Egypt', in D.M. Bailey (ed.) *Archaeological Research in Roman Egypt, Roman: Journal of Roman Archaeology, Supplementary Series* 19: 231–39.

Jones, B.W. (1979) *Domitian and the Senatorial Order. A Prosopographical Study of Domitian's Relationship with the Senate A.D. 81–96*, Philadelphia: American Philosophical Society.

Joshel, S.R. (1992) *Work, Identity and Legal Status at Rome*, Norman: University of Oklahoma Press.

Kampen, N. (1981) 'Biographical narration and Roman funerary art', *Journal of Roman Archaeology* 85: 47–58.

—— (1991) 'Reliefs of the Basilica Aemilia: a redating', *Klio* 2: 448–58.

Keaveney A. (1982) *Sulla: The Last Republican*, London: Croom Helm.

Kelly, K.C. (2000) *Performing Virginity and Testing Chastity in the Middle Ages*, Routledge: London.

Kelly, K.C. and Leslie, M. (1999) 'The epistemology of virginity', in K.C. Kelly and M. Leslie *Menacing Virgins: Representations of Virginity in the Middle Ages and Renaissance*, Newark, University of Delaware Press 15–25.

Kertzer, D.I. and Saller, R.P. (eds) (1991) *The Family in Italy from Antiquity to the Present*, New Haven: Yale University Press.

Kilmer, M.F. (1982) 'Genital phobia and depilation', *Journal of Hellenic Studies* 102: 104–12.

King, H. (1998) *Hippocrates' Woman: Reading the Female Body in Ancient Greece*, London: Routledge.

Kleiner, D.E.E. (1992) *Roman Sculpture*, New Haven: Yale University Press.

La Follette, L. (1994) 'The costume of the Roman bride', in J. Sebesta and L. Bonfante (eds) *The World of Roman Costume*, Wisconsin: University of Wisconsin Press, 54–64.

Lancaster, J.B. (1985) 'Evolutionary perspectives on sex difference in the higher primates', in A.S. Rossi (ed.) *Gender and the Life Course* New York: Aldine, 3–27.

Laurence, R. (1994) *Roman Pompeii: Space and Society*, Routledge: London.

—— (1994) 'Rumour and communication in Roman politics', *Greece and Rome* 41: 62–74.

—— (1997) 'History and female power at Rome', in T. Cornell and K. Lomas (eds) *Gender and Ethnicity in Ancient Italy* London: Accordia,129–39.

—— (2000) 'Metaphors, monuments and texts: the life-course in Roman culture', *World Archaeology* 31:442–56.

Levick, B. (1999) *Vespasian*, London: Routledge.

Lindsay, H. (1995) 'A fertile marriage: Agrippina and the chronology of her children by Germanicus', *Latomus* 54,1–2: 3–17.

Lintott, A. (1994) 'Political history 146–95BC', *in Cambridge Ancient History 9 (The Last Age of the Roman Republic 146–43BC)* second edition, Cambridge: Cambridge University Press, 40–103.

Levine, S. and Levine, R. (1985) 'Age, gender, and the demographic transition: the life course in Agrarian societies', in A.S. Rossi (ed.) *Gender and the Life Course*, New York: Aldine, 29–42.

Manson, M. (1983) 'The emergence of the small child at Rome', *History of Education* 12: 149–59.

Martin-Kilcher, S. (2000) '*Mors immatura* in the Roman World – a mirror of society and tradition' in J. Pearce, M. Millet and M. Strück (eds) *Burial, Society and Context in the Roman World*, Oxford: Oxbow Books, 63–77.

May, R.M. (1978) 'Human reproduction reconsidered', *Nature* 272: 491–5.

McGinn, T. (1999) 'Widows, orphans and social history', *Journal of Roman Archaeology* 12: 617–32.

Medina, J.J. (1996) *The Clock of Ages. Why we Age – How we Age – Winding Back the Clock*, Cambridge: Cambridge University Press.

Millar, F. (1998) *The Crowd in Rome in the Late Republic*, Ann Arbor, MI: Michigan University Press.

Minois, G. (1989) *History of Old Age*, Cambridge: Polity Press.

Molleson, T.I. (1993) 'The human remains', in D.E. Farwell and T.I. Molleson (ed.) *Poundbury Volume 2: The Cemetery, Dorchester*: Dorset Natural History and Archaeological Society Monograph 11: 142–206.

Mouritsen, H. (1998) The Album of Canusium and the town councils of Roman Italy, *Chiron* 28: 229–54.

Nardi, B.A. (1981) 'Modes of explanation in anthropological population theory: biological determinism vs. self-regulation in studies of population growth in Third World countries', *American Anthropologist* 83: 28–56.

Néraudau, J-P. (1984) *Etre Enfant à Rome*, Paris: Belles Lettres.

Nicolet, C. (1980) (English trans.) *The World of the Citizen in Republican Rome*, London: Batsford.

—— (1984) 'Augustus, government, and the propertied class', in F. Millar and E. Segal (eds) *Caesar Augustus: Seven Aspects*, Oxford: Clarendon, 89–128.

Nikolaidis, A.G. (1997) 'Plutarch on women and marriage', *Wiener Studien* 110: 27–88.

Parker, H.N. (1998) 'The Tetratogenic Grid', in J.P. Hallett and M.B. Skinner (eds) *Roman Sexualities*, Princeton, NJ: Princeton University Press.

Parkin, T. (1992) *Demography and Roman Society*, Baltimore, MB: John Hopkins.

—— (1997) 'Out of sight, out of mind: elderly members of the Roman family', in B. Rawson and P. Weaver (eds) *The Roman Family in Italy: Status, Sentiment and Space*, Oxford: Clarendon Press, 123–48.

—— (1998) 'Ageing in antiquity: status and participation', in P. Johnson and P. Thane (eds) *Old Age from Antiquity to Post Modernity*, London: Routledge 19–42.

Parkins, H. (1997) 'The "Consumer City" domesticated? The Roman city in elite economic strategies', in H.M. Parkins (ed.) *Roman Urbanism: Beyond the Consumer City*, London: Routledge, 83–111.

Patterson, O. (1981) *Slavery and Social Death: A Comparative Study*, Cambridge MA: Harvard University Press.

Petersen, J.M (1994) 'The education of girls in fourth-century Rome', in D. Wood (ed.) *The Church and Childhood (Studies in Church History* 31), Oxford: Blackwells pp. 29–37.

Pilcher, J. (1995) *Age and Generation in Modern Britain*, Oxford: Oxford University Press.

Pomeroy, S. (1991) *Women's History and Ancient History*, Chapel Hill: University of Carolina Press.

Postman, N. (1982) *The Disappearance of Childhood*, New York: Vintage.

Powell, J.G.F. 1988 (ed. and commentary) *Cicero: Cato Maior de Senectute*, Cambridge: Cambridge University Press.

Quadagno, J. (1999) *Ageing and the Life Course. An Introduction to Social Gerontology*, Boston: McGraw Hill College.

Ramage, N.H. and Ramage, A. (1991) *Roman Art*, London: Laurence King.

Rawson, B. (1966) 'Family life among the lower classes at Rome in the first two centuries of empire', *Classical Philology* 61: 71–183.

—— (ed.) (1986) *The Family in Ancient Rome*, London: Croom Helm.

—— (ed.) (1991) *Marriage, Divorce and Children in Ancient Rome*, Oxford: Clarendon Press.

—— (1997) 'The iconography of Roman childhood', in B. Rawson and P. Weaver (eds) *The Roman Family in Italy: Status, Sentiment, Space*, Clarendon: Oxford, 204–32.

Rawson, E. (1975) *Cicero: A Portrait*, Bristol Classical Press: London.

Richardson, D.W. and Short, R.V. (1978) 'Time and the onset of sperm production in boys', *Journal of Biosocial Science Suppl.* 5: 15–26.

Richlin, A. (1983) *The Garden of Priapus. Sexuality and Aggression in Roman Humour*, New Haven, CI and London: Yale University Press.

—— (1984) 'Invective against women in Roman satire', *Arethusa* 17: 67–80.

Riggsby, A.M. (1997) '"Public" and "private" in Roman culture: the case of the *cubiculum*', *Journal of Roman Archaeology* 10: 36–56.

Roberts, C. (1876) 'The physical requirements of factory children', *Journal of the Statistical Society* 39: 681–733.

Scullard, H.H. (1981) *Festivals and Ceremonies of the Roman Republic*, London: Thames and Hudson.

Toynbee, J.M.C. (1971) *Death and Burial in the Roman World*, London: John Hopkins.

Rose, H.J. (1923) 'Nocturnal funerals in Rome', *Classical Quarterly* 17: 191–4.

Rosivach, V. (1994) '*Anus*: some older women in Latin literature', *Classical World* 88,2: 107–17.

Rossi, A.S. (1985) *Gender and the Life Course*, New York: Aldine.

Rousselle A. (1988) Porneia: *On Desire and the Body in Antiquity* (English trans.), Oxford: Basil Blackwell.

Ryff, C.D. (1985) 'The subjective experience of life-span transitions', in A.S. Rossi (ed.) *Gender and the Life Course*, New York: Aldine, 97–113.

Saller, R. (1984) '*Familia, domus* and the Roman conception of family', *Phoenix* 38: 336–55.

—— (1987) 'Men's age at marriage and its consequences in the Roman family' *Classical Philology* 82: 21–34.

—— (1991) 'Roman heirship strategies in principle and in practice', in D.I. Kertzer and R.P. Saller (eds) *The Family in Italy from Antiquity to the Present*, New Haven: Yale University Press, 26–47.

—— (1993) 'The social dynamics of consent to marriage and sexual relations: the evidence of Roman comedy', in A. Laiou (ed.) *Consent and Coercion to Sex and Marriage in Ancient and Medieval Societies*, Washington: Dumbarton Oaks 83–104.

—— (1994) *Patriarchy, Property and Death in the Roman Family*, Cambridge: Cambridge University Press.

—— (1997) 'Symbols of gender and status hierarchies in the Roman household', in S. Murnaghan and S. Joshel (eds) *Women and Slaves in Graeco-Roman Culture*, London: Routledge.

—— (1998) '*Pater familias, mater familias*, and the gendered semantics of the Roman household', *Classical Philology* 94: 182–97.

Scullard, H.H. (1981) *Festivals and Ceremonies of the Roman Republic*, London: Thames and Hudson.

Sebesta, J. (1998) 'Women's costume and feminine civic morality in Augustan Rome', in M. Wyke (ed.) *Gender and the Body in the Ancient Mediterranean*, Oxford: Blackwells, 81–104.

—— (1994) 'Symbolism in the costume of the Roman woman', in J. Sebesta and L. Bonfante (eds) *The World of Roman Costume*, Wisconsin: University of Wisconsin Press, 46–53.

Sebesta, J. and Bonfante, L. (1994) *The World of Roman Costume*, Wisconsin: University of Wisconsin Press.

Shackleton-Bailey, D.R. (1971) *Cicero*, London: Duckworth.

—— (1965–70) *Cicero's Letters to Atticus*, vols 1–7, Cambridge: Cambridge University Press.

—— (1977) *Cicero: Epistulae Ad Familiaries*, vols 1 and 2, Cambridge: Cambridge University Press.

Shahar, S. (1998) 'Old age in the high and late Middle Ages: image, expectation and status', in P. Johnson and P. Thane (eds) *Old Age from Antiquity to Post-Modernity*, London: Routledge, 43–63.

Shaw, A. (1987) 'The age of Roman girls at marriage: some reconsiderations', *Journal of Roman Studies* 77: 30–46.

Shaw, B. (1991) 'The cultural meaning of death: age and gender in the Roman family', in D.I. Kertzer and R.P. Saller (eds) *The Family in Italy from Antiquity to the Present*, New Haven, CT: Yale University Press, 66–90.

Shelton, J-A. (1988) *As the Romans Did: A Source Book in Roman Social History*, Oxford: Oxford University Press.

—— (1990) 'Pliny the Younger and the ideal wife', *Classica et Medievalia* 41: 163–86.

Sherwin-White, A.N. (1966) *The Letters of Pliny: A Historical and Social Commentary*, Oxford: Clarendon Press.

Short, R.V. (1976) 'The evolution of human reproduction', *Proceedings of the Royal Society B*, 195: 3–24.

Skinner, M.B. (1983) 'Clodia Metelli', *Transactions of the American Philological Association* 113: 273–87.

Stockton, D. (1971) *Cicero: A Political Biography*, Oxford: Oxford University Press.

Suder, W. (1978) 'On age classification in Roman Imperial literature', *The Classical Bulletin* 55: 5–8.

Syme, R. (1958) *Tacitus*, Oxford: Clarendon.

—— (1986) *The Augustan Aristocracy*, Oxford: Clarendon.

Talbert, R.J.A. (1984) *The Senate of Imperial Rome*, Princeton, NJ: Princeton University Press.

Thomas, Y. (1986) 'A Rome, pères citoyens et cité des pères: IIe siècle av. J-C – IIe siècle ap. J-C', in A. Burguère *et al.* (eds) *Histoire de la Famille,* Paris: Armand Colin, 195–229.

Toner, J.P. (1995) *Leisure and Ancient Rome*, Oxford: Polity Press.

Toynbee, J.M.C. (1971) *Death and Burial in the Roman World*, London: John Hopkins.

Treggiari, S. (1991a) *Roman Marriage*, Oxford: Clarendon Press.

—— (1991b) 'Divorce Roman style: how easy and how frequent was it?', in B. Rawson (ed.) *Marriage, Divorce and Children in Ancient Rome*, Oxford: Clarendon, 7–30.

—— (1994) 'Putting the bride to bed', *Echoes du Monde Classique* 38 n.s.13: 311–31.

172

—— (1999) 'The upper-class house as a symbol and focus of emotion in Cicero', *Journal of Roman Archaeology* 12: 33–56.

Van Hooff, A.J.L. (1990) *From Autothanasia to Suicide. Self-killing in Classical Antiquity*, London: Routledge.

Veyne, P. (1960) 'Iconographie de la "transvectio equitum" et des lupercales', *Revue Etudes Anciennes* 62: 100–110.

—— (1987) (ed.) *History of Private Life*, Cambridge, MA and London: Belknap Press.

Walcot, P. (1991) 'On widows and their reputation in antiquity', *Symbolae Osloenses* 66: 5–26.

Wallace-Hadrill, A. (1994) *Houses and Society in Pompeii and Herculaneum*, Princeton: Princeton University Press.

Wallace-Hadrill, A. (1997) 'Rethinking the *atrium* house', in R. Laurence and A. Wallace-Hadrill (eds) *Domestic Space in the Roman World: Pompeii and Beyond*, Journal of Roman Archaeology, Supplementary Series 22.

Walter, A. (1979) '*The dextrarum iunctio* of Lepcis Magna in relationship to the iconography of marriage', *Antiquités Africaines* 6:14, 271–83.

Warde Fowler, W. (1908) *The Roman Festivals of the Period of the Republic*, London: MacMillan.

Watson, P.A. (1994) *Ancient Stepmothers, Myth, Misogyny and Reality*, Leiden: E.J. Brill.

Wiedemann, T. (1989) *Adults and Children in the Roman Empire*, London: Routledge.

Williams, C.A. (1999) *Roman Homosexuality. Ideologies of Masculinity in Classical Antiquity*, Oxford: Oxford University Press.

Williams, G. (1958) 'Some aspects of Roman marriage ceremonies and ideals', *Journal of Roman Studies* 48: 16–29.

Wilson, A. (1980) 'The infancy of the history of childhood: an appraisal of Ariès', *History and Theory* 19: 132–53.

Wiseman, T.P. (1985) *Catullus and his World: A Reappraisal*, Cambridge: Cambridge University Press.

Wyke, M. and Biddiss, M. (1999) 'Introduction: using and abusing antiquity', in M. Wyke and M. Biddiss (eds) *The Uses and Abuses of Antiquity*, Bern: Peter Lang, 13–18.

Zanker P. (1988) *The Power of Images in the Age of Augustus,* Michigan, Ann Arbor, MI.

Ziolkowski, A. (1995) '*Urbs direptio*, or how the Romans sacked cities', in J. Rich and G. Shipley (eds) *War and Society in the Roman World*, London: Routledge, 69–91.

INDEX